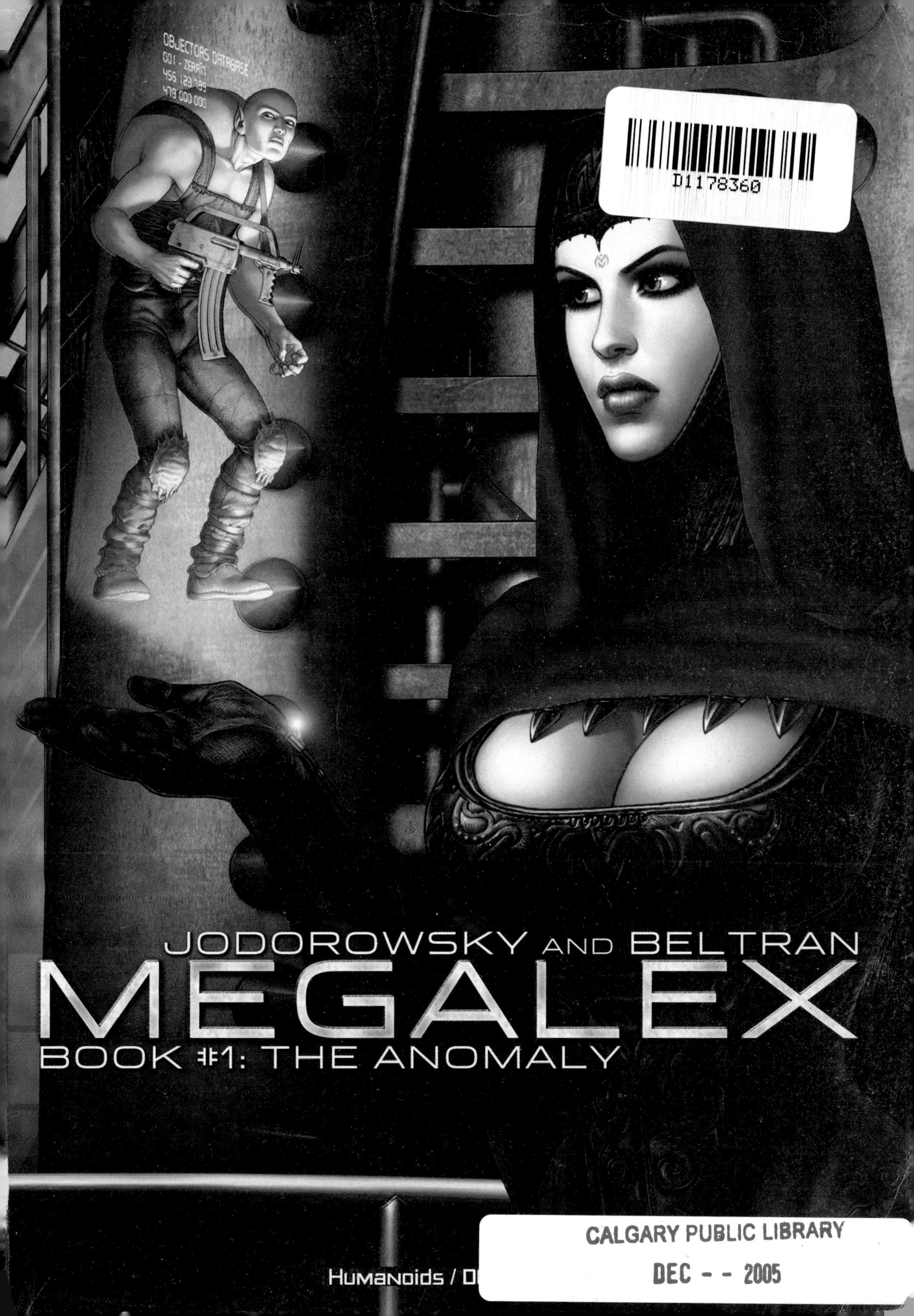
OBJECTORS DATABASE

JODOROWSKY AND BELTRAN

MEGALEX

BOOK #1: THE ANOMALY

Humanoids / DC

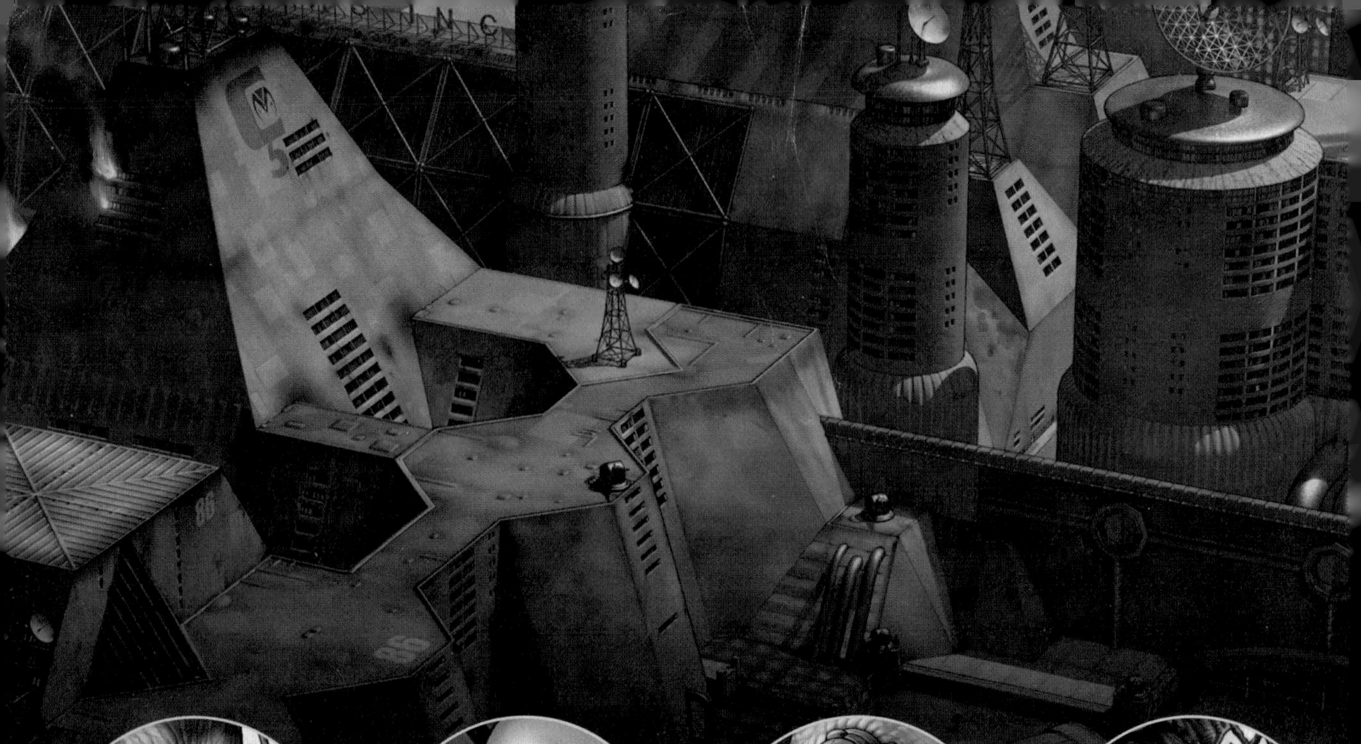

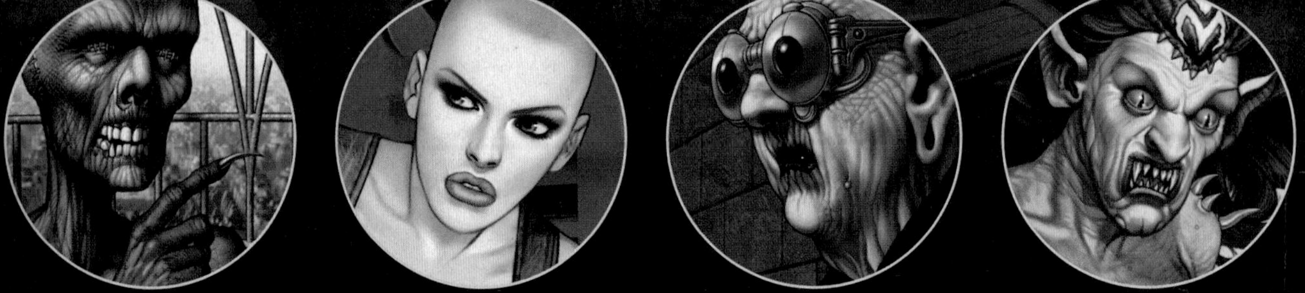

ALEXANDRO JODOROWSKY, writer
FRED BELTRAN, artist
SASHA WATSON, translator

THIERRY FRISSEN, BOOK DESIGNER & LETTERER
FRANCIS LOMBARD, EDITOR, COLLECTED EDITION
BRUNO LECIGNE & FABRICE GIGER, EDITORS, ORIGINAL EDITION

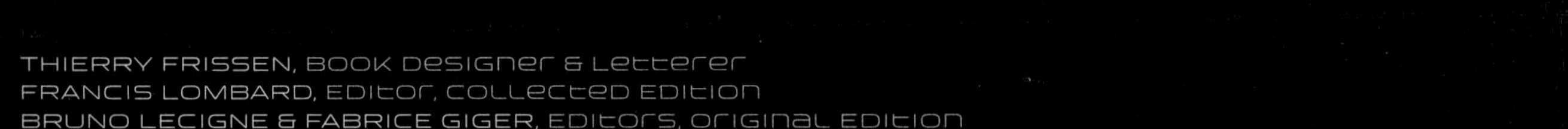

DC COMICS:

PAUL LEVITZ, President & Publisher
GEORG BREWER, VP-Design & Retail Product Development
RICHARD BRUNING, Senior VP-Creative Director
PATRICK CALDON, Senior VP-Finance & Operations
CHRIS CARAMALIS, VP-Finance
TERRI CUNNINGHAM, VP-Managing Editor
ALISON GILL, VP-Manufacturing
RICH JOHNSON, VP-Book Trade Sales
HANK KANALZ, VP-General Manager, WildStorm
LILLIAN LASERSON, Senior VP & General Counsel
JIM LEE, Editorial Director-WildStorm
DAVID MCKILLIPS, VP-Advertising & Custom Publishing
JOHN NEE, VP-Business Development
GREGORY NOVECK, Senior VP-Creative Affairs
CHERYL RUBIN, Senior VP-Brand Management
BOB WAYNE, VP-Sales & Marketing

MEGALEX BOOK #1: THE ANOMALY, Humanoids Publishing. PO Box 931658, Hollywood, CA 90093. This is a publication of DC Comics, 1700 Broadway, New York, NY 10019.

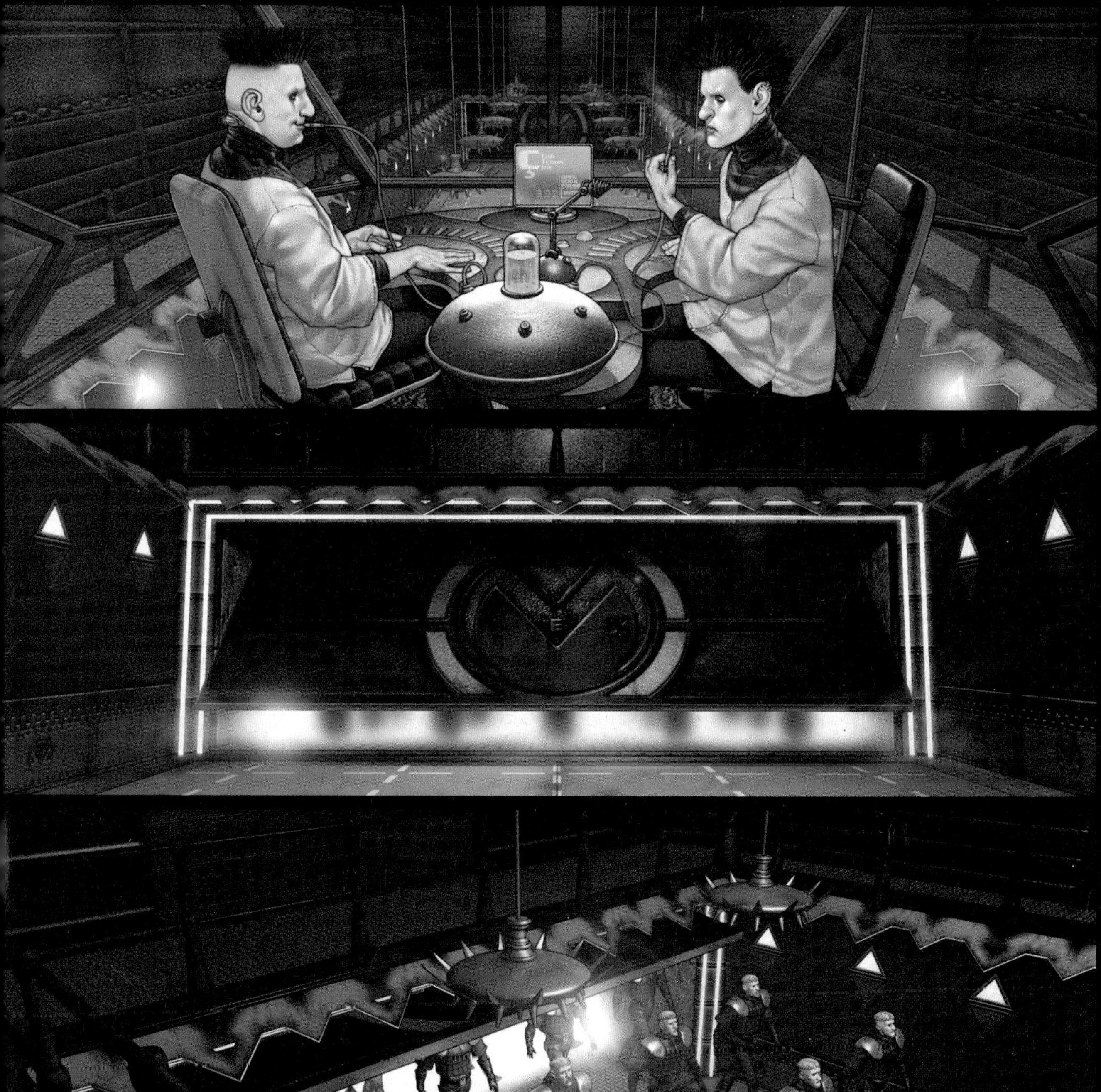

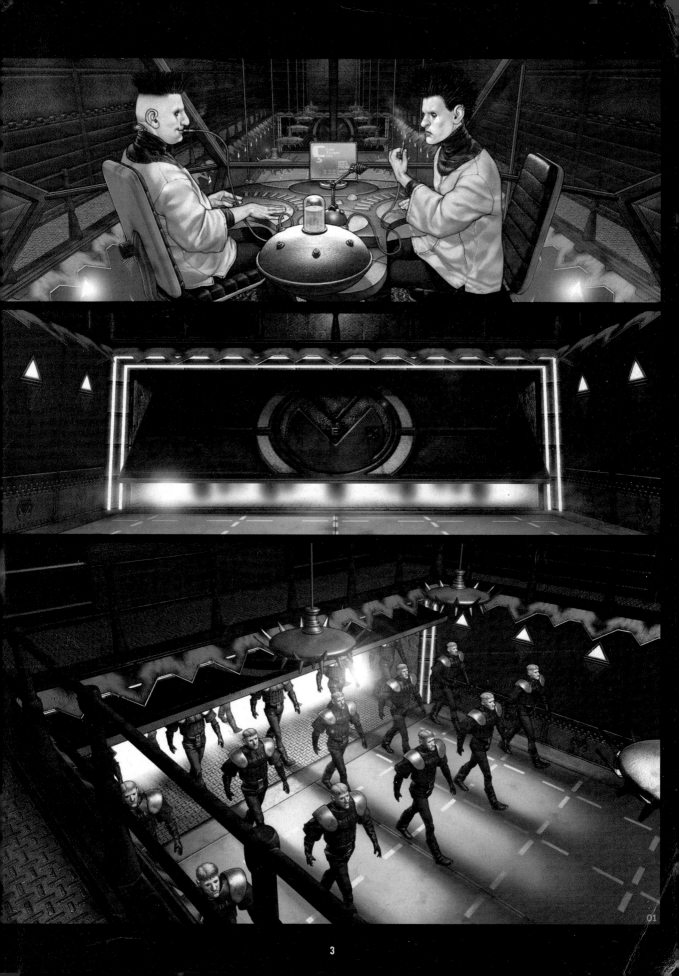

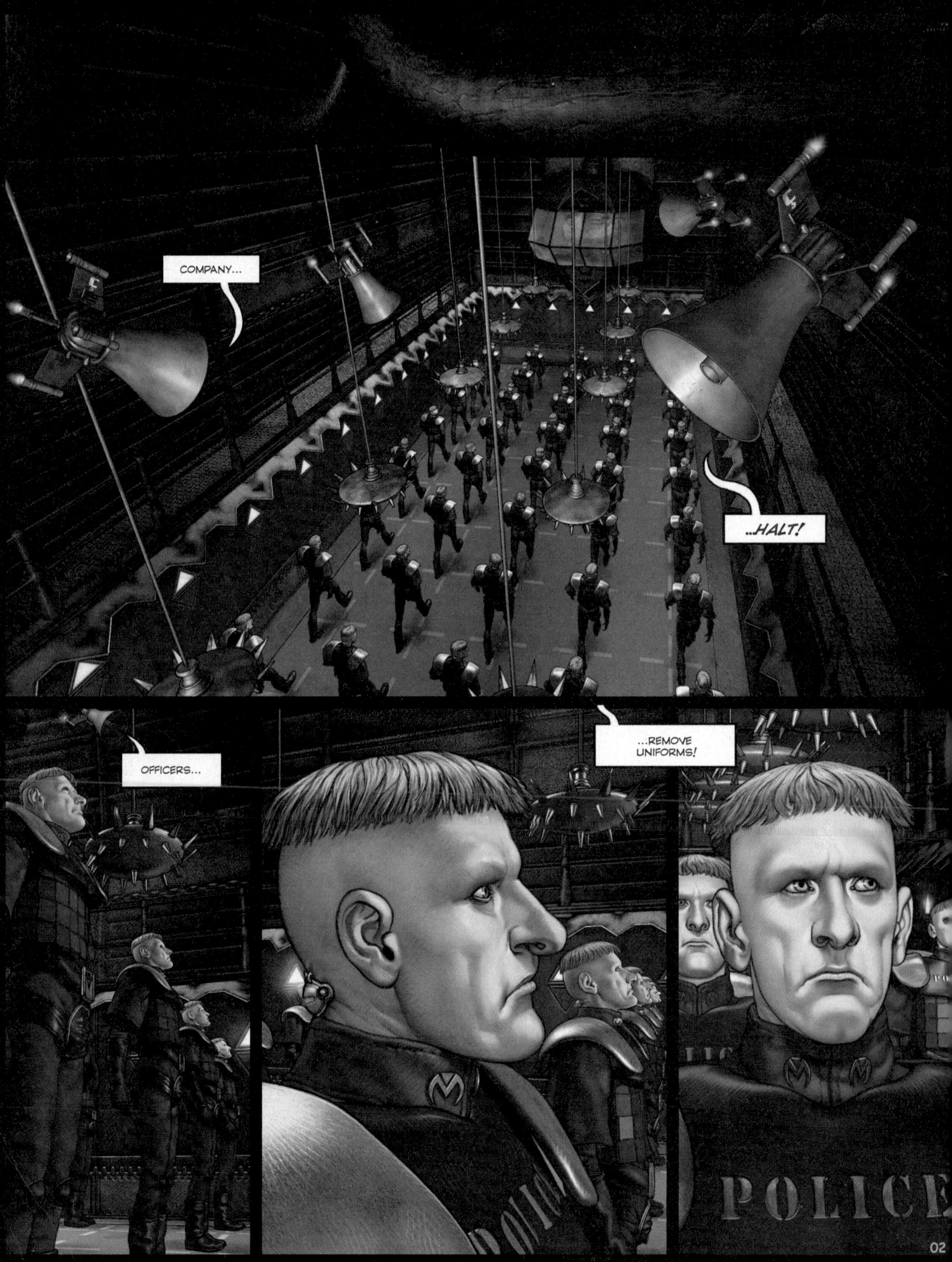
COMPANY...
...HALT!
OFFICERS...
...REMOVE UNIFORMS!
POLICE
02

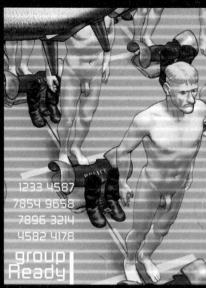

group
Ready

1233 4587
7854 9658
7896 3214
4582 4178

BRING OUT THE FABRIC-FEEDERS!

ENTER

03

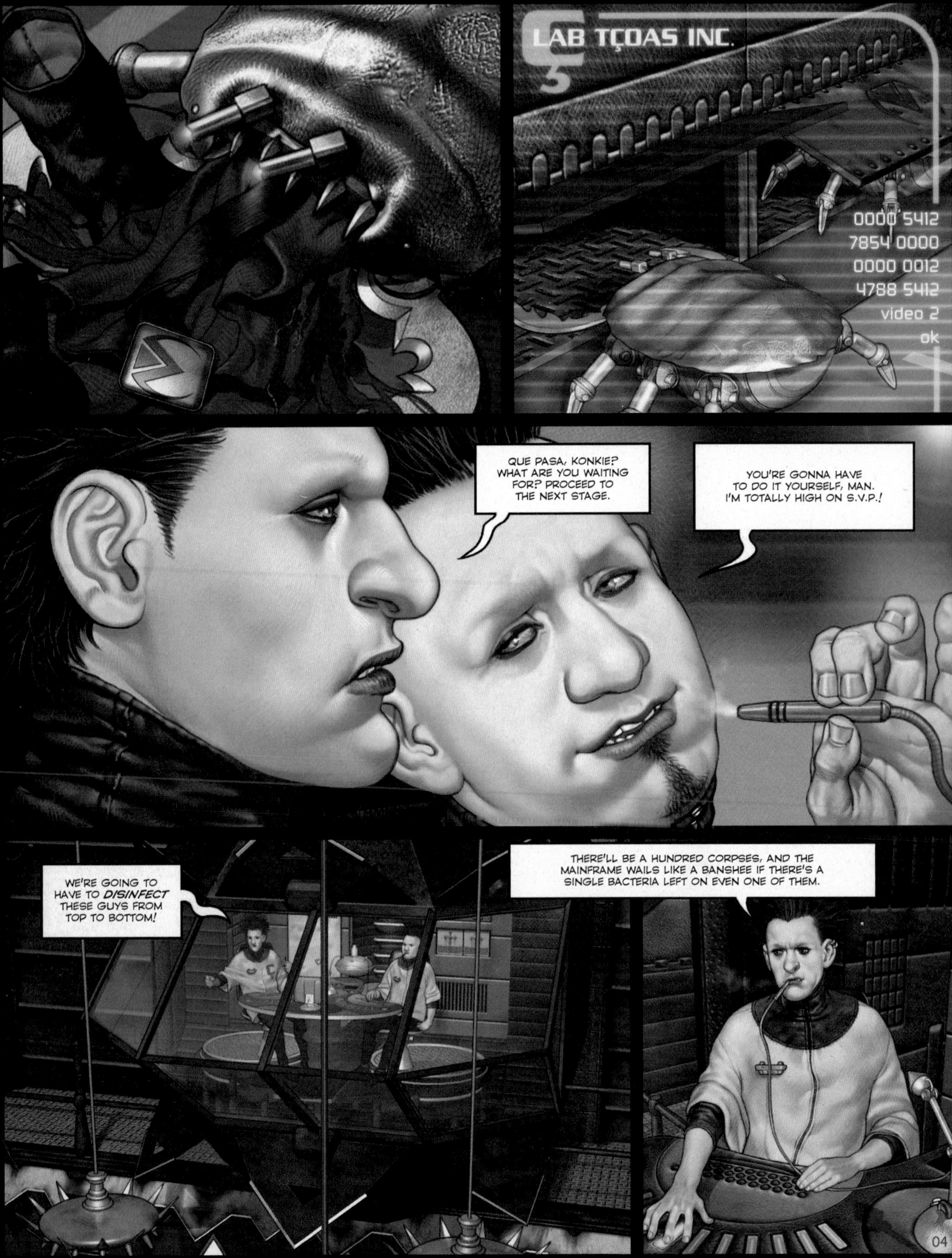
LAB TÇOAS INC.
0000 5412
7854 0000
0000 0012
4788 5412
video 2
ok
QUE PASA, KONKIE? WHAT ARE YOU WAITING FOR? PROCEED TO THE NEXT STAGE.
YOU'RE GONNA HAVE TO DO IT YOURSELF, MAN. I'M TOTALLY HIGH ON S.V.P.!
WE'RE GOING TO HAVE TO *DISINFECT* THESE GUYS FROM TOP TO BOTTOM!
THERE'LL BE A HUNDRED CORPSES, AND THE MAINFRAME WAILS LIKE A BANSHEE IF THERE'S A SINGLE BACTERIA LEFT ON EVEN ONE OF THEM.
04

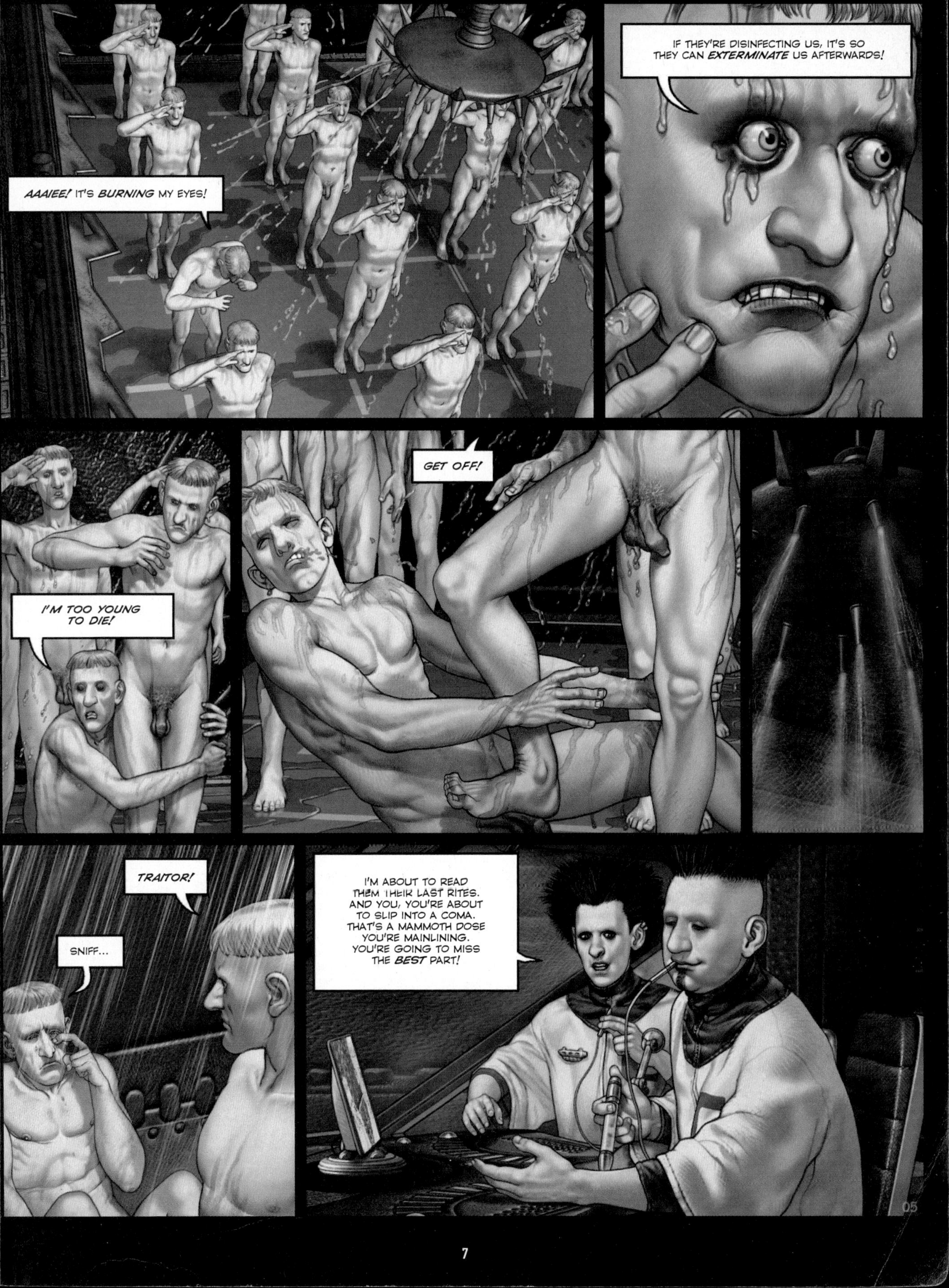
AAAIEE! IT'S BURNING MY EYES!
IF THEY'RE DISINFECTING US, IT'S SO THEY CAN EXTERMINATE US AFTERWARDS!
I'M TOO YOUNG TO DIE!
GET OFF!
TRAITOR!
SNIFF...
I'M ABOUT TO READ THEM THEIR LAST RITES. AND YOU, YOU'RE ABOUT TO SLIP INTO A COMA. THAT'S A MAMMOTH DOSE YOU'RE MAINLINING. YOU'RE GOING TO MISS THE BEST PART!

ATTENTION! BRAVE AND LOYAL SERVANTS, THE TIME THAT HAS BEEN GRANTED TO YOU HAS EXPIRED.

IN A FEW MOMENTS, THE 400 DAYS OF LIFE THAT WERE ALLOTTED TO YOU, WHICH YOU SPENT SERVING MEGALEX, OUR BELOVED HOMELAND, AND ITS QUEEN MOTHER MAREA, WILL COME TO AN END.

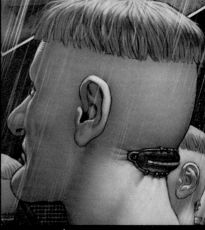

THE TIME HAS COME FOR YOUR FINAL ACT OF HEROISM. THE CONTROL TABS IMPLANTED AT THE BASE OF YOUR SKULLS WILL SOON COMPLETE THEIR SACRED FUNCTION.

LONG LIVE QUEEN MOTHER MAREA!

LONG LIVE MAREA!

LONG LIVE PRINCESS KAVATAH!

LONG LIVE KAVATAH!

LONG LIVE MEGALEX!

LONG LIVE MEGALEX!

DEEEAAATH! DEATH TO THE QUEEN! LET 'EM ALL DIE! LET US OUT OF HERE, YOU MURDERERS! IT ISN'T FAIR! 400 DAYS IS NOTHING! A PITTANCE! WE WANT TO LIVE LONGER THAN THAT! WE WANT TO LIVE! LIVE!

HE'S RIGHT!

400 DAYS IS HARDLY ANYTHING!

WE DON'T WANT TO DIE!

06

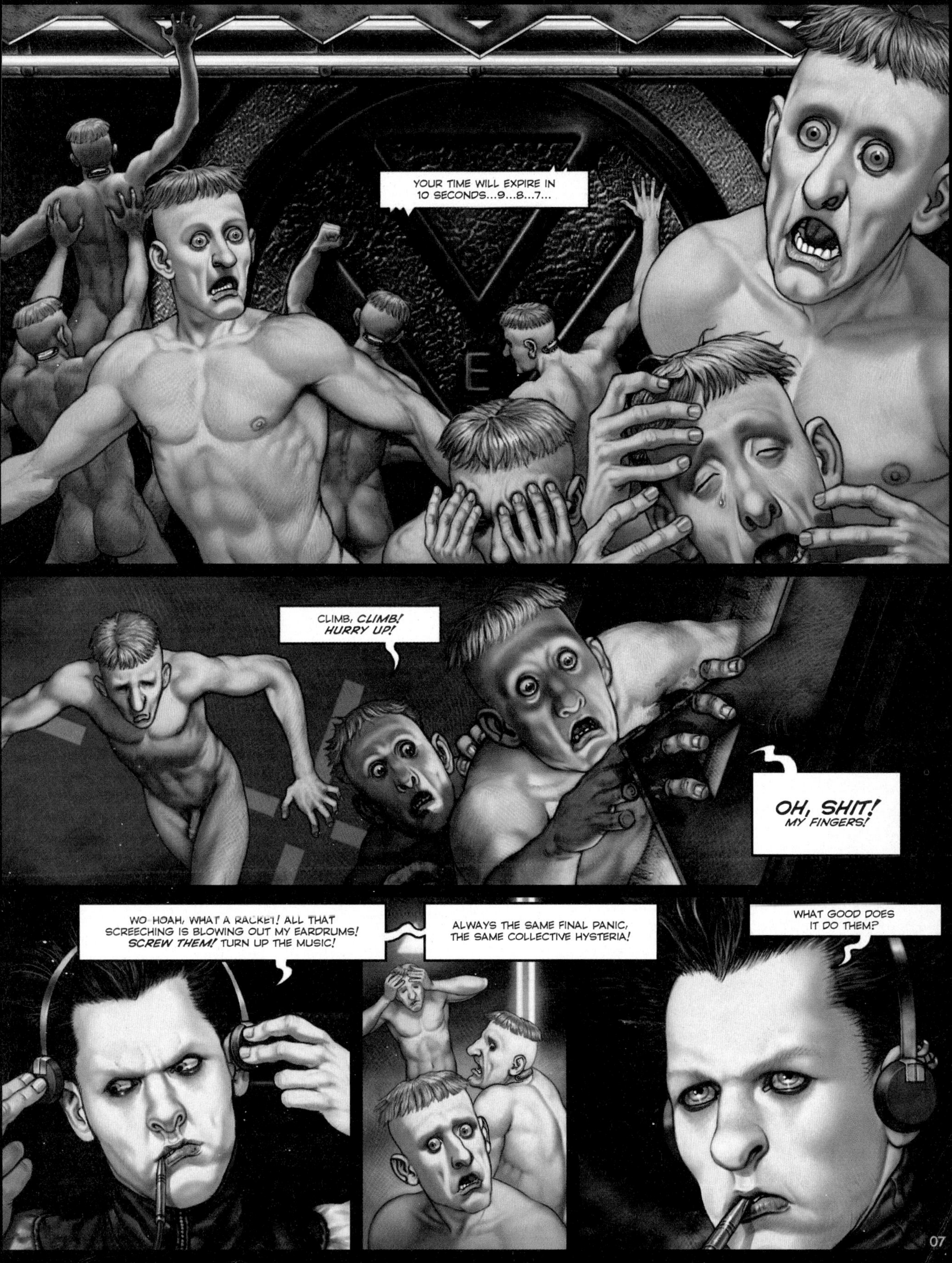
YOUR TIME WILL EXPIRE IN 10 SECONDS...9...8...7...
CLIMB, CLIMB! HURRY UP!
OH, SHIT! MY FINGERS!
WO-HOAH, WHAT A RACKET! ALL THAT SCREECHING IS BLOWING OUT MY EARDRUMS! SCREW THEM! TURN UP THE MUSIC!
ALWAYS THE SAME FINAL PANIC, THE SAME COLLECTIVE HYSTERIA!
WHAT GOOD DOES IT DO THEM?
07

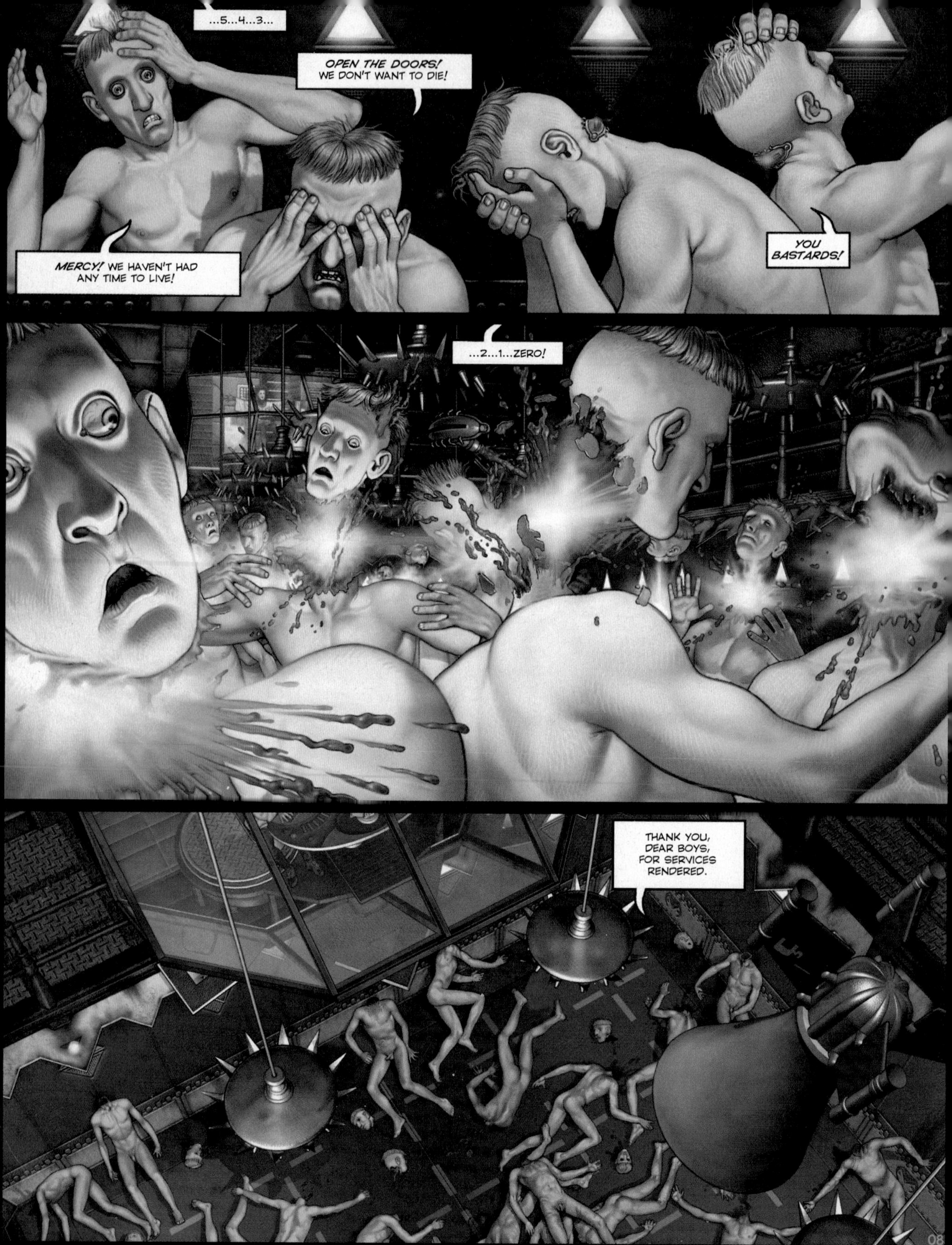

...5...4...3...
OPEN THE DOORS! WE DON'T WANT TO DIE!
MERCY! WE HAVEN'T HAD ANY TIME TO LIVE!
YOU BASTARDS!
...2...1...ZERO!
THANK YOU, DEAR BOYS, FOR SERVICES RENDERED.
08

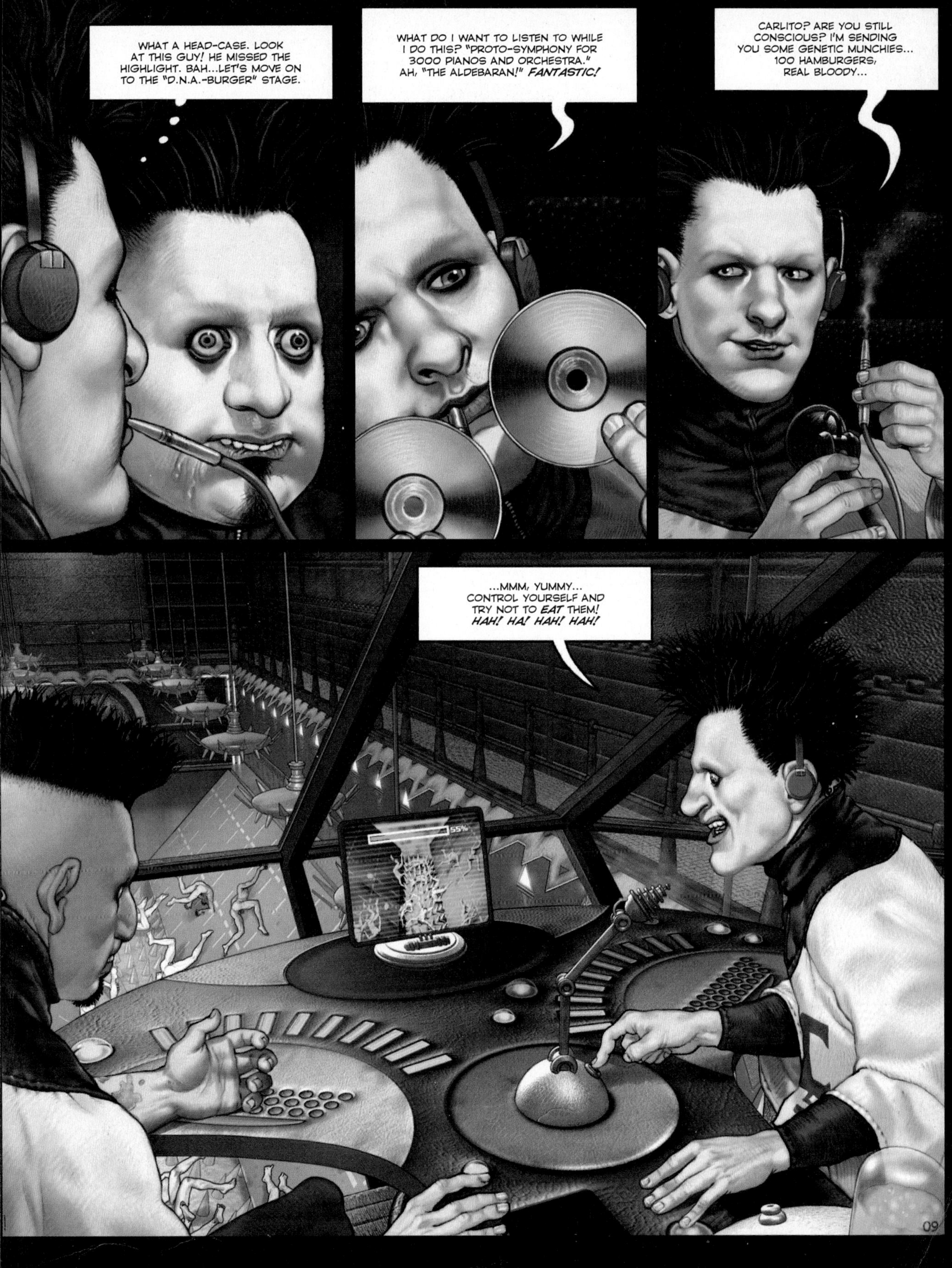
WHAT A HEAD-CASE. LOOK AT THIS GUY! HE MISSED THE HIGHLIGHT. BAH...LET'S MOVE ON TO THE "D.N.A.-BURGER" STAGE.
WHAT DO I WANT TO LISTEN TO WHILE I DO THIS? "PROTO-SYMPHONY FOR 3000 PIANOS AND ORCHESTRA." AH, "THE ALDEBARAN!" FANTASTIC!
CARLITO? ARE YOU STILL CONSCIOUS? I'M SENDING YOU SOME GENETIC MUNCHIES... 100 HAMBURGERS, REAL BLOODY...
55%
...MMM, YUMMY... CONTROL YOURSELF AND TRY NOT TO EAT THEM! HAH! HA! HAH! HAH!
09

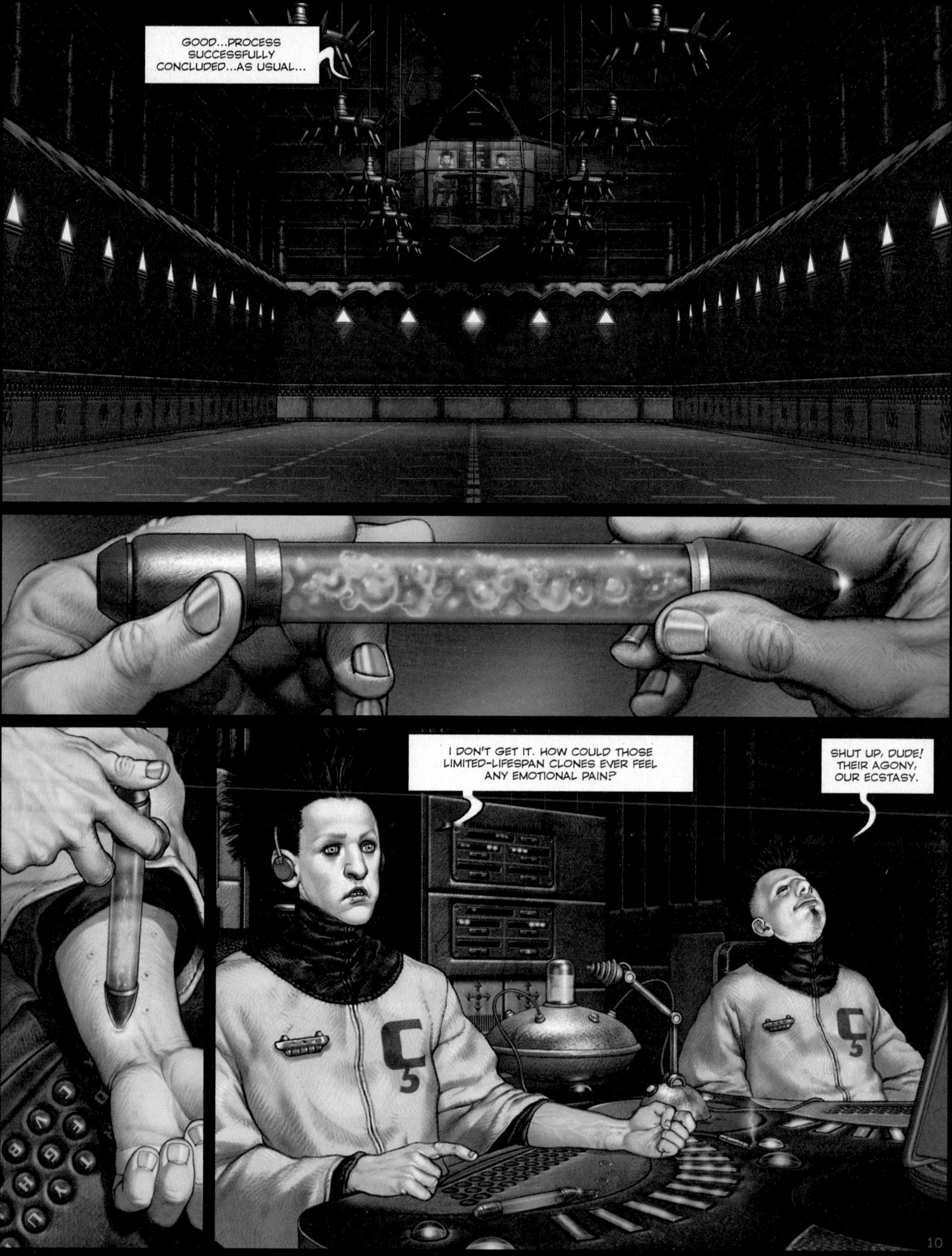
GOOD...PROCESS SUCCESSFULLY CONCLUDED...AS USUAL...
I DON'T GET IT. HOW COULD THOSE LIMITED-LIFESPAN CLONES EVER FEEL ANY EMOTIONAL PAIN?
SHUT UP, DUDE! THEIR AGONY, OUR ECSTASY.
10

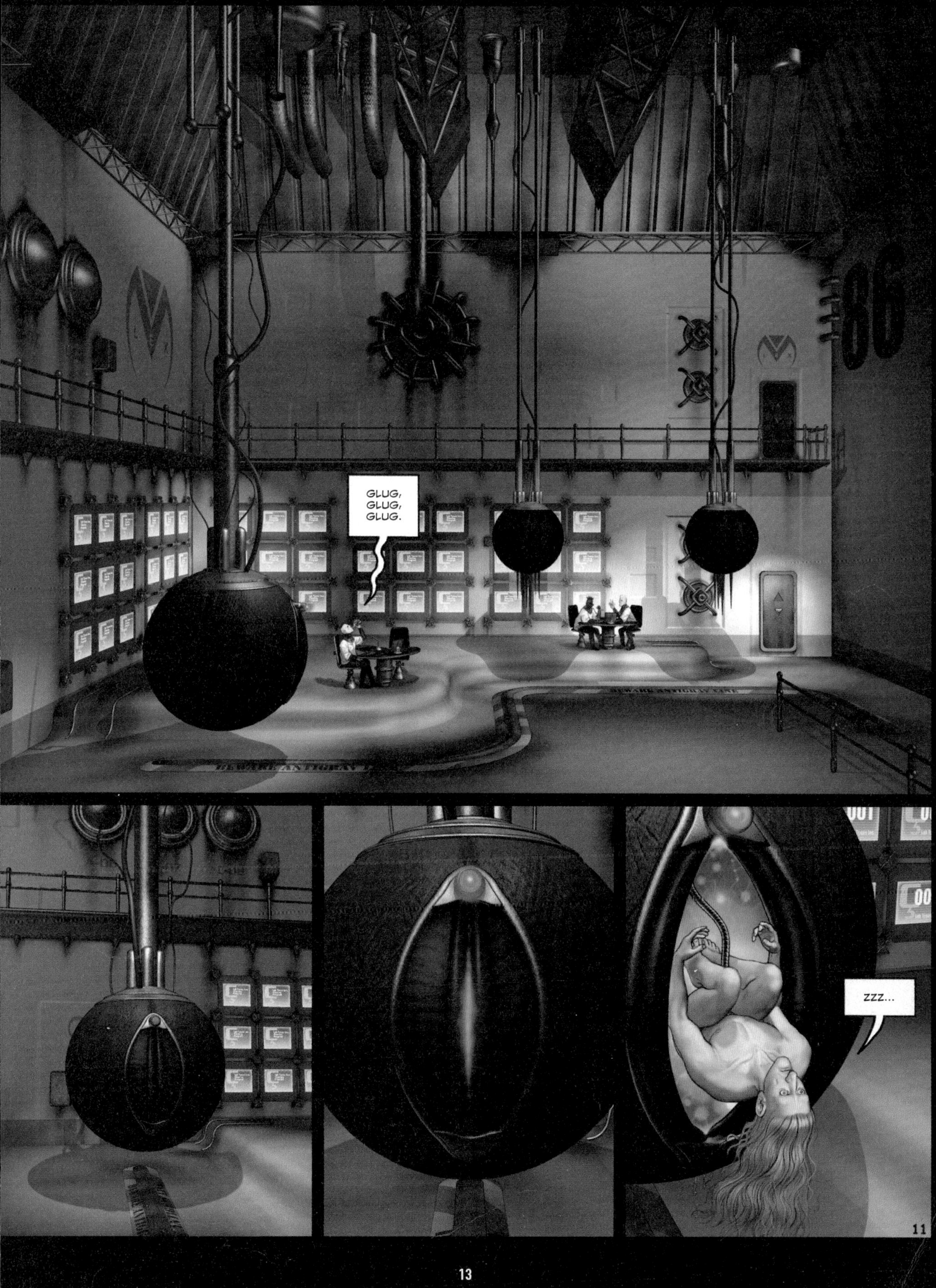
GLUG,
GLUG,
GLUG.
ZZZ...

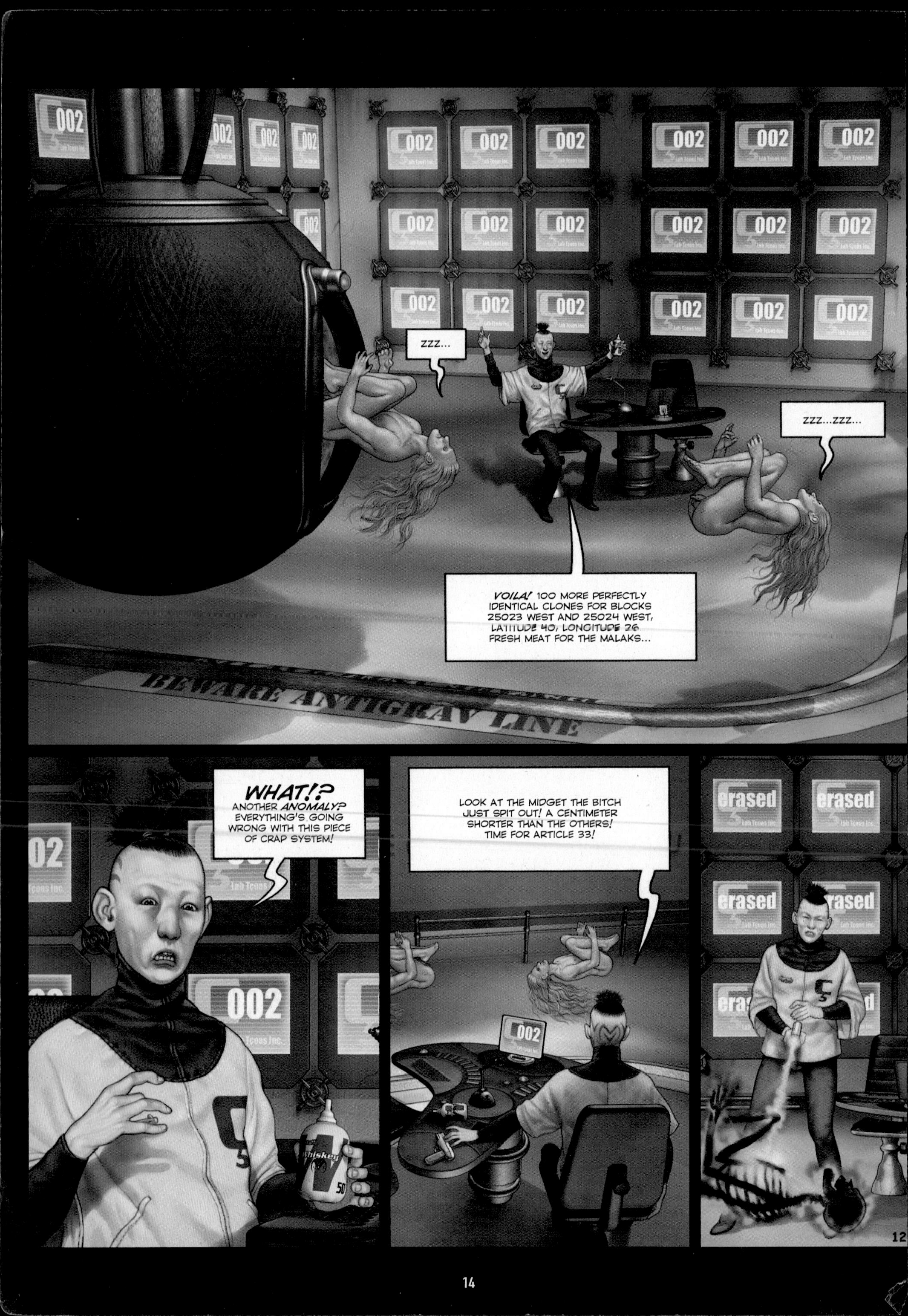
ZZZ...
ZZZ...ZZZ...
VOILA! 100 MORE PERFECTLY IDENTICAL CLONES FOR BLOCKS 25023 WEST AND 25024 WEST, LATITUDE 40, LONGITUDE 26 FRESH MEAT FOR THE MALAKS...
BEWARE ANTIGRAV LINE
WHAT!? ANOTHER ANOMALY? EVERYTHING'S GOING WRONG WITH THIS PIECE OF CRAP SYSTEM!
LOOK AT THE MIDGET THE BITCH JUST SPIT OUT! A CENTIMETER SHORTER THAN THE OTHERS! TIME FOR ARTICLE 33!
erased
erased

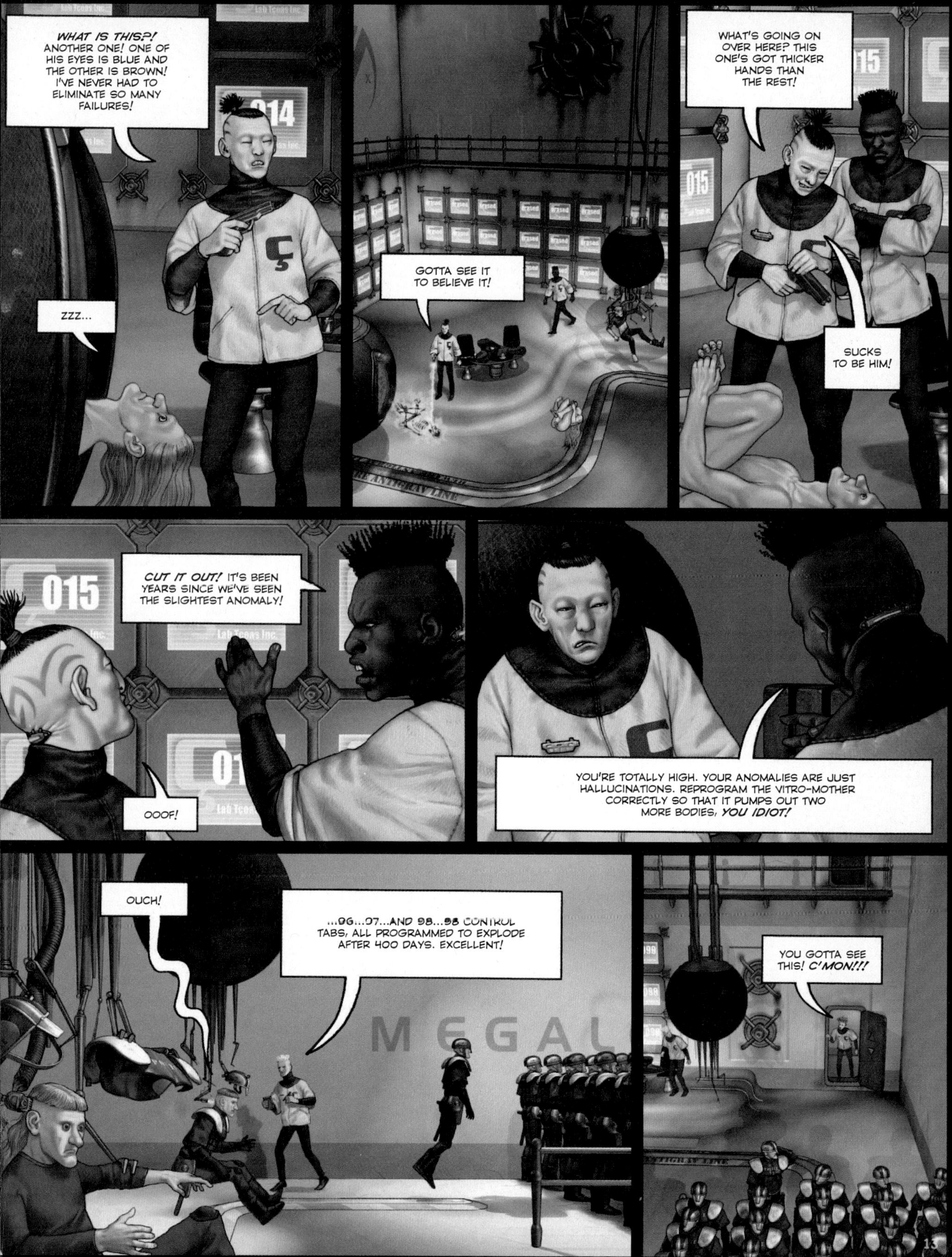
WHAT IS THIS?! ANOTHER ONE! ONE OF HIS EYES IS BLUE AND THE OTHER IS BROWN! I'VE NEVER HAD TO ELIMINATE SO MANY FAILURES!
ZZZ...
GOTTA SEE IT TO BELIEVE IT!
WHAT'S GOING ON OVER HERE? THIS ONE'S GOT THICKER HANDS THAN THE REST!
SUCKS TO BE HIM!
CUT IT OUT! IT'S BEEN YEARS SINCE WE'VE SEEN THE SLIGHTEST ANOMALY!
OOOF!
YOU'RE TOTALLY HIGH. YOUR ANOMALIES ARE JUST HALLUCINATIONS. REPROGRAM THE VITRO-MOTHER CORRECTLY SO THAT IT PUMPS OUT TWO MORE BODIES, YOU IDIOT!
OUCH!
...96...97...AND 98...98 CONTROL TABS, ALL PROGRAMMED TO EXPLODE AFTER 400 DAYS. EXCELLENT!
YOU GOTTA SEE THIS! C'MON!!!

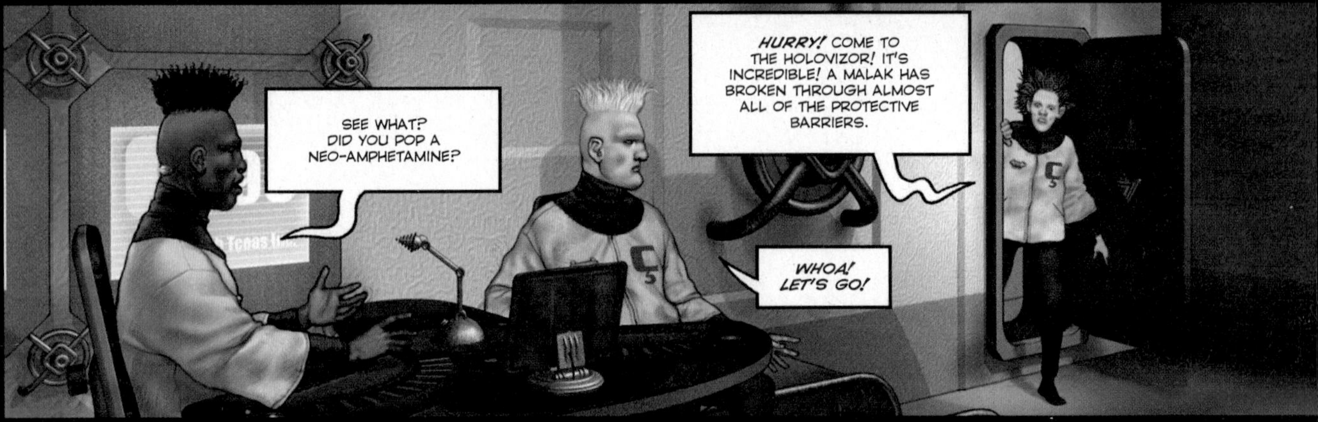
SEE WHAT? DID YOU POP A NEO-AMPHETAMINE?
HURRY! COME TO THE HOLOVIZOR! IT'S INCREDIBLE! A MALAK HAS BROKEN THROUGH ALMOST ALL OF THE PROTECTIVE BARRIERS.
WHOA! LET'S GO!

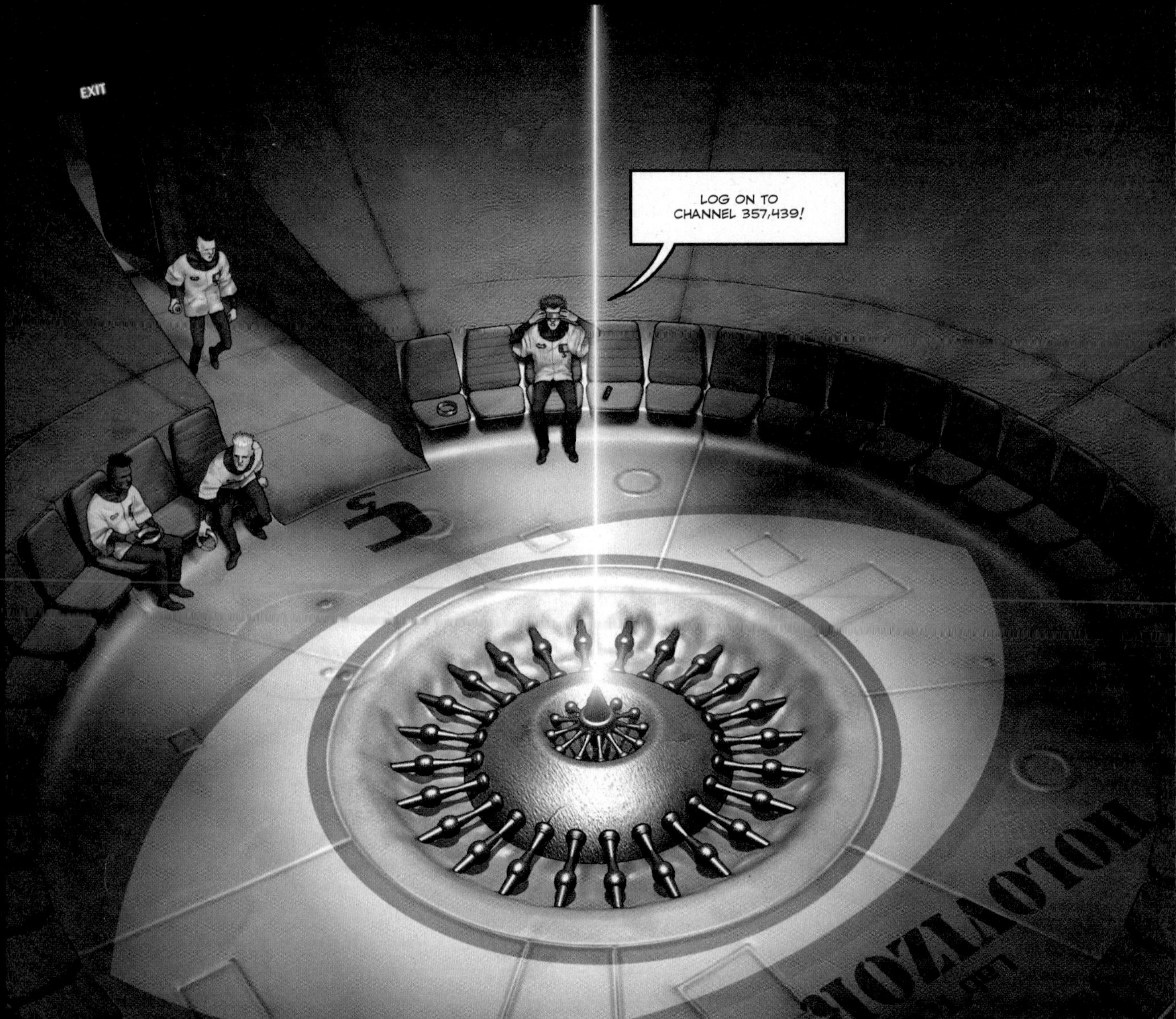
EXIT
LOG ON TO CHANNEL 357,439!

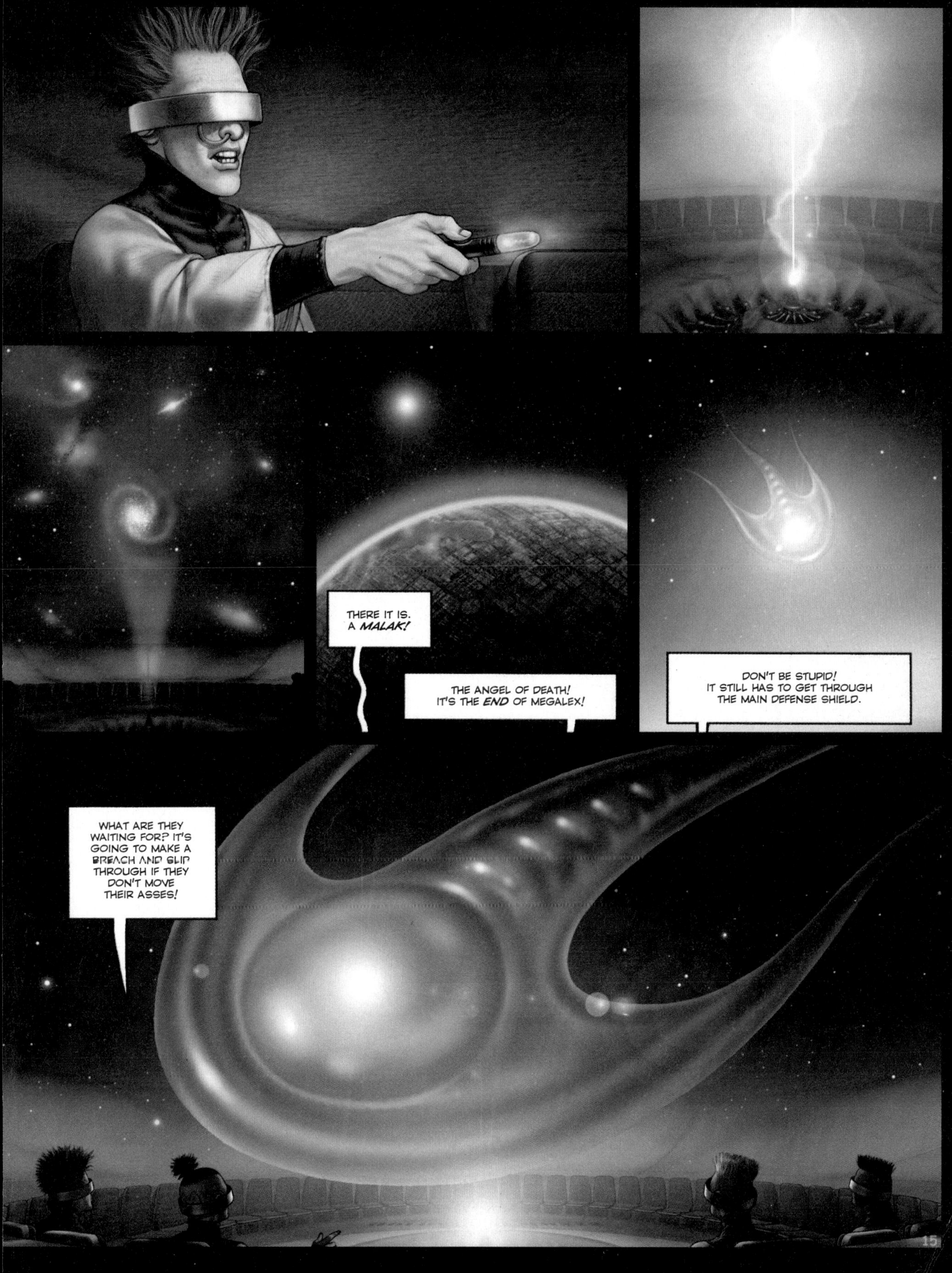
THERE IT IS.
A *MALAK!*
THE ANGEL OF DEATH!
IT'S THE *END* OF MEGALEX!
DON'T BE STUPID!
IT STILL HAS TO GET THROUGH
THE MAIN DEFENSE SHIELD.
WHAT ARE THEY WAITING FOR? IT'S GOING TO MAKE A BREACH AND SLIP THROUGH IF THEY DON'T MOVE THEIR ASSES!

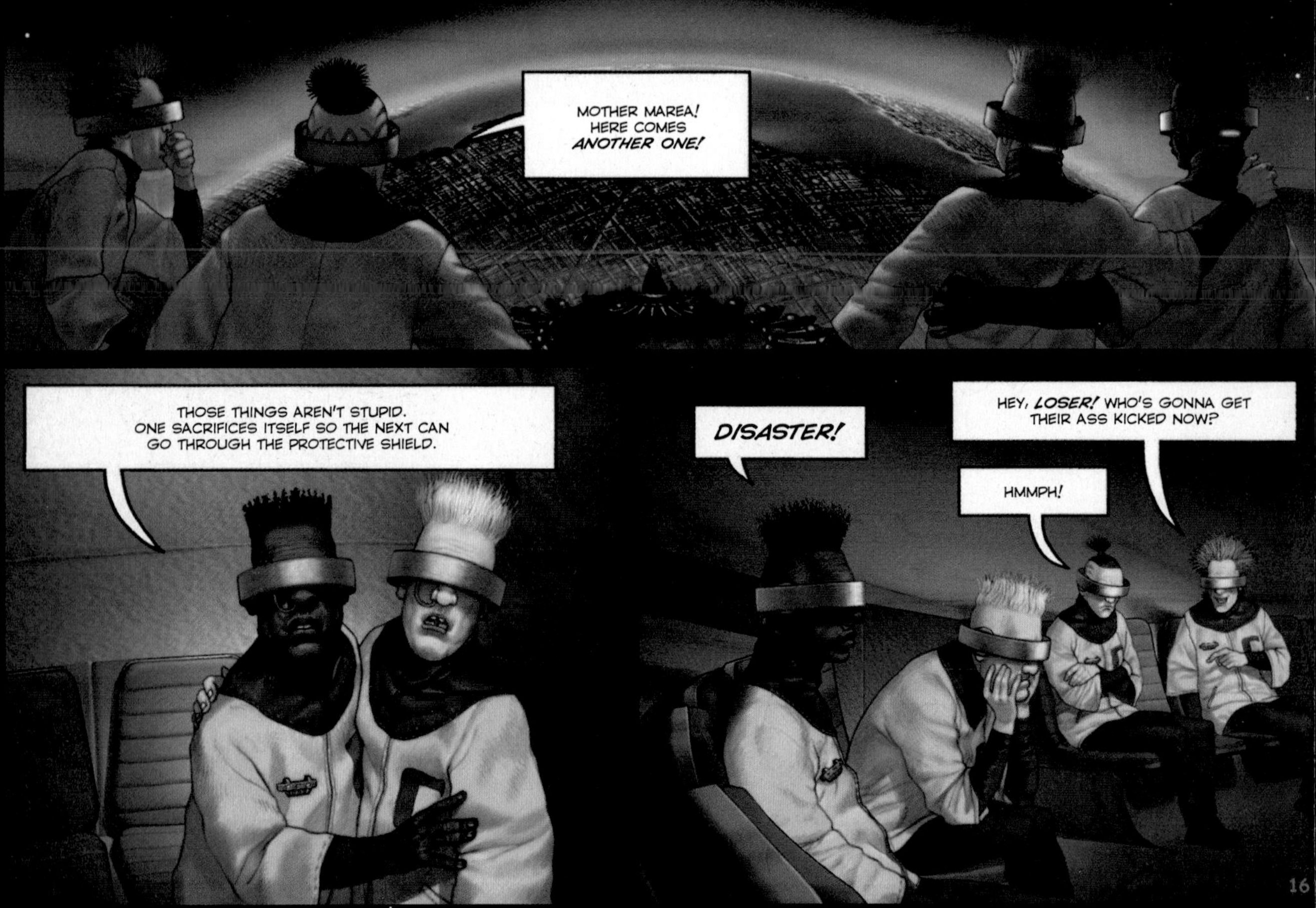
MOTHER MAREA! HERE COMES ANOTHER ONE!
THOSE THINGS AREN'T STUPID. ONE SACRIFICES ITSELF SO THE NEXT CAN GO THROUGH THE PROTECTIVE SHIELD.
DISASTER!
HEY, LOSER! WHO'S GONNA GET THEIR ASS KICKED NOW?
HMMPH!
16

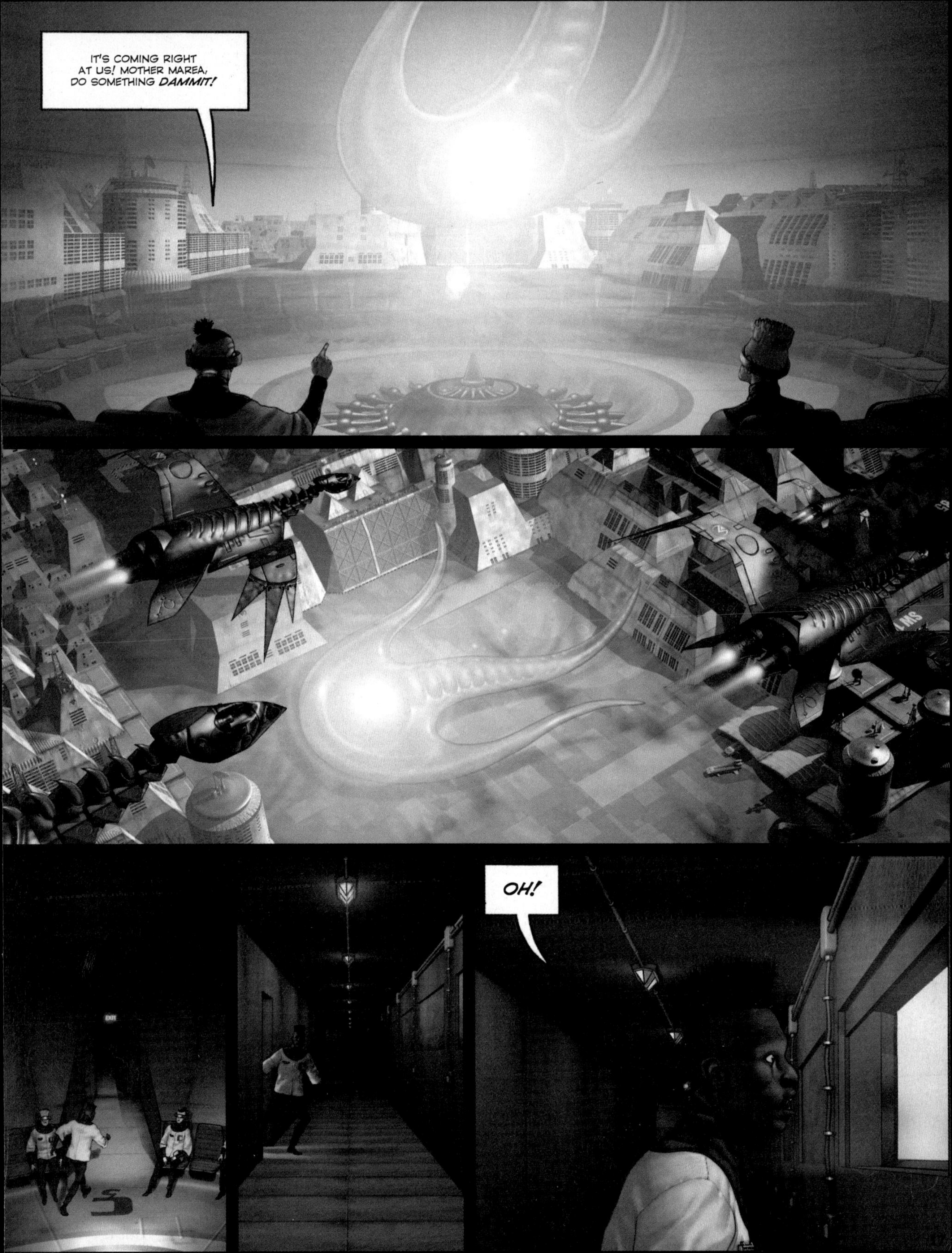
IT'S COMING RIGHT AT US! MOTHER MAREA, DO SOMETHING *DAMMIT!*
OH!

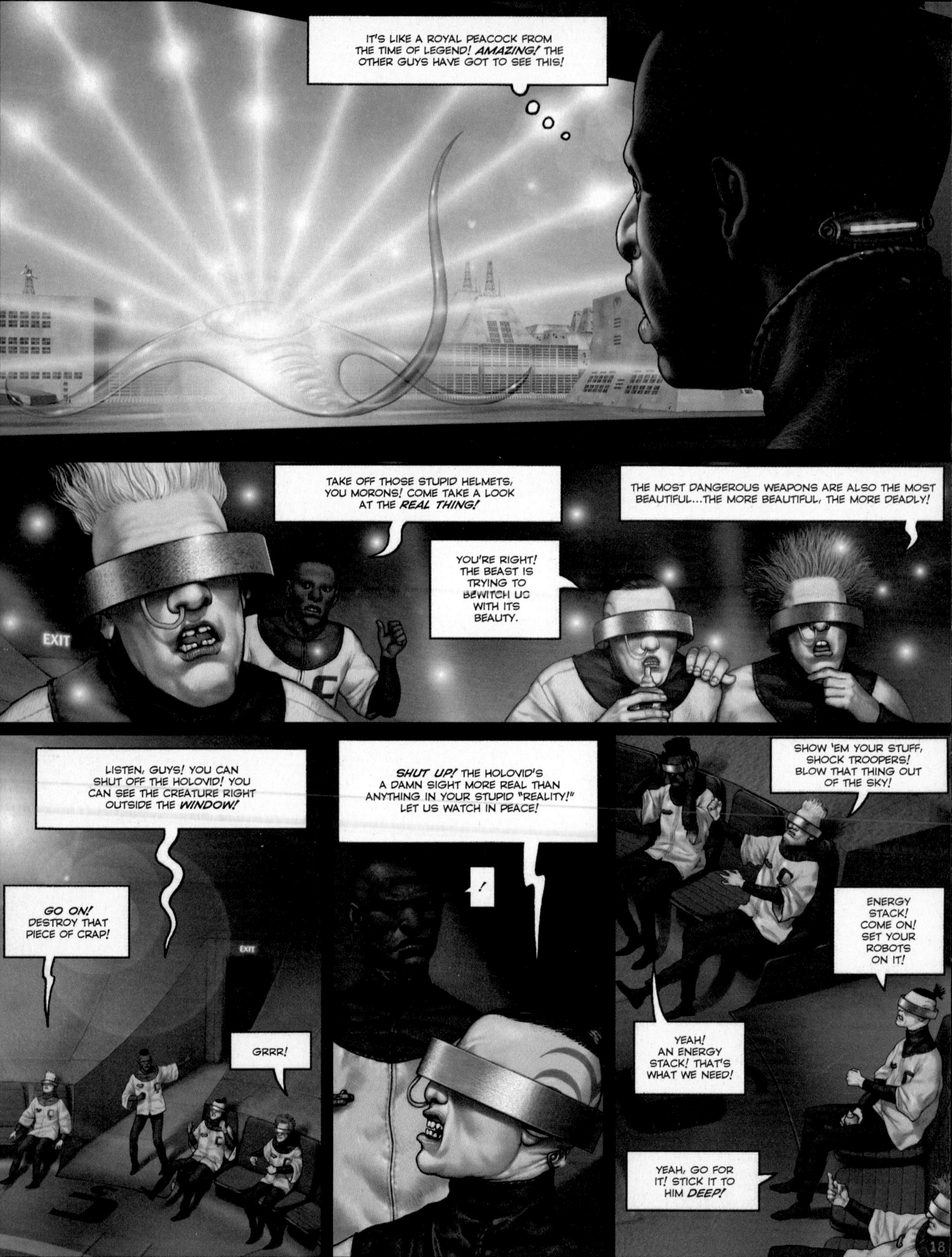

IT'S LIKE A ROYAL PEACOCK FROM THE TIME OF LEGEND! AMAZING! THE OTHER GUYS HAVE GOT TO SEE THIS!
TAKE OFF THOSE STUPID HELMETS, YOU MORONS! COME TAKE A LOOK AT THE REAL THING!
EXIT
YOU'RE RIGHT! THE BEAST IS TRYING TO BEWITCH US WITH ITS BEAUTY.
THE MOST DANGEROUS WEAPONS ARE ALSO THE MOST BEAUTIFUL...THE MORE BEAUTIFUL, THE MORE DEADLY!
LISTEN, GUYS! YOU CAN SHUT OFF THE HOLOVID! YOU CAN SEE THE CREATURE RIGHT OUTSIDE THE WINDOW!
GO ON! DESTROY THAT PIECE OF CRAP!
EXIT
GRRR!
SHUT UP! THE HOLOVID'S A DAMN SIGHT MORE REAL THAN ANYTHING IN YOUR STUPID "REALITY!" LET US WATCH IN PEACE!
!
SHOW 'EM YOUR STUFF, SHOCK TROOPERS! BLOW THAT THING OUT OF THE SKY!
ENERGY STACK! COME ON! SET YOUR ROBOTS ON IT!
YEAH! AN ENERGY STACK! THAT'S WHAT WE NEED!
YEAH, GO FOR IT! STICK IT TO HIM DEEP!

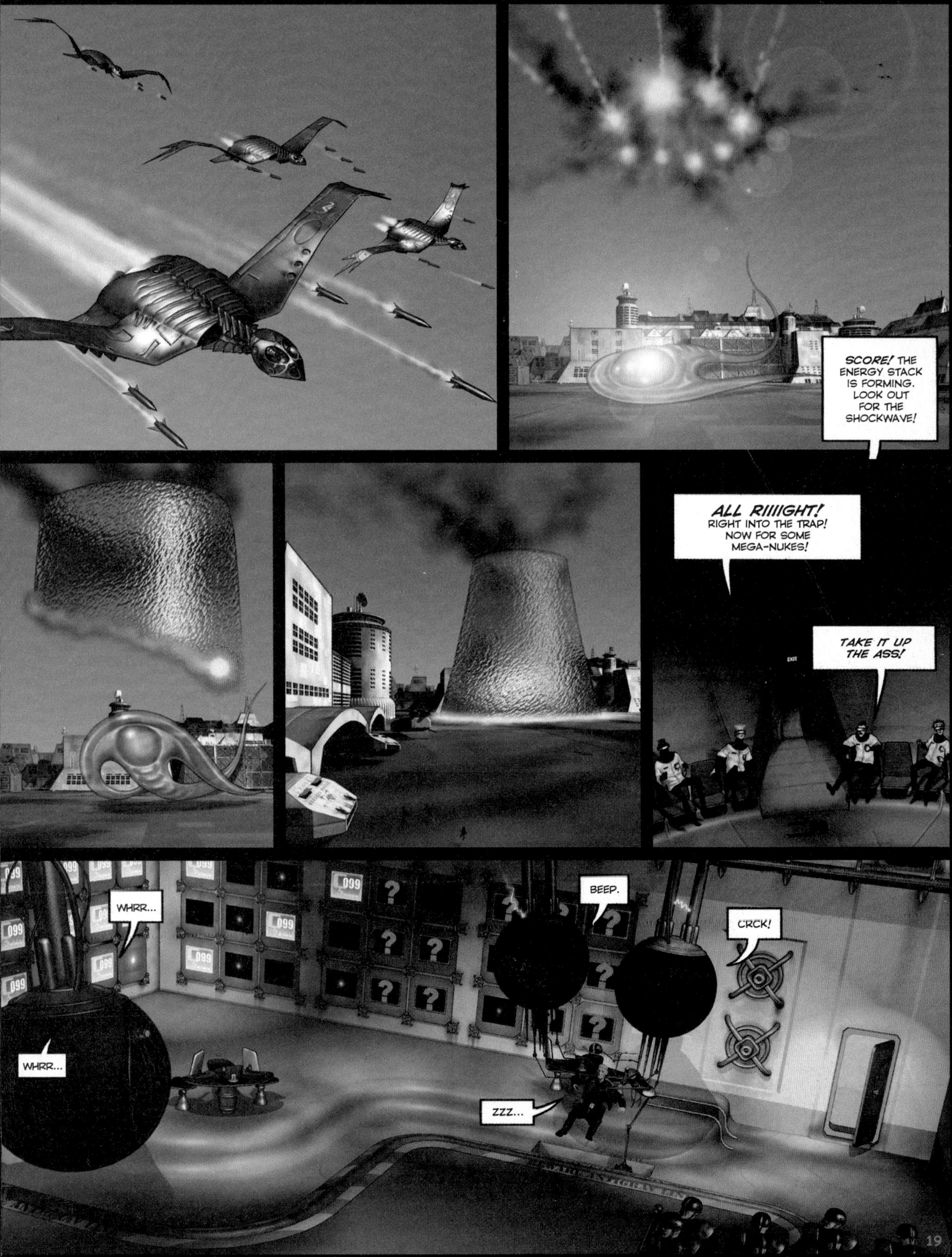
SCORE! THE ENERGY STACK IS FORMING. LOOK OUT FOR THE SHOCKWAVE!
ALL RIIIIGHT! RIGHT INTO THE TRAP! NOW FOR SOME MEGA-NUKES!
TAKE IT UP THE ASS!
EXIT
WHRR...
WHRR...
BEEP.
CRCK!
ZZZ...

TAKE IT UP THE--

SHUT UP, YOU *IDIOT!* CAN'T YOU SEE WE'RE NOT BEATING IT?

THEY'RE GONNA BE FORCED TO DROP THE *ULTRAMEGA-NUKE!*

WHOA! THE ULTRAMEGA! THAT'LL FINISH IT OFF!

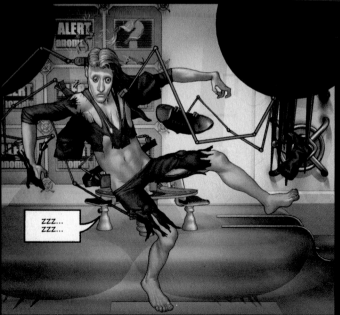

ZZZ... ZZZ....

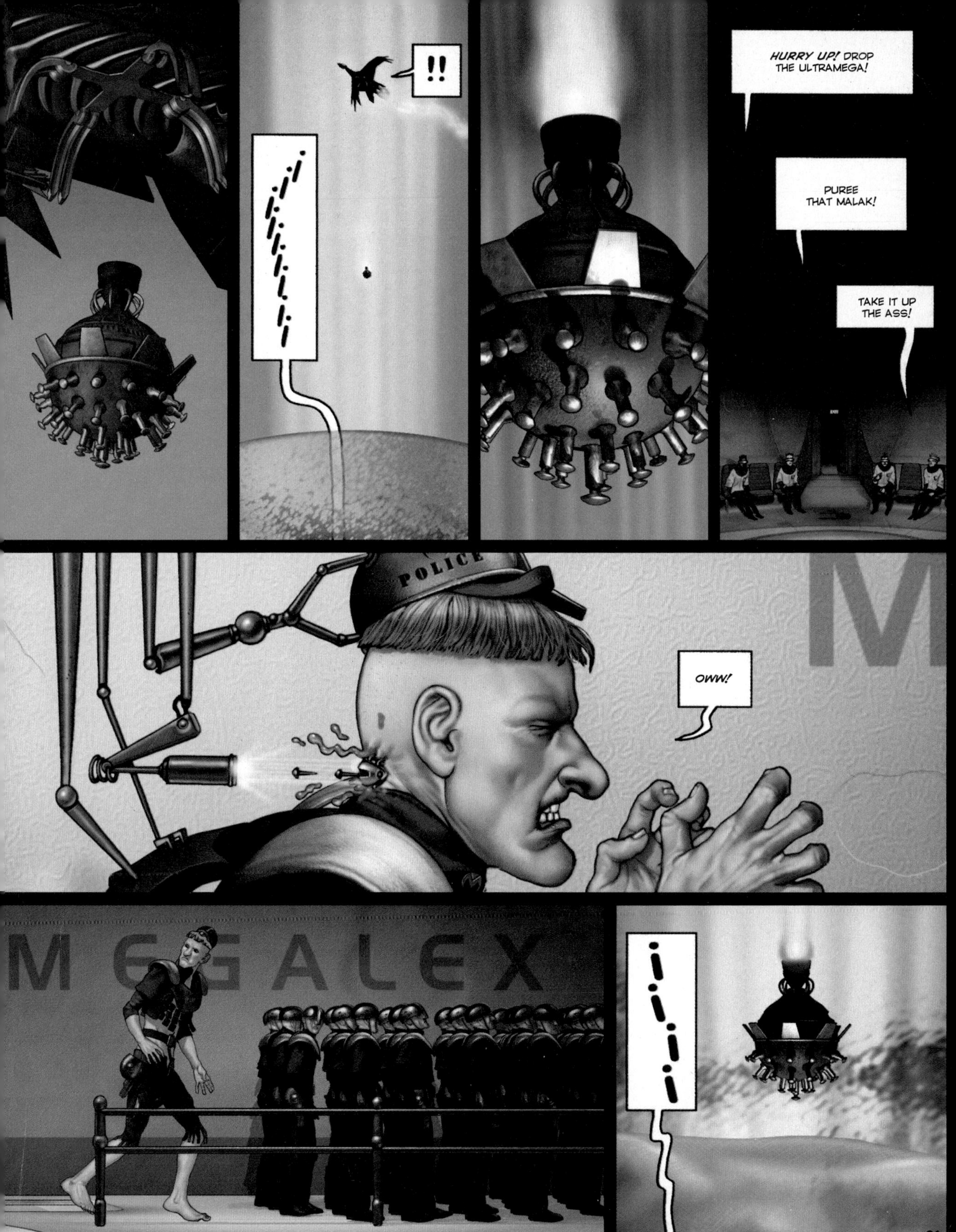
!!
HURRY UP! DROP THE ULTRAMEGA!
PUREE THAT MALAK!
TAKE IT UP THE ASS!
POLICE
OWW!
MEGALEX

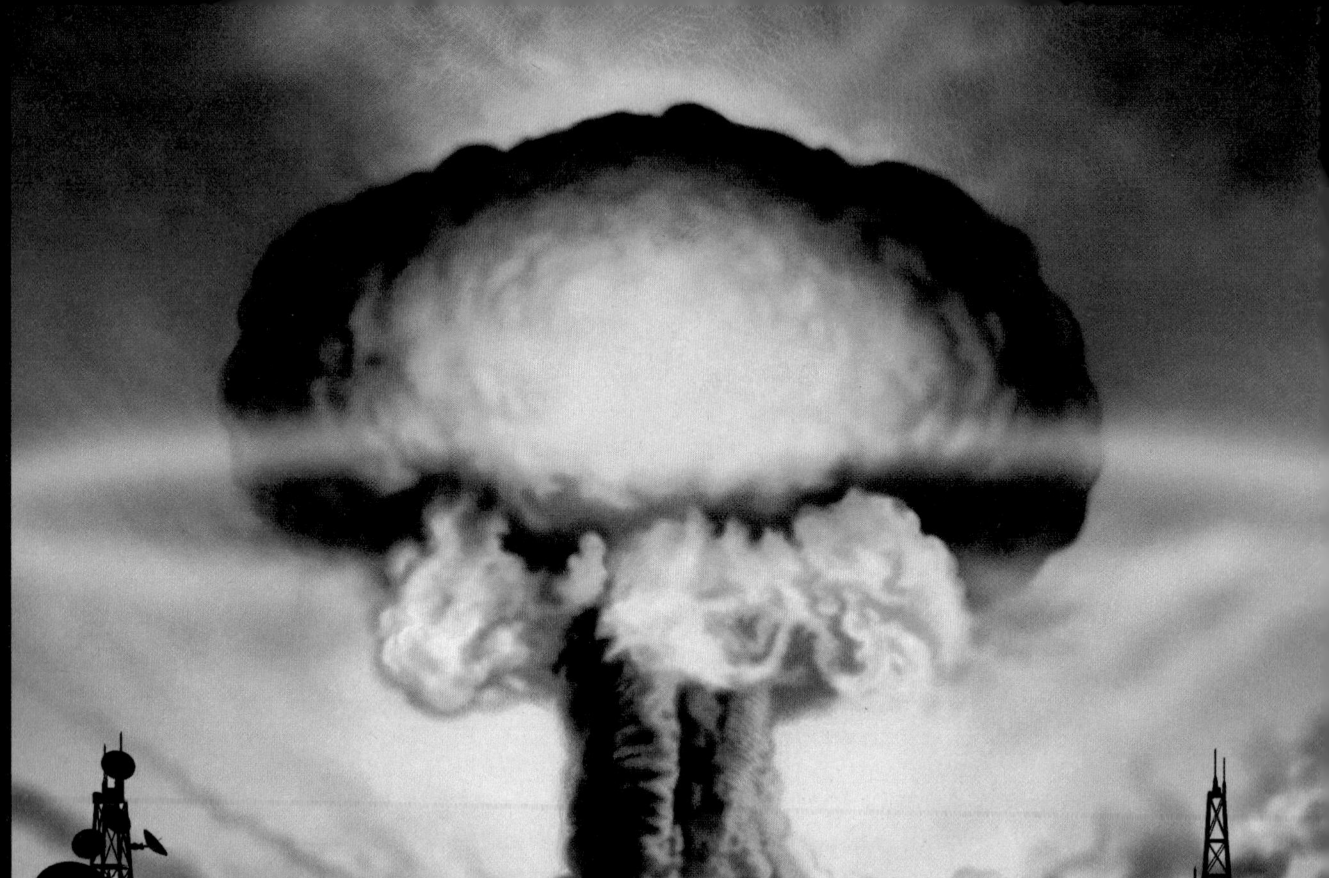

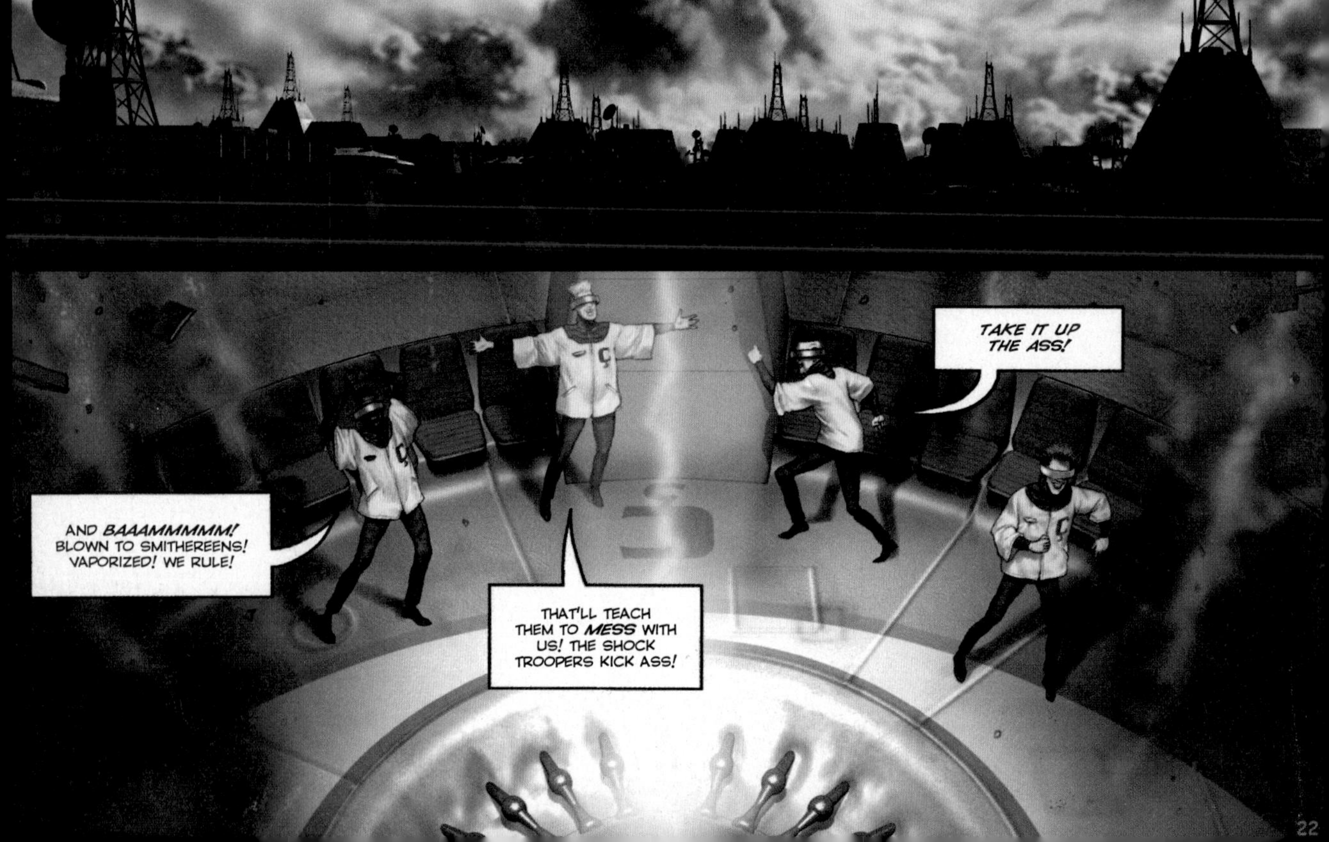

AND BAAAMMMMM! BLOWN TO SMITHEREENS! VAPORIZED! WE RULE!
THAT'LL TEACH THEM TO MESS WITH US! THE SHOCK TROOPERS KICK ASS!
TAKE IT UP THE ASS!

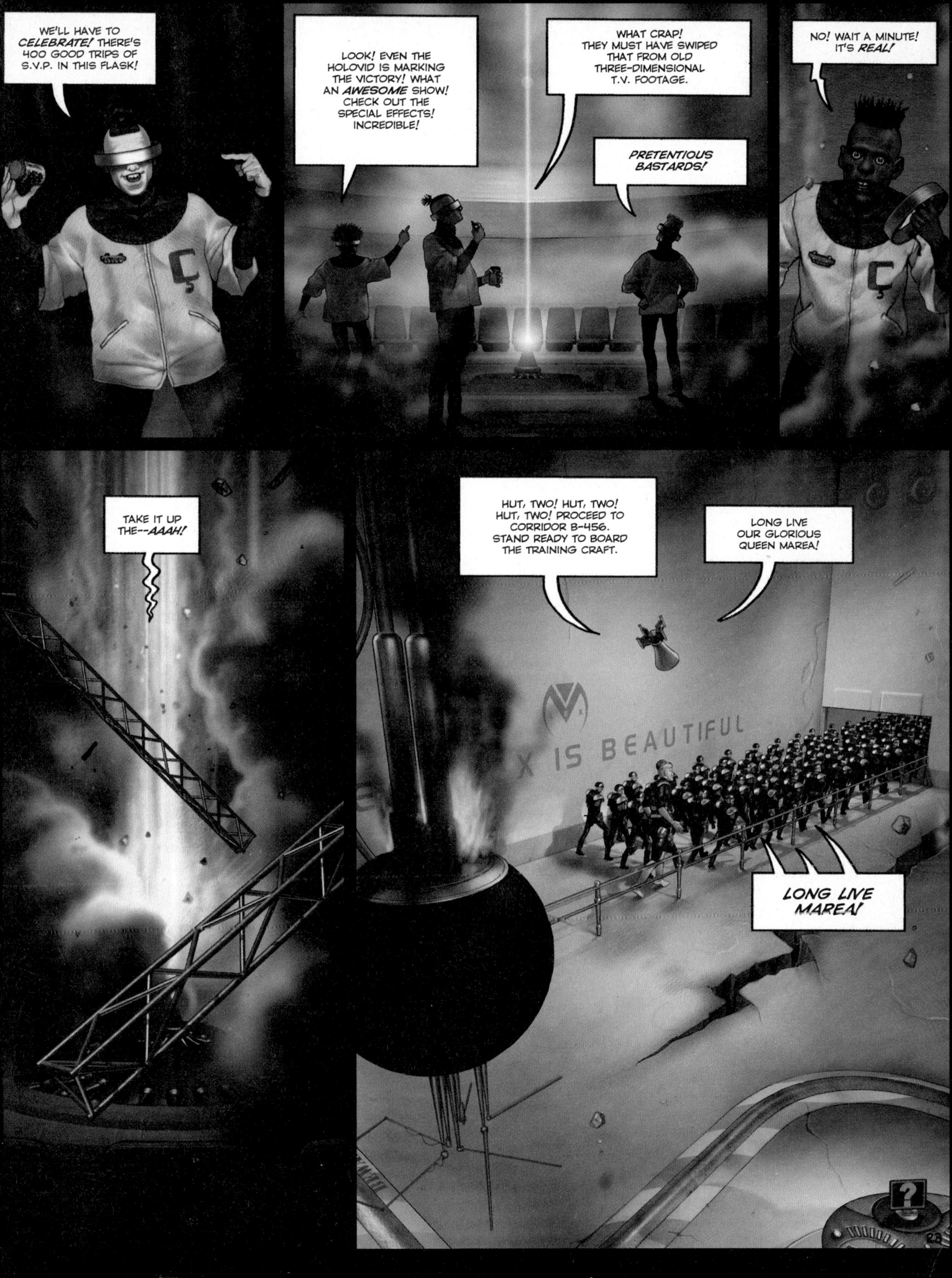

WE'LL HAVE TO CELEBRATE! THERE'S 400 GOOD TRIPS OF S.V.P. IN THIS FLASK!
LOOK! EVEN THE HOLOVID IS MARKING THE VICTORY! WHAT AN AWESOME SHOW! CHECK OUT THE SPECIAL EFFECTS! INCREDIBLE!
WHAT CRAP! THEY MUST HAVE SWIPED THAT FROM OLD THREE-DIMENSIONAL T.V. FOOTAGE.
PRETENTIOUS BASTARDS!
NO! WAIT A MINUTE! IT'S REAL!
TAKE IT UP THE--AAAH!
HUT, TWO! HUT, TWO! HUT, TWO! PROCEED TO CORRIDOR B-456. STAND READY TO BOARD THE TRAINING CRAFT.
LONG LIVE OUR GLORIOUS QUEEN MAREA!
X IS BEAUTIFUL
LONG LIVE MAREA!

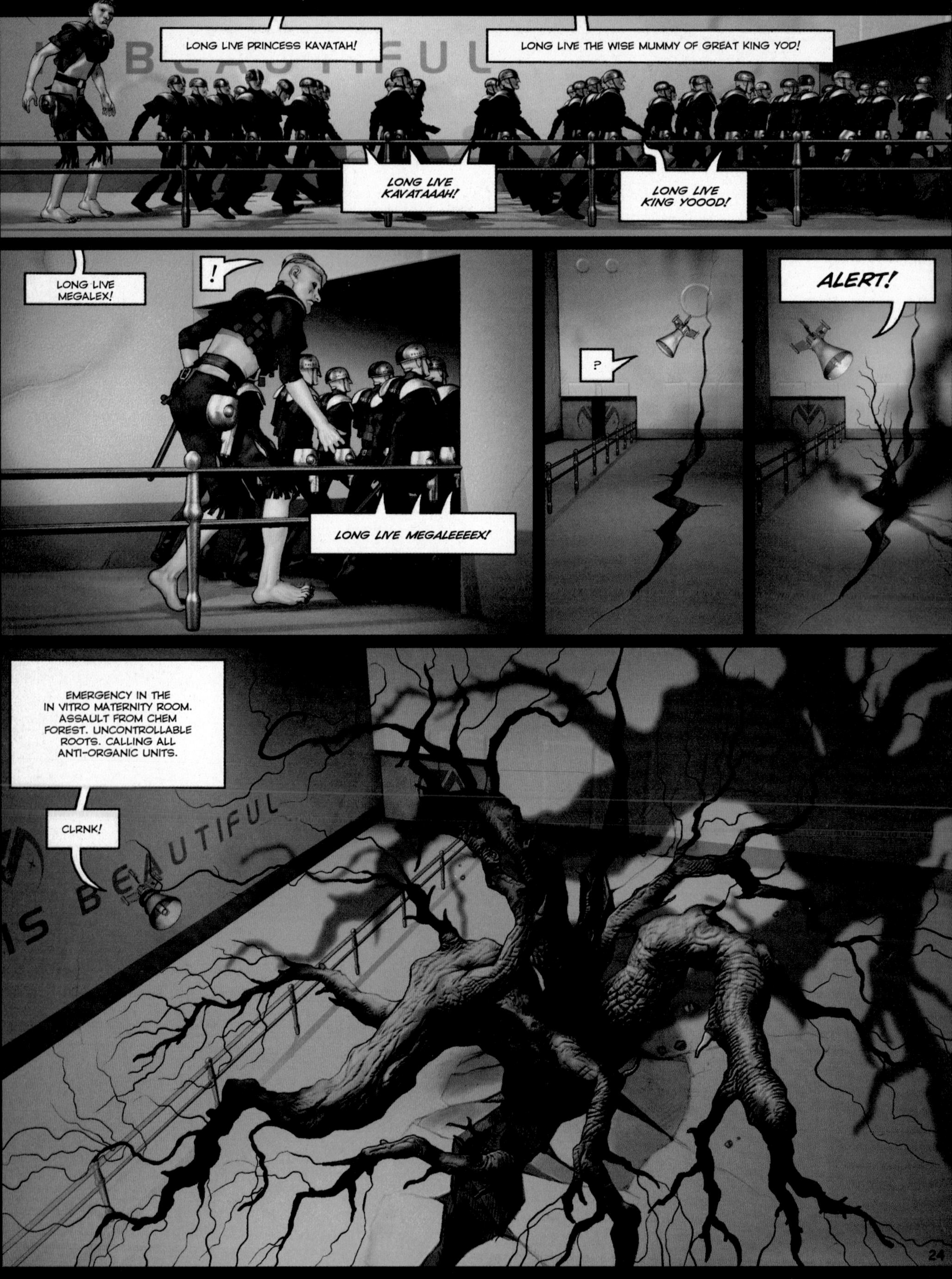

LONG LIVE PRINCESS KAVATAH!
LONG LIVE THE WISE MUMMY OF GREAT KING YOD!
LONG LIVE KAVATAAAH!
LONG LIVE KING YOOOD!
LONG LIVE MEGALEX!
!
LONG LIVE MEGALEEEEX!
?
ALERT!
EMERGENCY IN THE IN VITRO MATERNITY ROOM. ASSAULT FROM CHEM FOREST. UNCONTROLLABLE ROOTS. CALLING ALL ANTI-ORGANIC UNITS.
CLRNK!
IS BEAUTIFUL
24

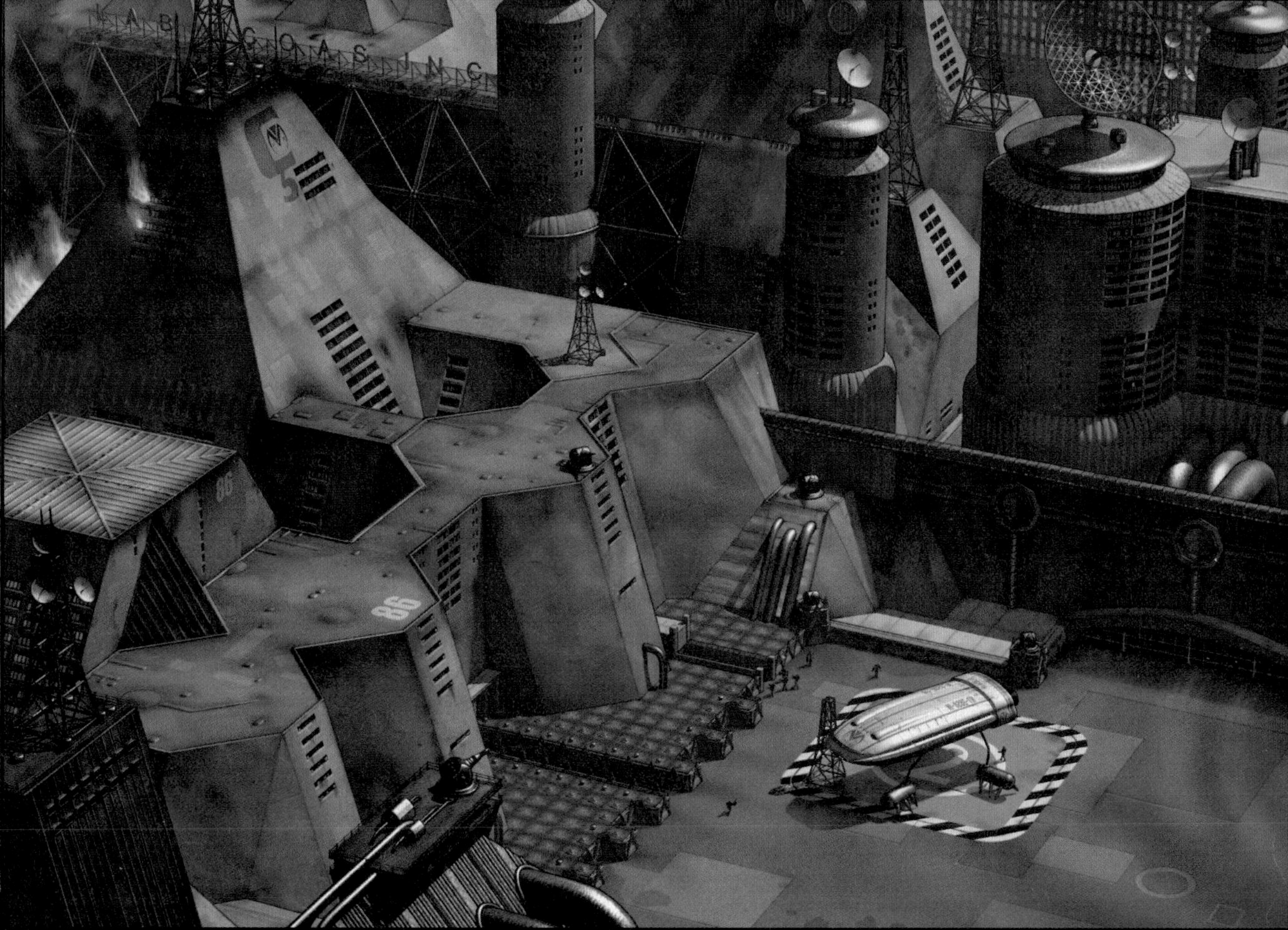

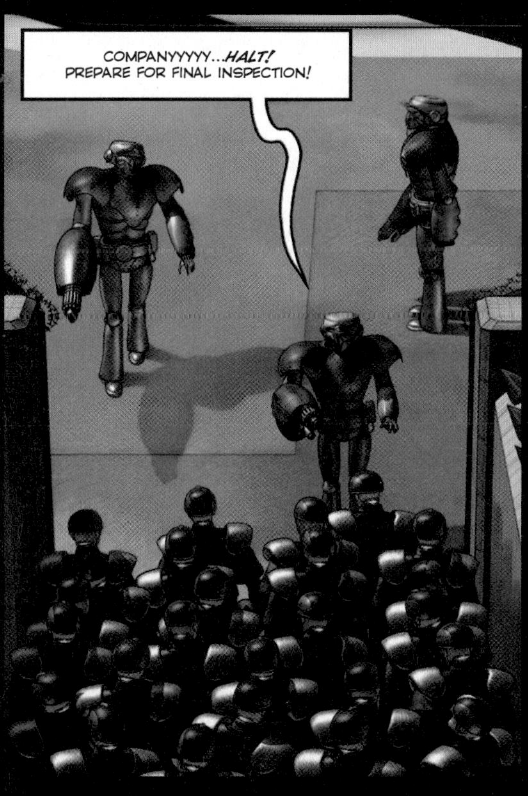
COMPANYYYYY...**HALT!**
PREPARE FOR FINAL INSPECTION!

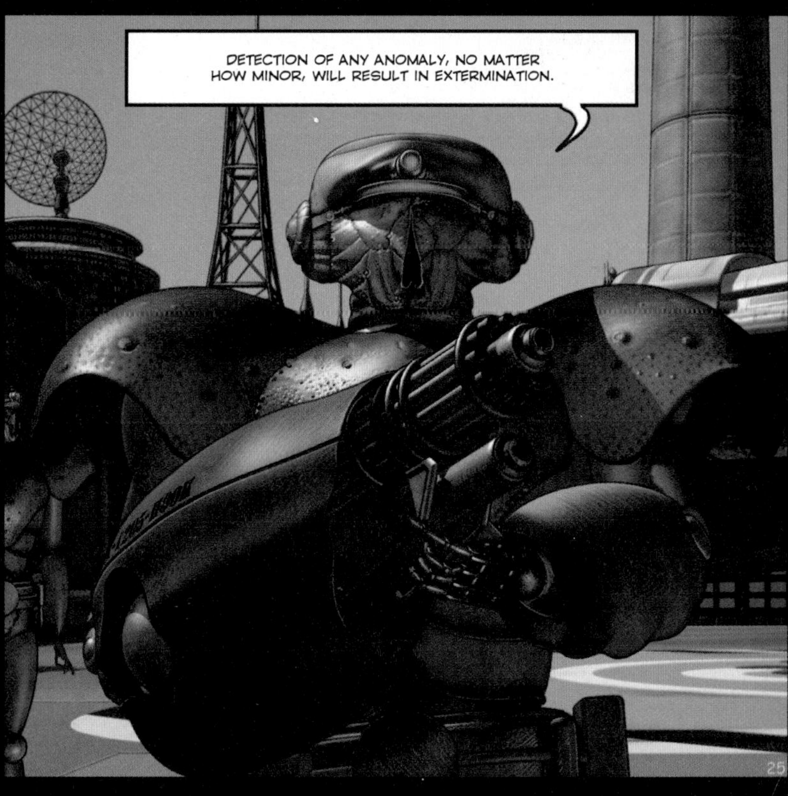
DETECTION OF ANY ANOMALY, NO MATTER HOW MINOR, WILL RESULT IN EXTERMINATION.

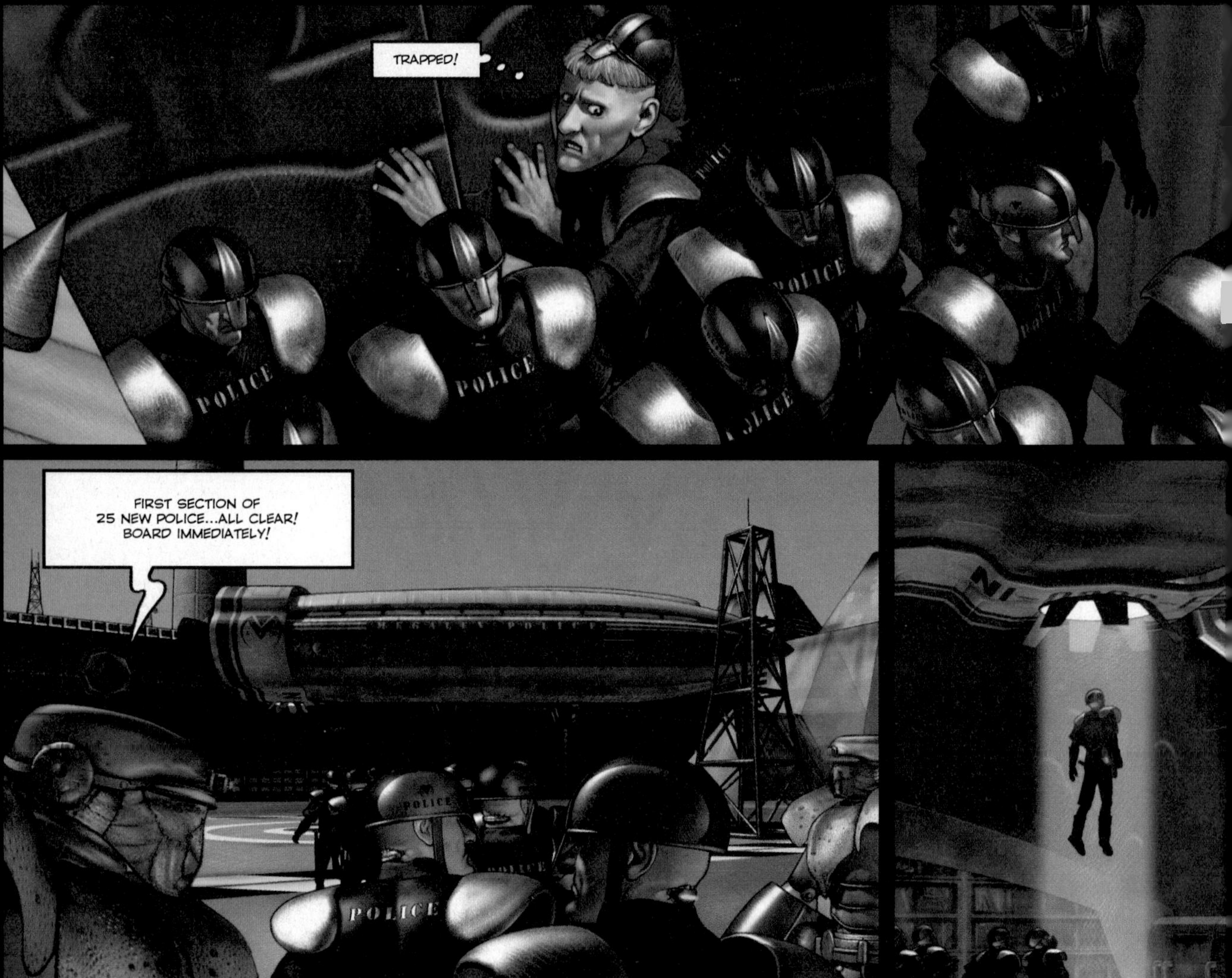
TRAPPED!
POLICE
POLICE
POLICE
FIRST SECTION OF 25 NEW POLICE...ALL CLEAR! BOARD IMMEDIATELY!
POLICE
POLICE
WELCOME TO MY WOMB. PLEASE FILL SEATS 1 TO 25. THANK YOU.
26

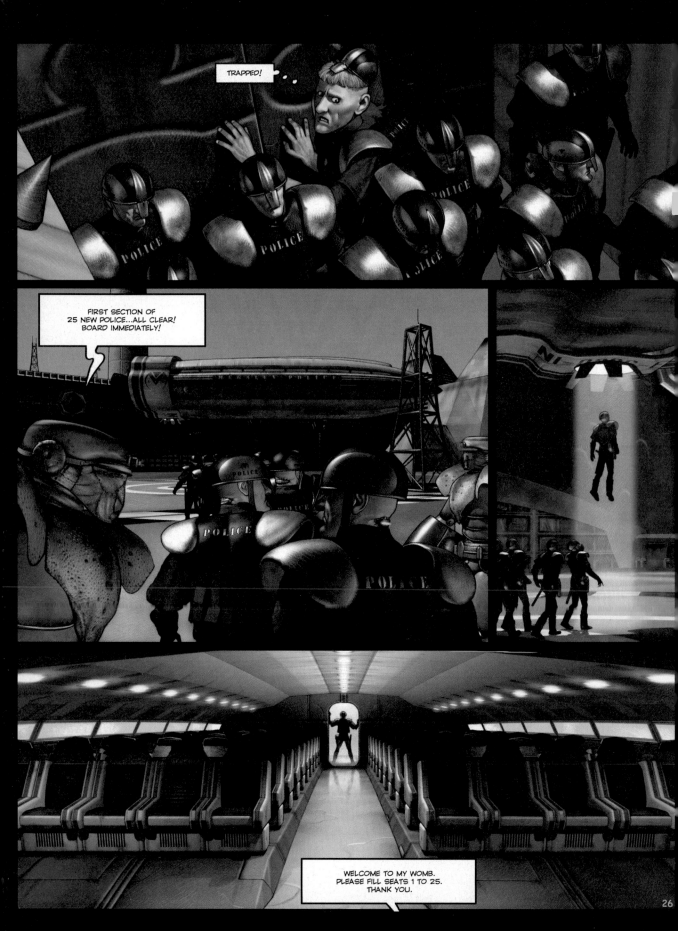

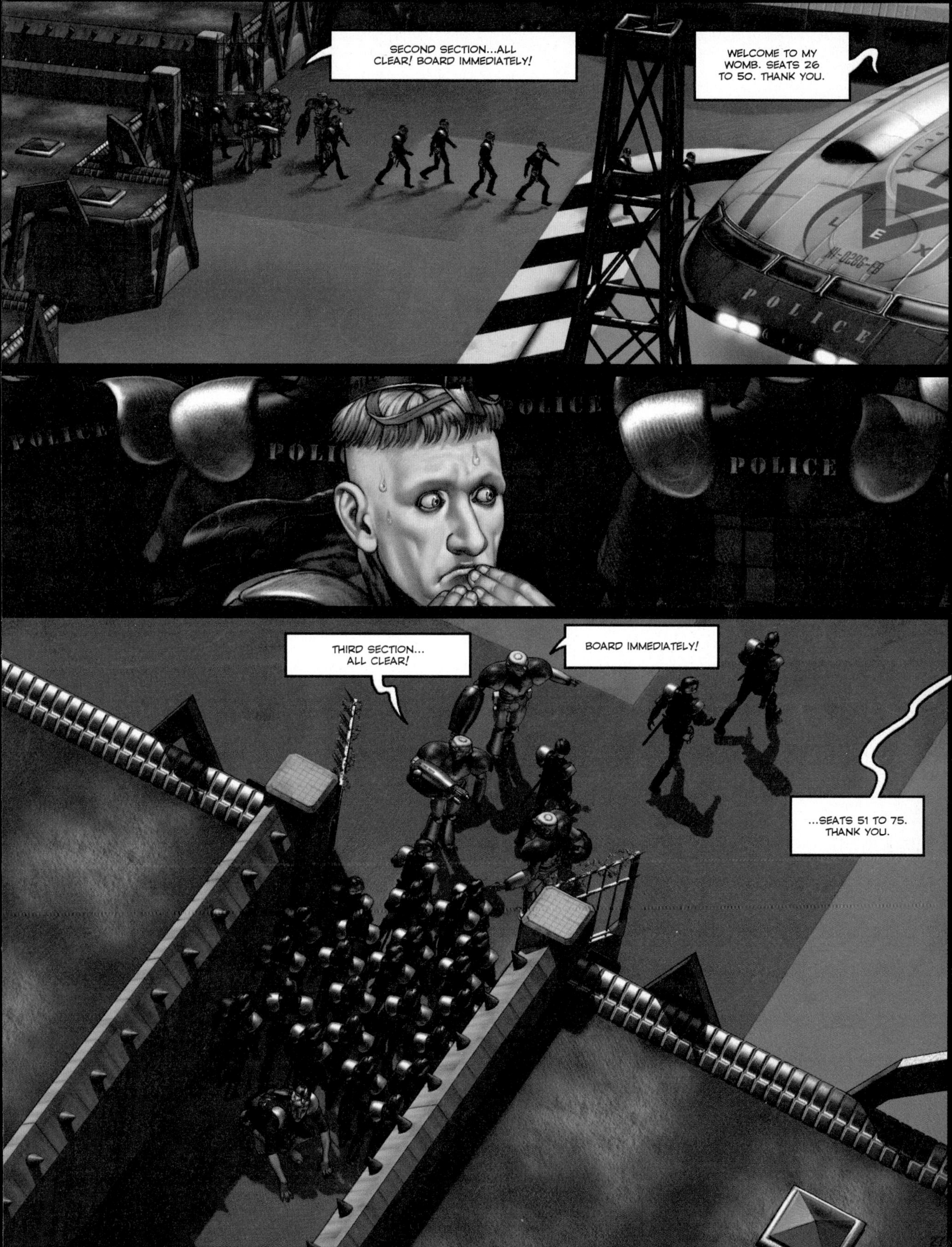
SECOND SECTION...ALL CLEAR! BOARD IMMEDIATELY!
WELCOME TO MY WOMB. SEATS 26 TO 50. THANK YOU.
POLICE
POLICE
POLICE
THIRD SECTION... ALL CLEAR!
BOARD IMMEDIATELY!
...SEATS 51 TO 75. THANK YOU.

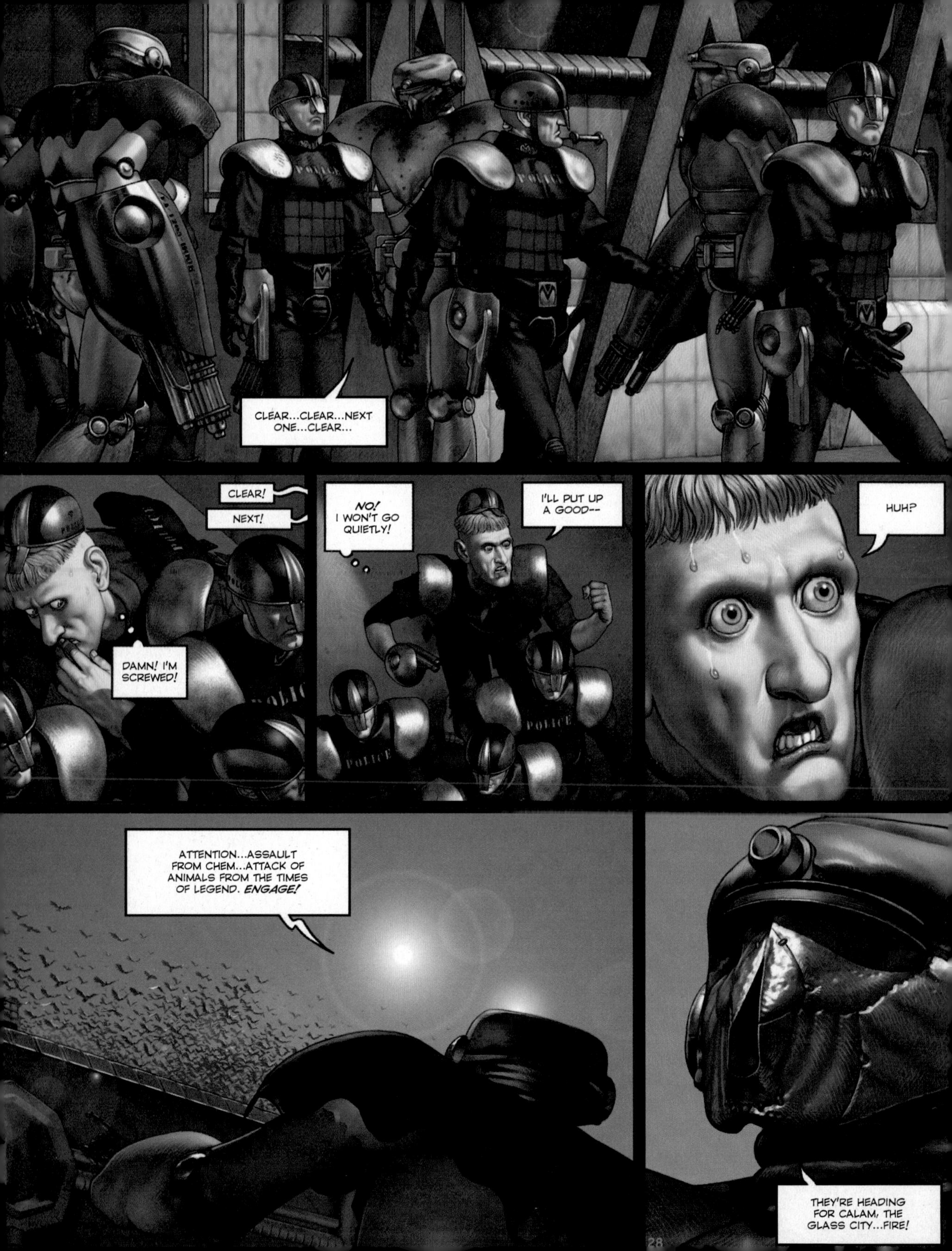
CLEAR...CLEAR...NEXT ONE...CLEAR...
CLEAR!
NEXT!
DAMN! I'M SCREWED!
NO! I WON'T GO QUIETLY!
I'LL PUT UP A GOOD--
HUH?
ATTENTION...ASSAULT FROM CHEM...ATTACK OF ANIMALS FROM THE TIMES OF LEGEND. ENGAGE!
THEY'RE HEADING FOR CALAM, THE GLASS CITY...FIRE!

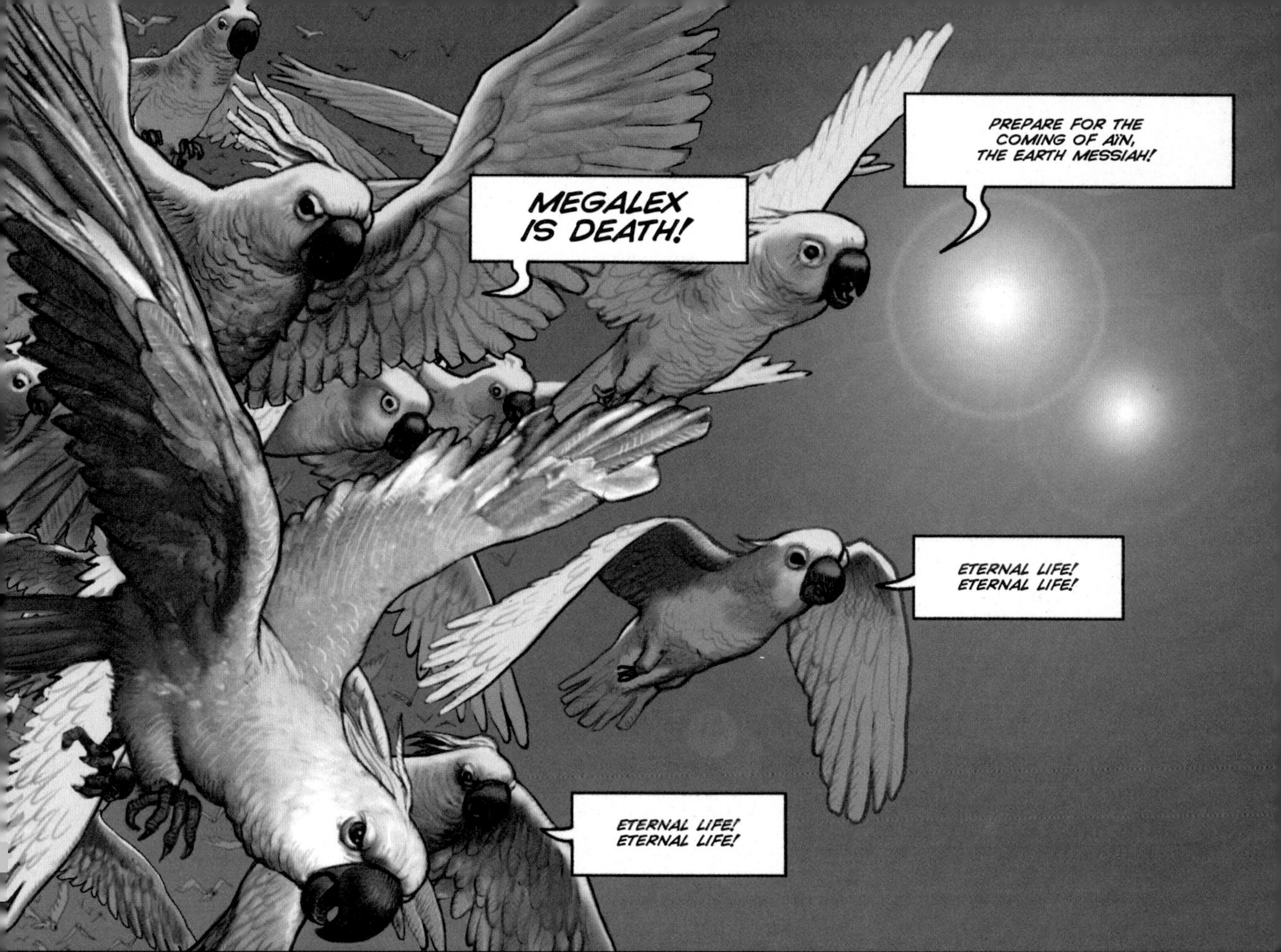
MEGALEX IS DEATH!
PREPARE FOR THE COMING OF AÏN, THE EARTH MESSIAH!
ETERNAL LIFE! ETERNAL LIFE!
ETERNAL LIFE! ETERNAL LIFE!

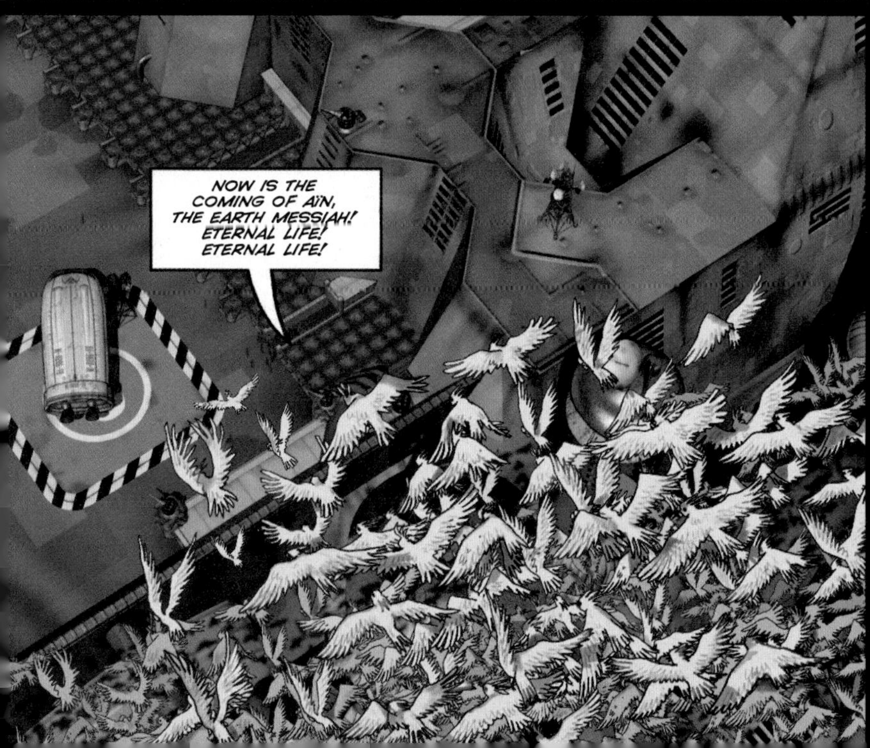
NOW IS THE COMING OF AÏN, THE EARTH MESSIAH! ETERNAL LIFE! ETERNAL LIFE!

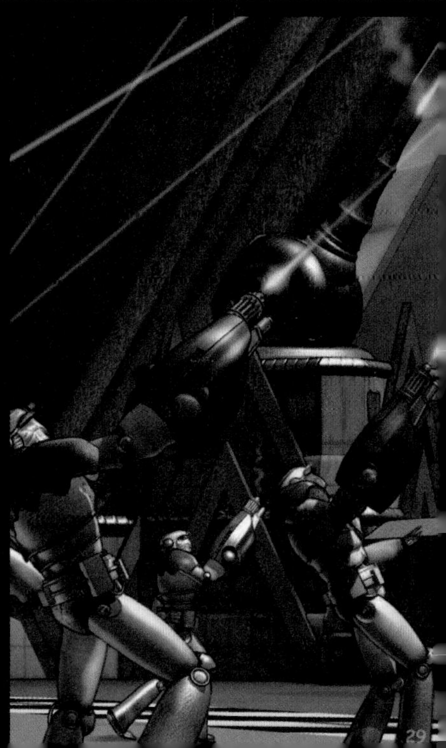

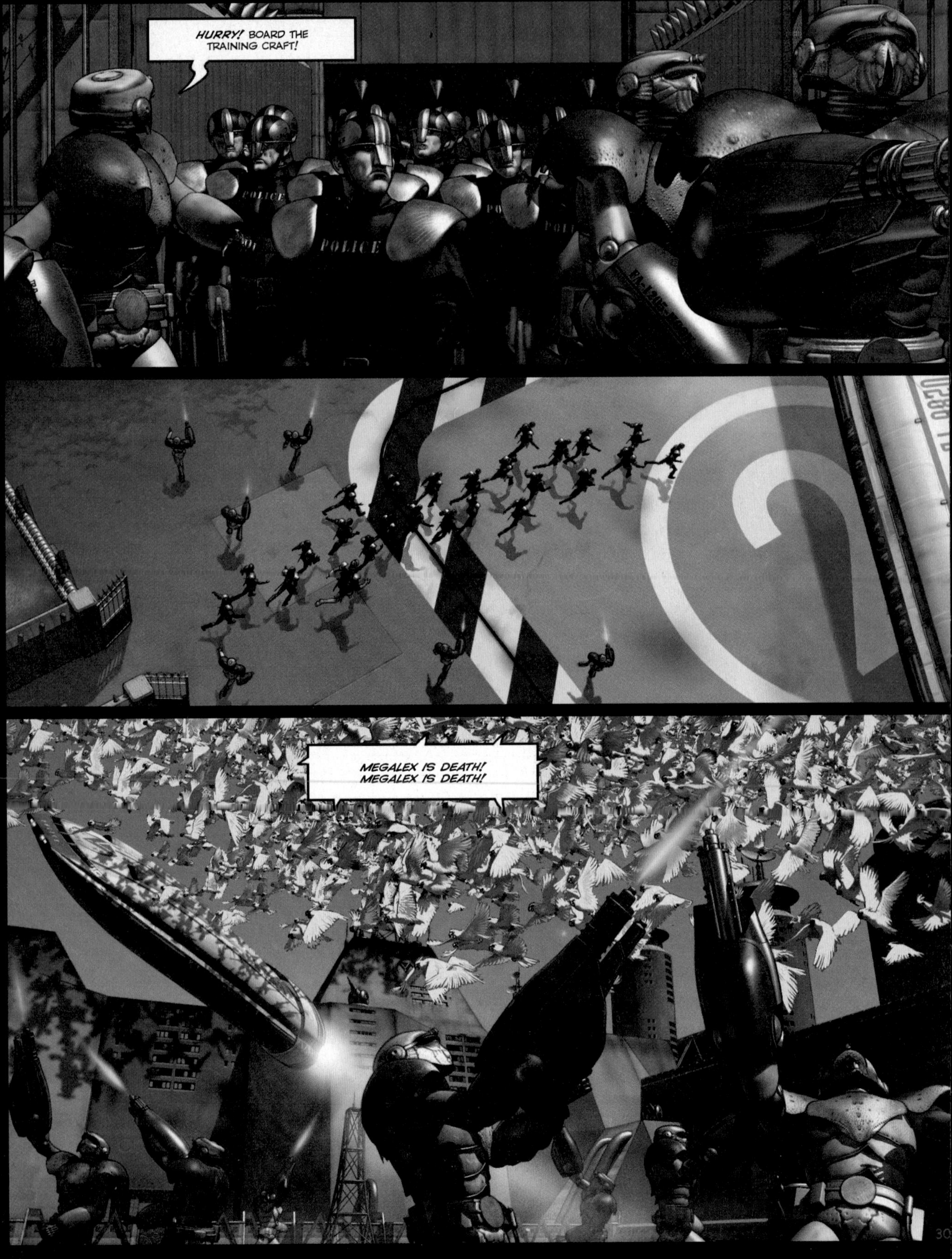
HURRY! BOARD THE TRAINING CRAFT!
MEGALEX IS DEATH! MEGALEX IS DEATH!

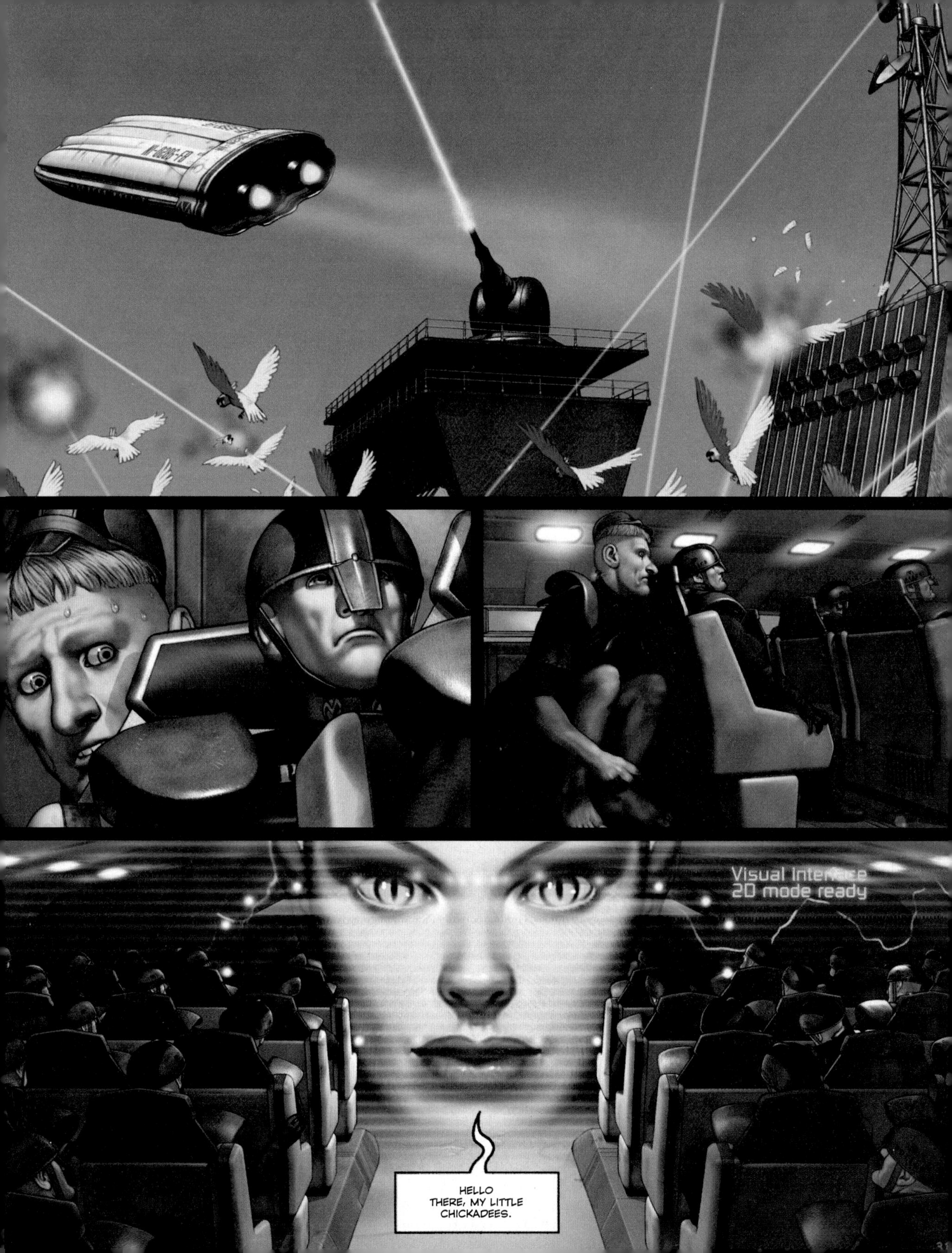
Visual Interface
2D mode ready
HELLO THERE, MY LITTLE CHICKADEES.

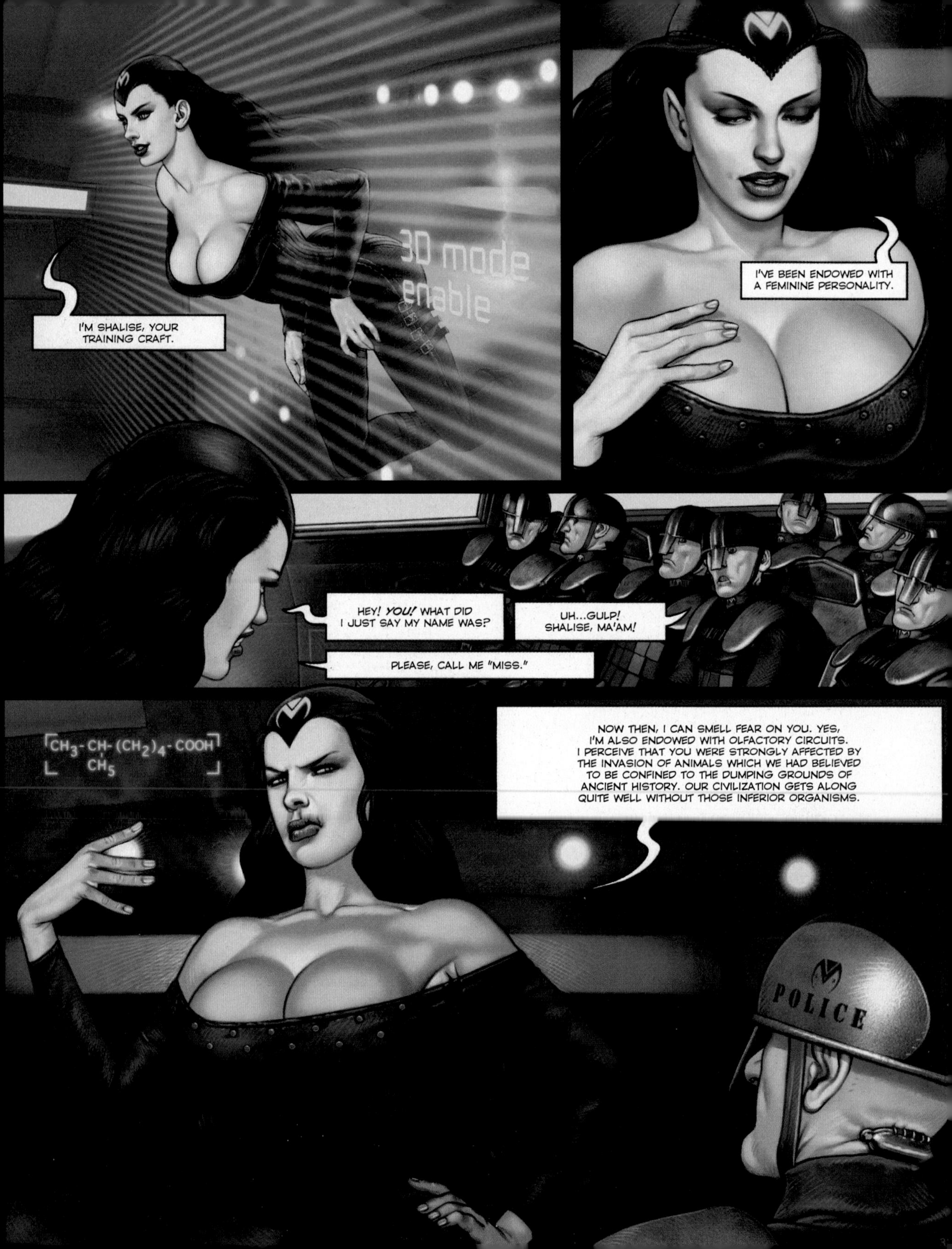
3D mode enable
I'M SHALISE, YOUR TRAINING CRAFT.
I'VE BEEN ENDOWED WITH A FEMININE PERSONALITY.
HEY! *YOU!* WHAT DID I JUST SAY MY NAME WAS?
UH...GULP! SHALISE, MA'AM!
PLEASE, CALL ME "MISS."
CH_3-CH-$(CH_2)_4$-COOH
CH_5
NOW THEN, I CAN SMELL FEAR ON YOU. YES, I'M ALSO ENDOWED WITH OLFACTORY CIRCUITS. I PERCEIVE THAT YOU WERE STRONGLY AFFECTED BY THE INVASION OF ANIMALS WHICH WE HAD BELIEVED TO BE CONFINED TO THE DUMPING GROUNDS OF ANCIENT HISTORY. OUR CIVILIZATION GETS ALONG QUITE WELL WITHOUT THOSE INFERIOR ORGANISMS.
POLICE

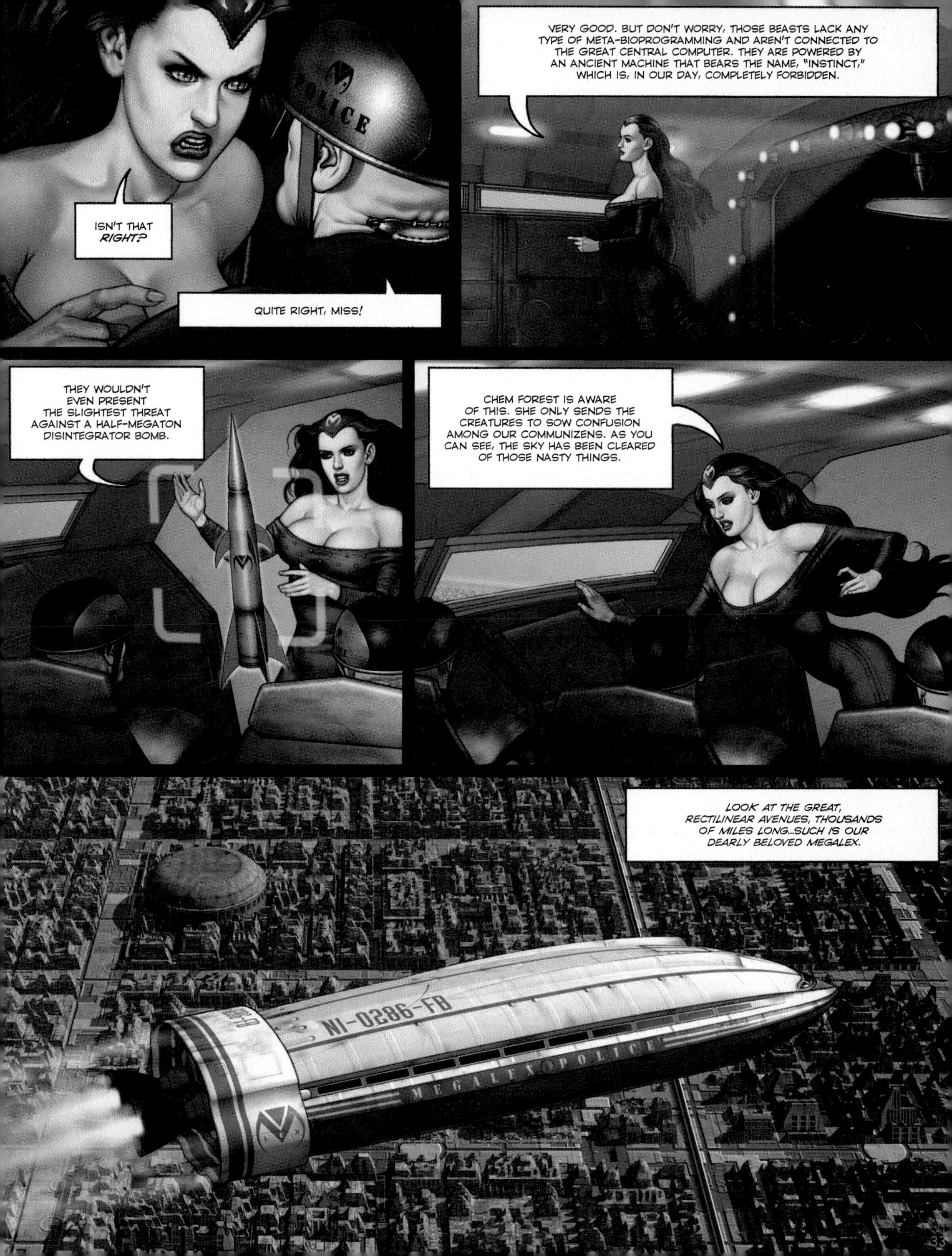

ISN'T THAT *RIGHT?*
QUITE RIGHT, MISS!
VERY GOOD. BUT DON'T WORRY, THOSE BEASTS LACK ANY TYPE OF META-BIOPROGRAMMING AND AREN'T CONNECTED TO THE GREAT CENTRAL COMPUTER. THEY ARE POWERED BY AN ANCIENT MACHINE THAT BEARS THE NAME, "INSTINCT," WHICH IS, IN OUR DAY, COMPLETELY FORBIDDEN.
POLICE
THEY WOULDN'T EVEN PRESENT THE SLIGHTEST THREAT AGAINST A HALF-MEGATON DISINTEGRATOR BOMB.
CHEM FOREST IS AWARE OF THIS. SHE ONLY SENDS THE CREATURES TO SOW CONFUSION AMONG OUR COMMUNIZENS. AS YOU CAN SEE, THE SKY HAS BEEN CLEARED OF THOSE NASTY THINGS.
LOOK AT THE GREAT, RECTILINEAR AVENUES, THOUSANDS OF MILES LONG...SUCH IS OUR DEARLY BELOVED MEGALEX.
NI-0286-FB
MEGALEX POLICE

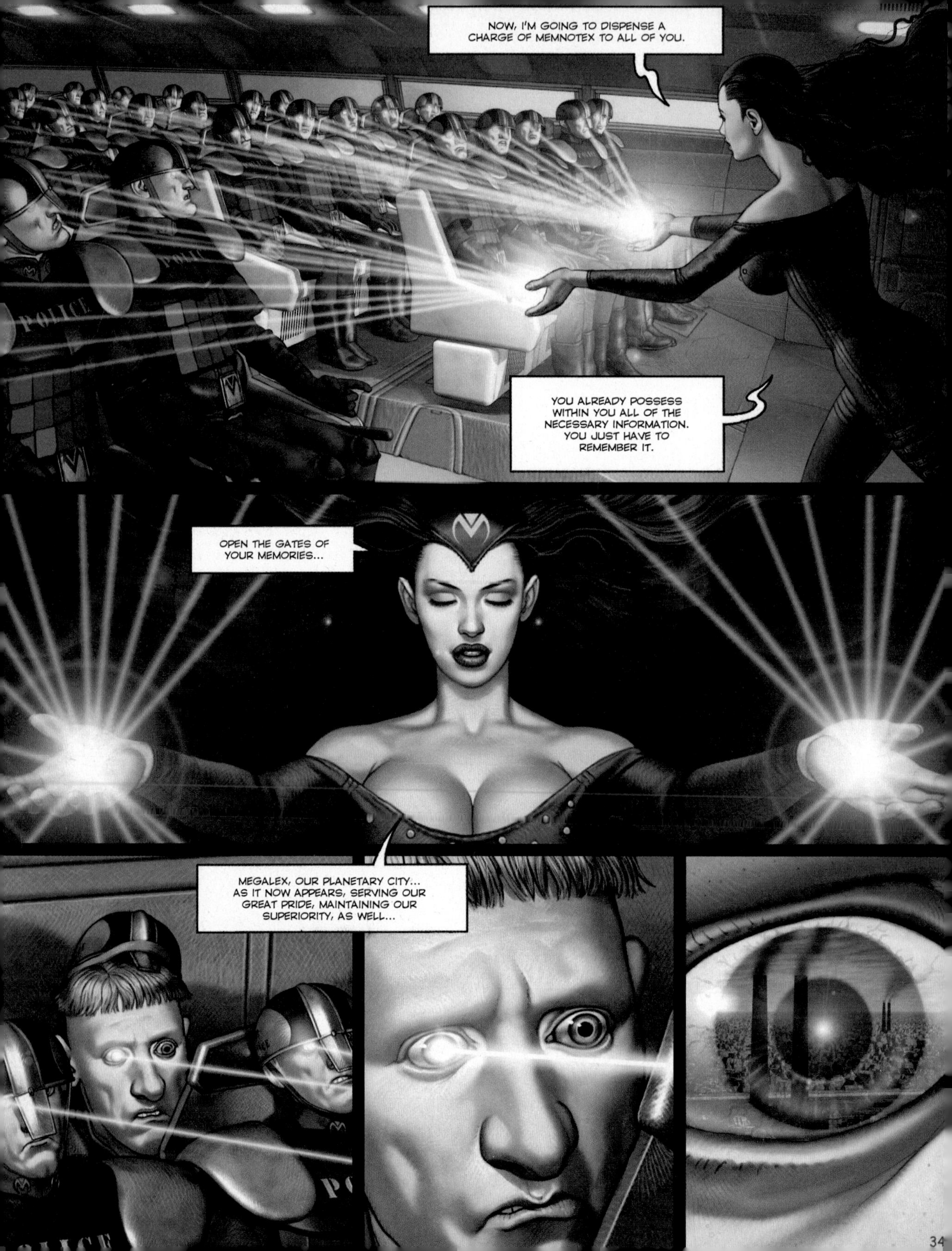
NOW, I'M GOING TO DISPENSE A CHARGE OF MEMNOTEX TO ALL OF YOU.
YOU ALREADY POSSESS WITHIN YOU ALL OF THE NECESSARY INFORMATION. YOU JUST HAVE TO REMEMBER IT.
OPEN THE GATES OF YOUR MEMORIES...
MEGALEX, OUR PLANETARY CITY... AS IT NOW APPEARS, SERVING OUR GREAT PRIDE, MAINTAINING OUR SUPERIORITY, AS WELL...

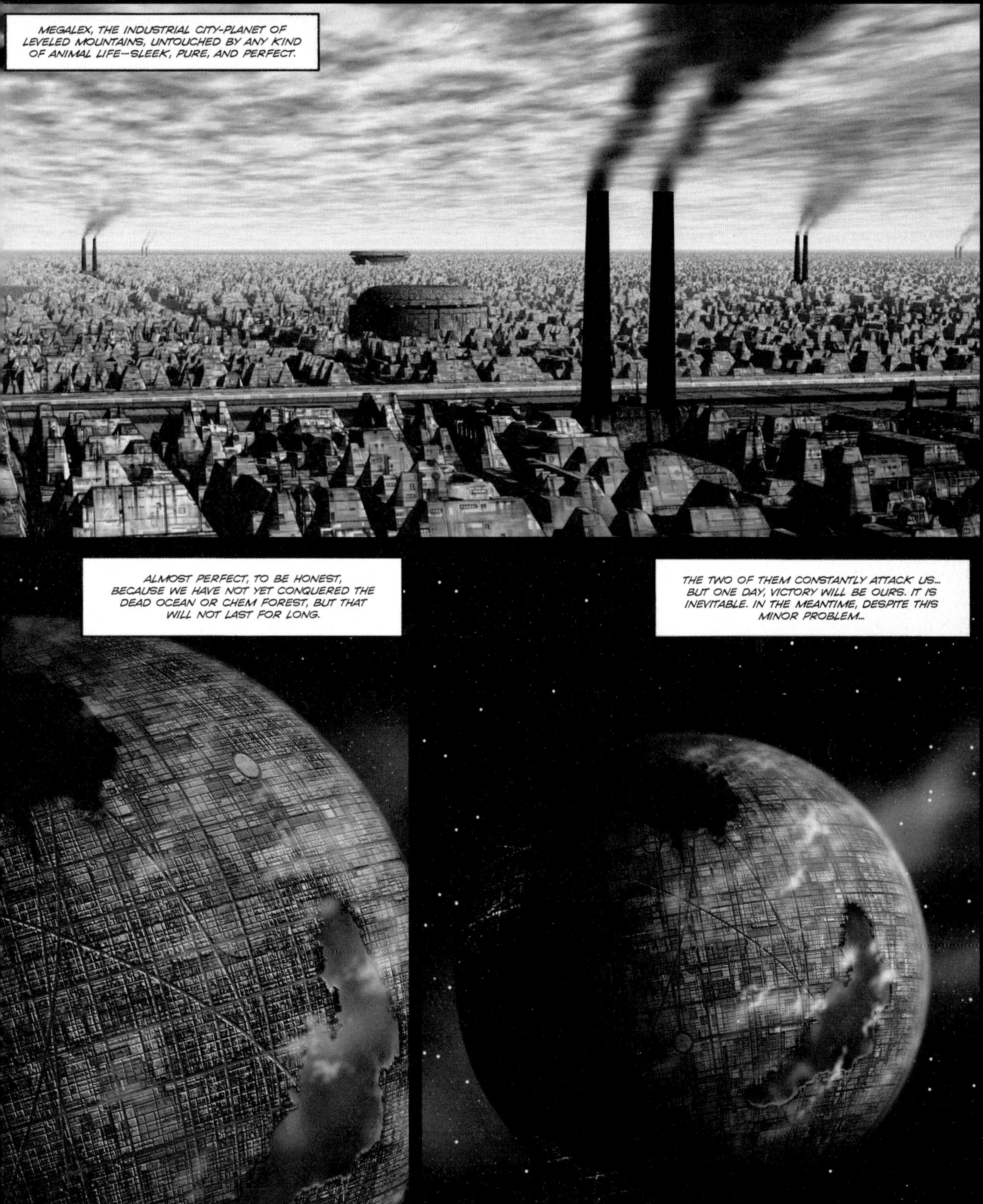
MEGALEX, THE INDUSTRIAL CITY-PLANET OF LEVELED MOUNTAINS, UNTOUCHED BY ANY KIND OF ANIMAL LIFE—SLEEK, PURE, AND PERFECT.
ALMOST PERFECT, TO BE HONEST, BECAUSE WE HAVE NOT YET CONQUERED THE DEAD OCEAN OR CHEM FOREST, BUT THAT WILL NOT LAST FOR LONG.
THE TWO OF THEM CONSTANTLY ATTACK US... BUT ONE DAY, VICTORY WILL BE OURS. IT IS INEVITABLE. IN THE MEANTIME, DESPITE THIS MINOR PROBLEM...

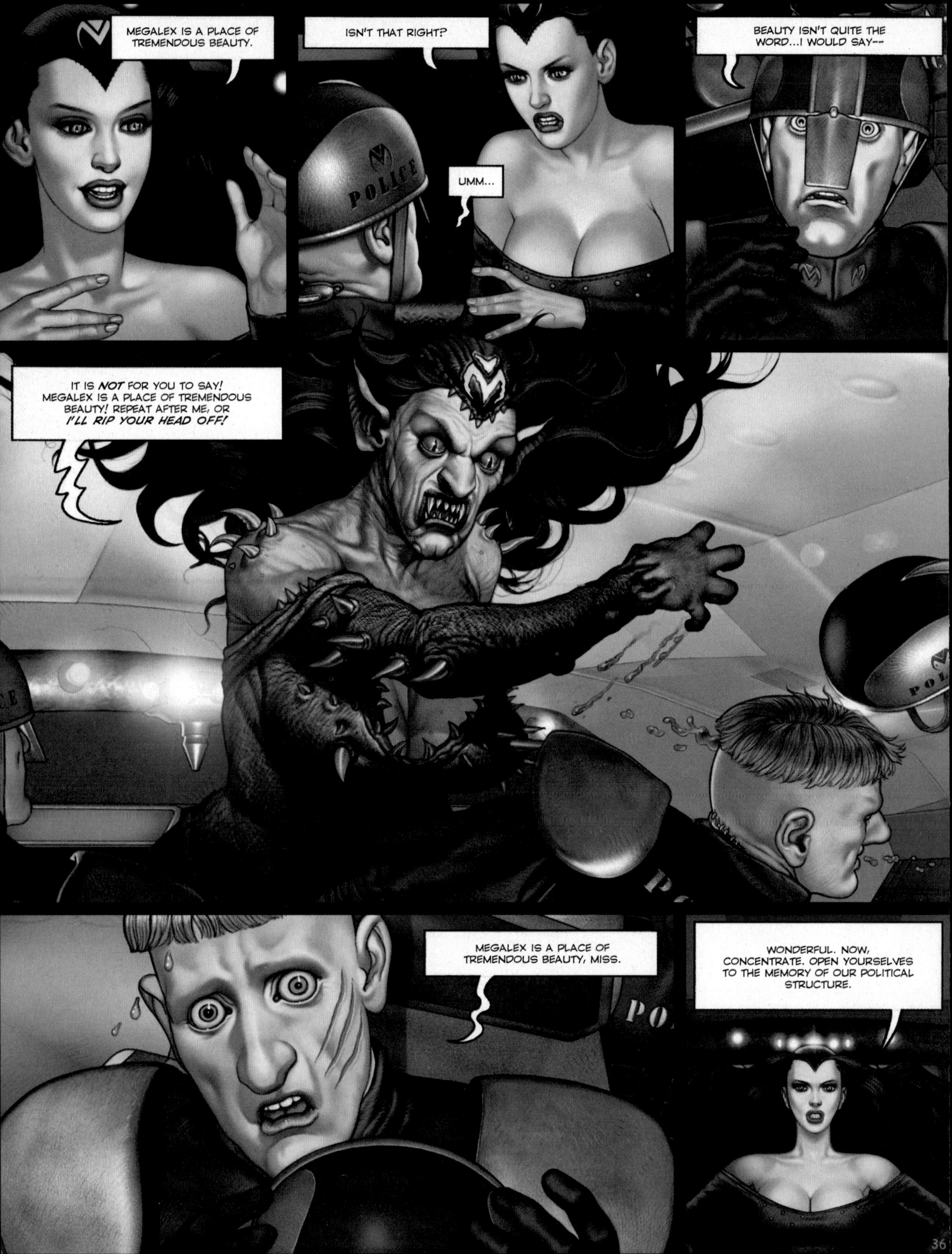

MEGALEX IS A PLACE OF TREMENDOUS BEAUTY.
ISN'T THAT RIGHT?
UMM...
BEAUTY ISN'T QUITE THE WORD...I WOULD SAY--
IT IS *NOT* FOR YOU TO SAY! MEGALEX IS A PLACE OF TREMENDOUS BEAUTY! REPEAT AFTER ME, OR *I'LL RIP YOUR HEAD OFF!*
MEGALEX IS A PLACE OF TREMENDOUS BEAUTY, MISS.
WONDERFUL. NOW, CONCENTRATE. OPEN YOURSELVES TO THE MEMORY OF OUR POLITICAL STRUCTURE.

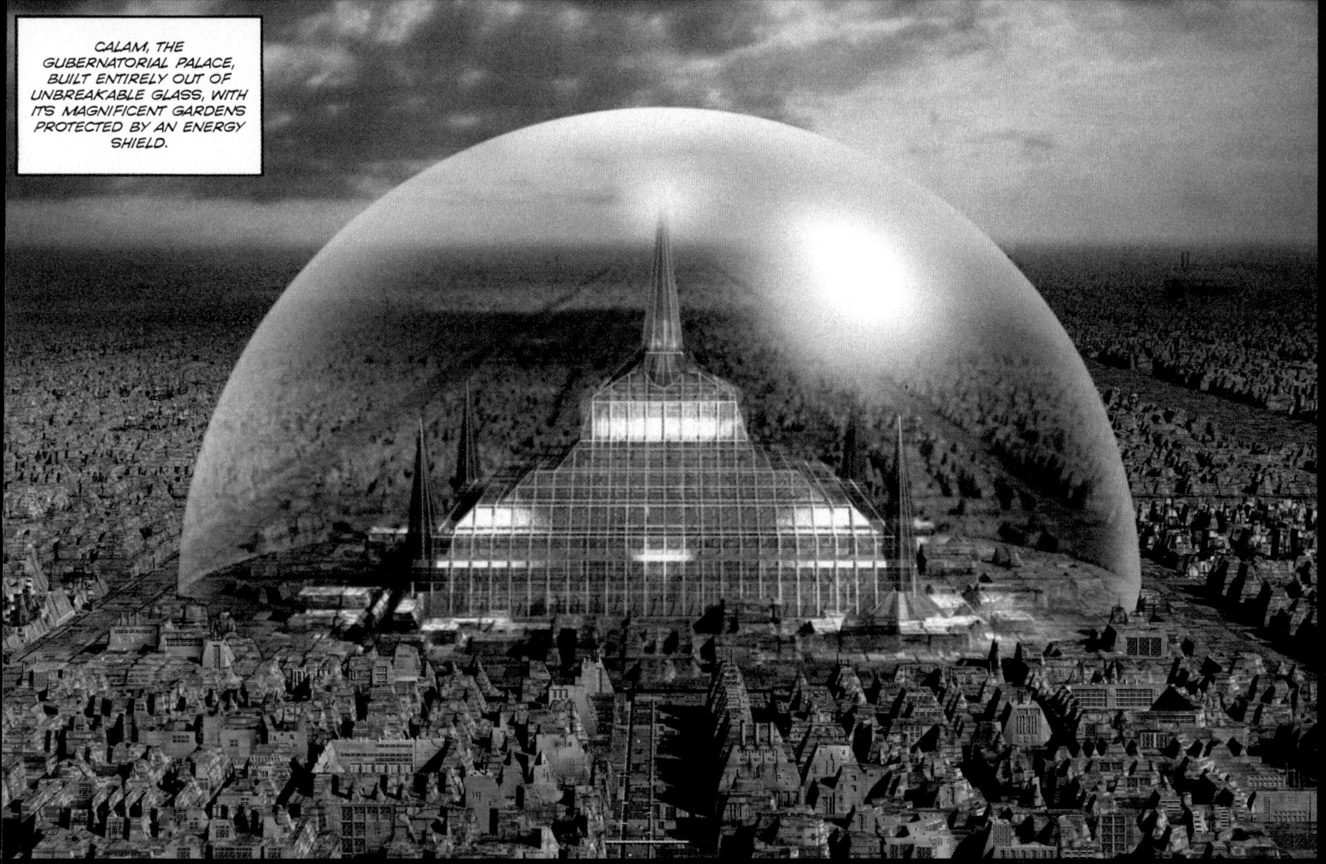
CALAM, THE GUBERNATORIAL PALACE, BUILT ENTIRELY OUT OF UNBREAKABLE GLASS, WITH ITS MAGNIFICENT GARDENS PROTECTED BY AN ENERGY SHIELD.

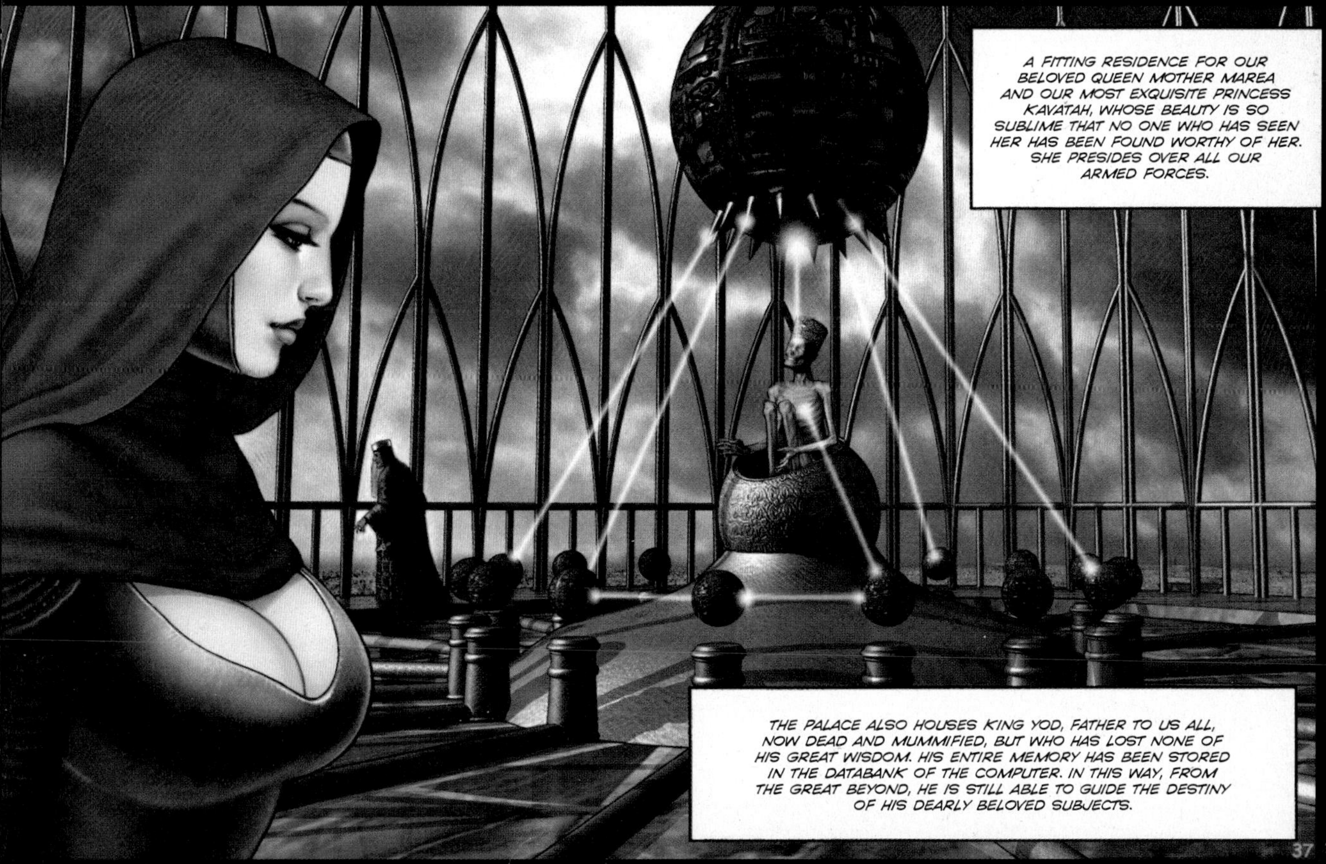
A FITTING RESIDENCE FOR OUR BELOVED QUEEN MOTHER MAREA AND OUR MOST EXQUISITE PRINCESS KAVATAH, WHOSE BEAUTY IS SO SUBLIME THAT NO ONE WHO HAS SEEN HER HAS BEEN FOUND WORTHY OF HER. SHE PRESIDES OVER ALL OUR ARMED FORCES.
THE PALACE ALSO HOUSES KING YOD, FATHER TO US ALL, NOW DEAD AND MUMMIFIED, BUT WHO HAS LOST NONE OF HIS GREAT WISDOM. HIS ENTIRE MEMORY HAS BEEN STORED IN THE DATABANK OF THE COMPUTER. IN THIS WAY, FROM THE GREAT BEYOND, HE IS STILL ABLE TO GUIDE THE DESTINY OF HIS DEARLY BELOVED SUBJECTS.
37

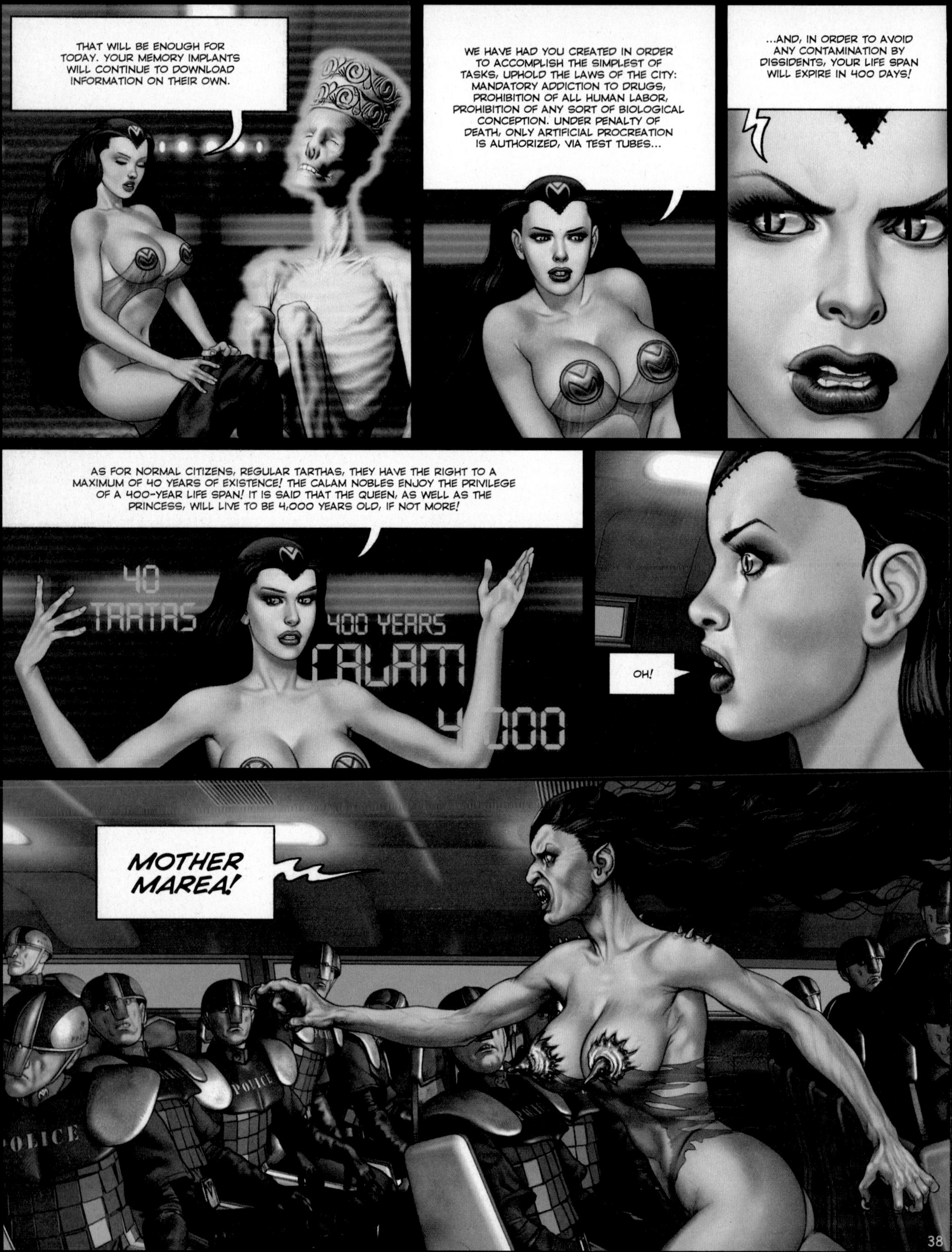
THAT WILL BE ENOUGH FOR TODAY. YOUR MEMORY IMPLANTS WILL CONTINUE TO DOWNLOAD INFORMATION ON THEIR OWN.
WE HAVE HAD YOU CREATED IN ORDER TO ACCOMPLISH THE SIMPLEST OF TASKS, UPHOLD THE LAWS OF THE CITY: MANDATORY ADDICTION TO DRUGS, PROHIBITION OF ALL HUMAN LABOR, PROHIBITION OF ANY SORT OF BIOLOGICAL CONCEPTION. UNDER PENALTY OF DEATH, ONLY ARTIFICIAL PROCREATION IS AUTHORIZED, VIA TEST TUBES...
...AND, IN ORDER TO AVOID ANY CONTAMINATION BY DISSIDENTS, YOUR LIFE SPAN WILL EXPIRE IN 400 DAYS!
AS FOR NORMAL CITIZENS, REGULAR TARTHAS, THEY HAVE THE RIGHT TO A MAXIMUM OF 40 YEARS OF EXISTENCE! THE CALAM NOBLES ENJOY THE PRIVILEGE OF A 400-YEAR LIFE SPAN! IT IS SAID THAT THE QUEEN, AS WELL AS THE PRINCESS, WILL LIVE TO BE 4,000 YEARS OLD, IF NOT MORE!
40
TARTAS
400 YEARS
CALAM
OH!
MOTHER MAREA!
POLICE

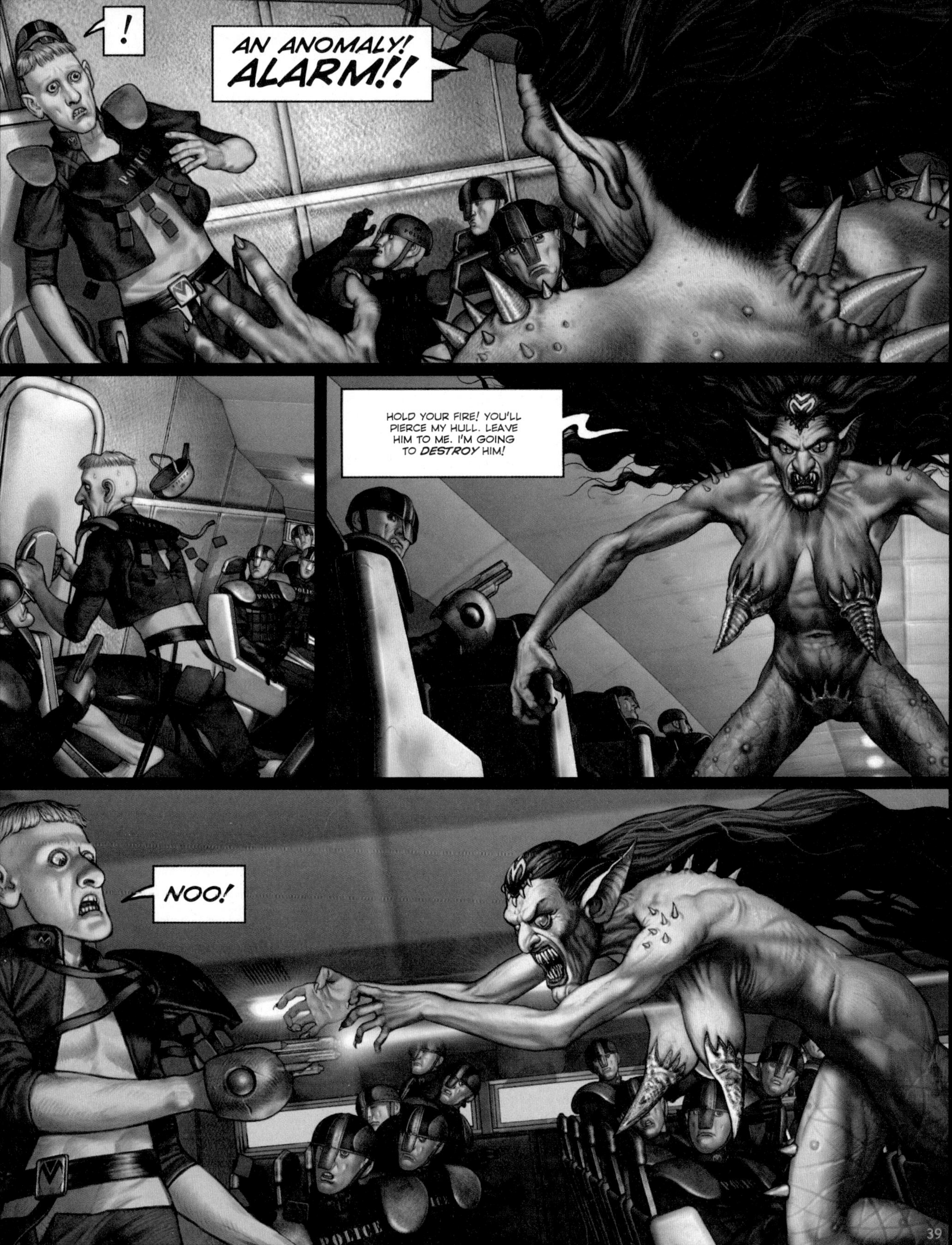
!
AN ANOMALY! ALARM!!
HOLD YOUR FIRE! YOU'LL PIERCE MY HULL. LEAVE HIM TO ME. I'M GOING TO *DESTROY* HIM!
NOO!
POLICE
39

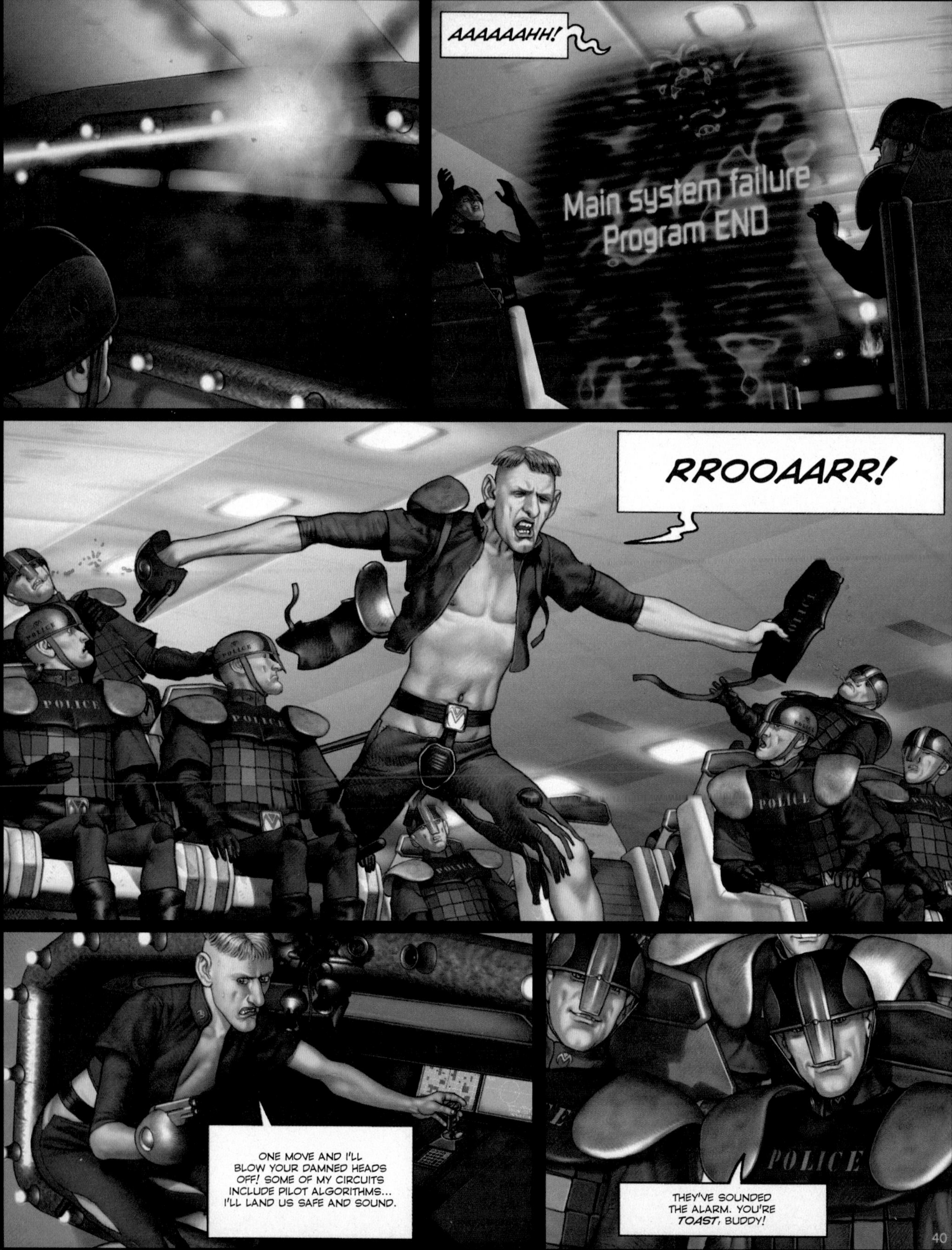
AAAAAAHH!
Main system failure
Program END
RROOAARR!
ONE MOVE AND I'LL BLOW YOUR DAMNED HEADS OFF! SOME OF MY CIRCUITS INCLUDE PILOT ALGORITHMS... I'LL LAND US SAFE AND SOUND.
THEY'VE SOUNDED THE ALARM. YOU'RE *TOAST*, BUDDY!
40

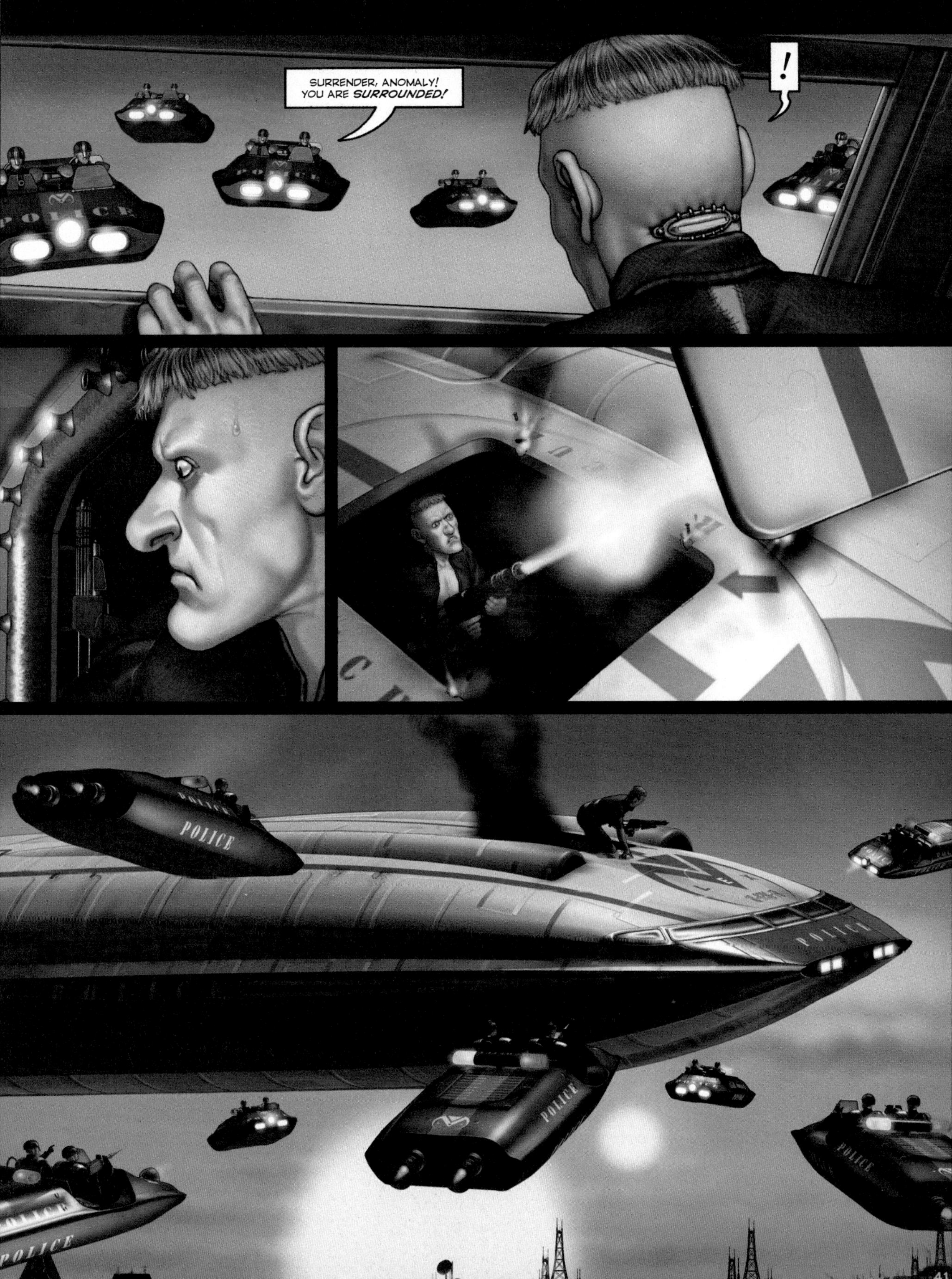
SURRENDER, ANOMALY! YOU ARE SURROUNDED!
!
POLICE
POLICE
POLICE
POLICE

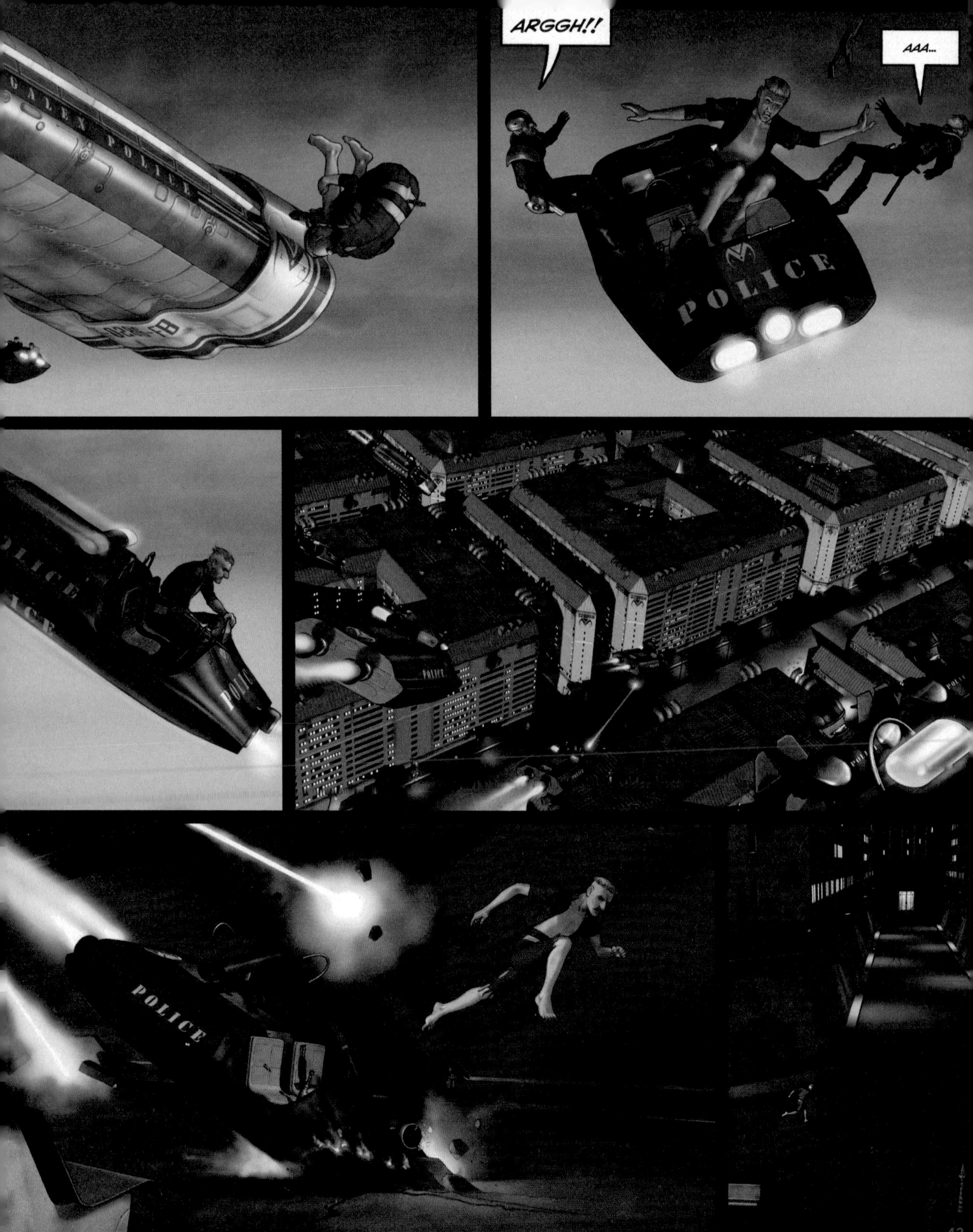
ARGGH!!
AAA...

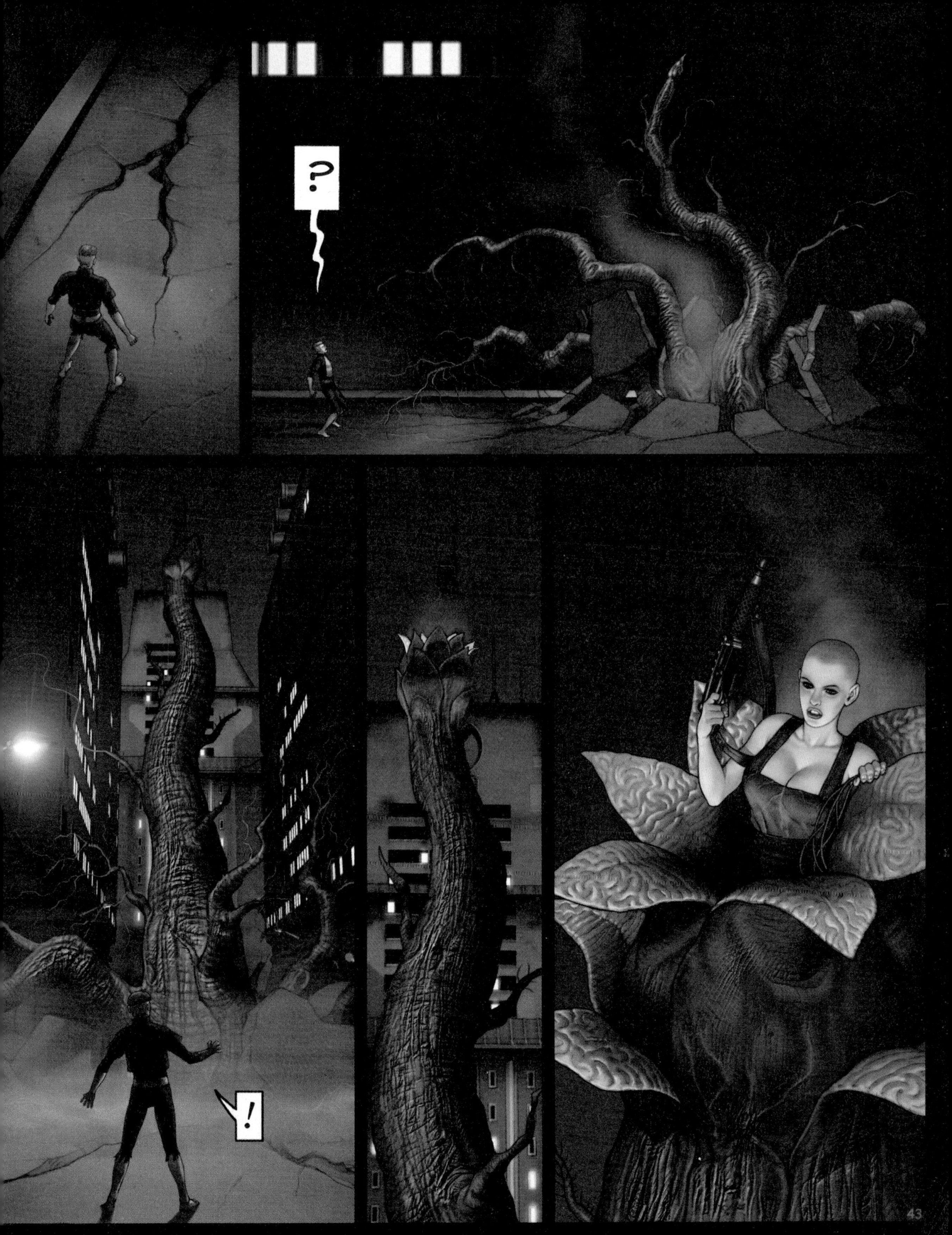
?
!

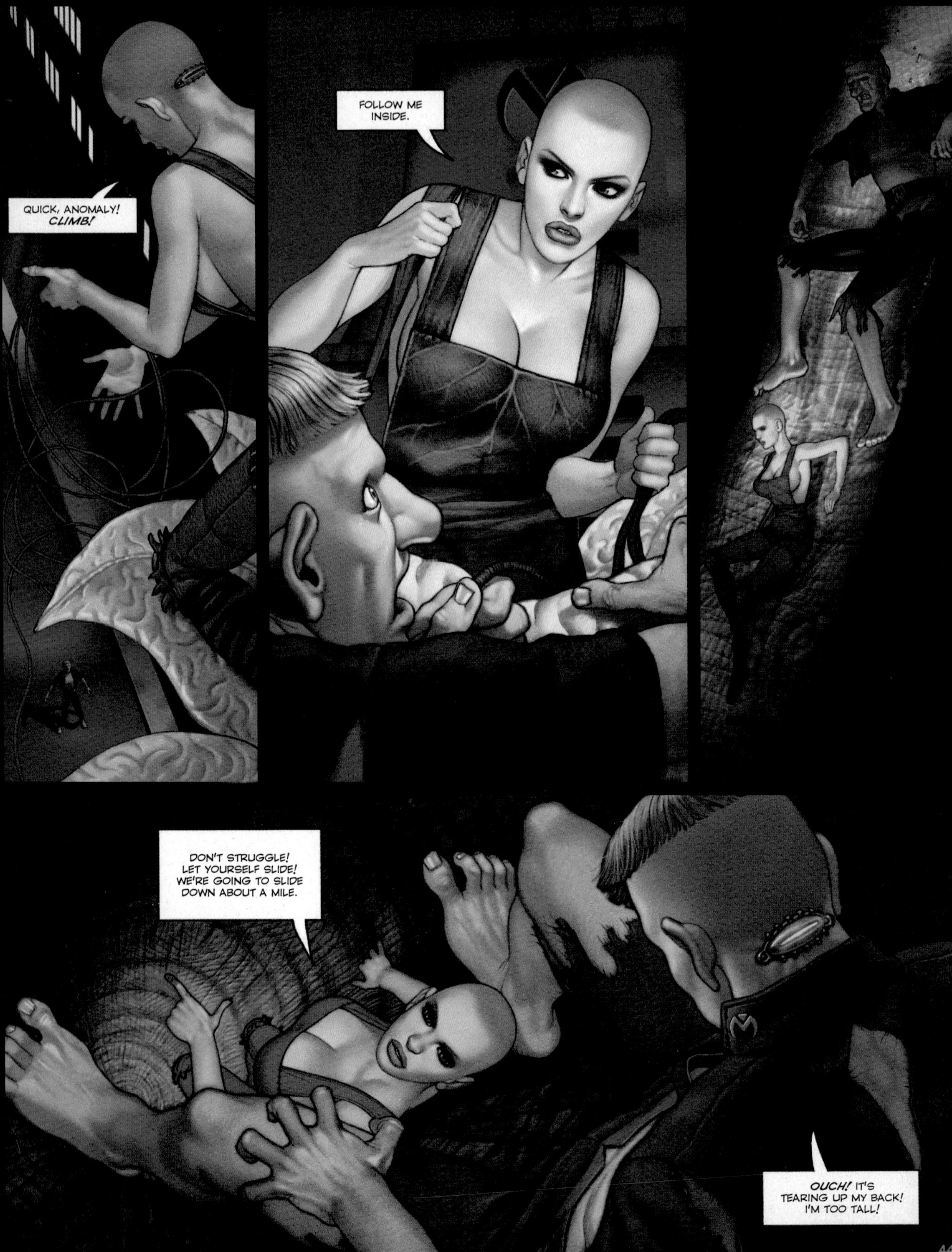
QUICK, ANOMALY! *CLIMB!*
FOLLOW ME INSIDE.
DON'T STRUGGLE! LET YOURSELF SLIDE! WE'RE GOING TO SLIDE DOWN ABOUT A MILE.
OUCH! IT'S TEARING UP MY BACK! I'M TOO TALL!

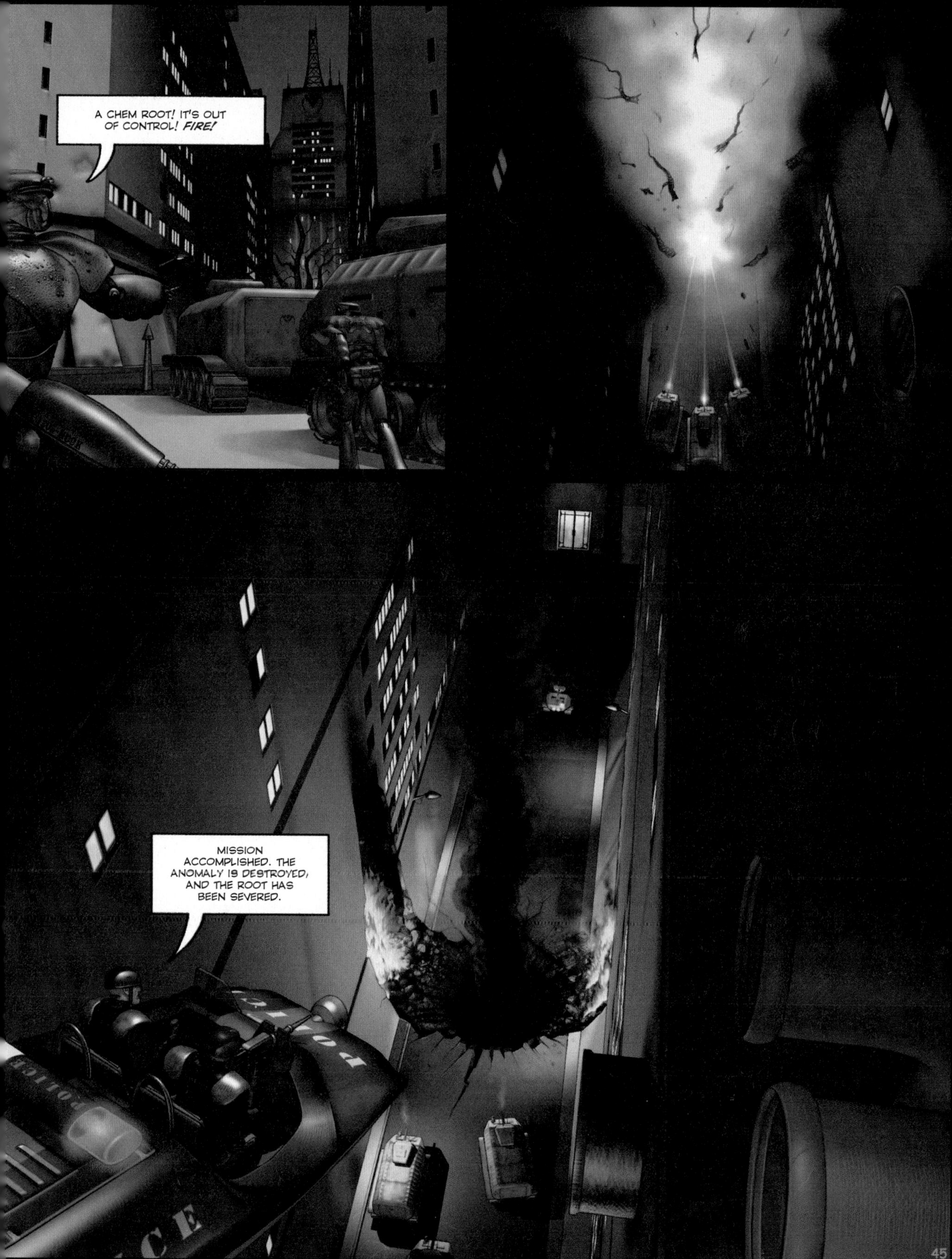
A CHEM ROOT! IT'S OUT OF CONTROL! *FIRE!*
MISSION ACCOMPLISHED. THE ANOMALY IS DESTROYED, AND THE ROOT HAS BEEN SEVERED.

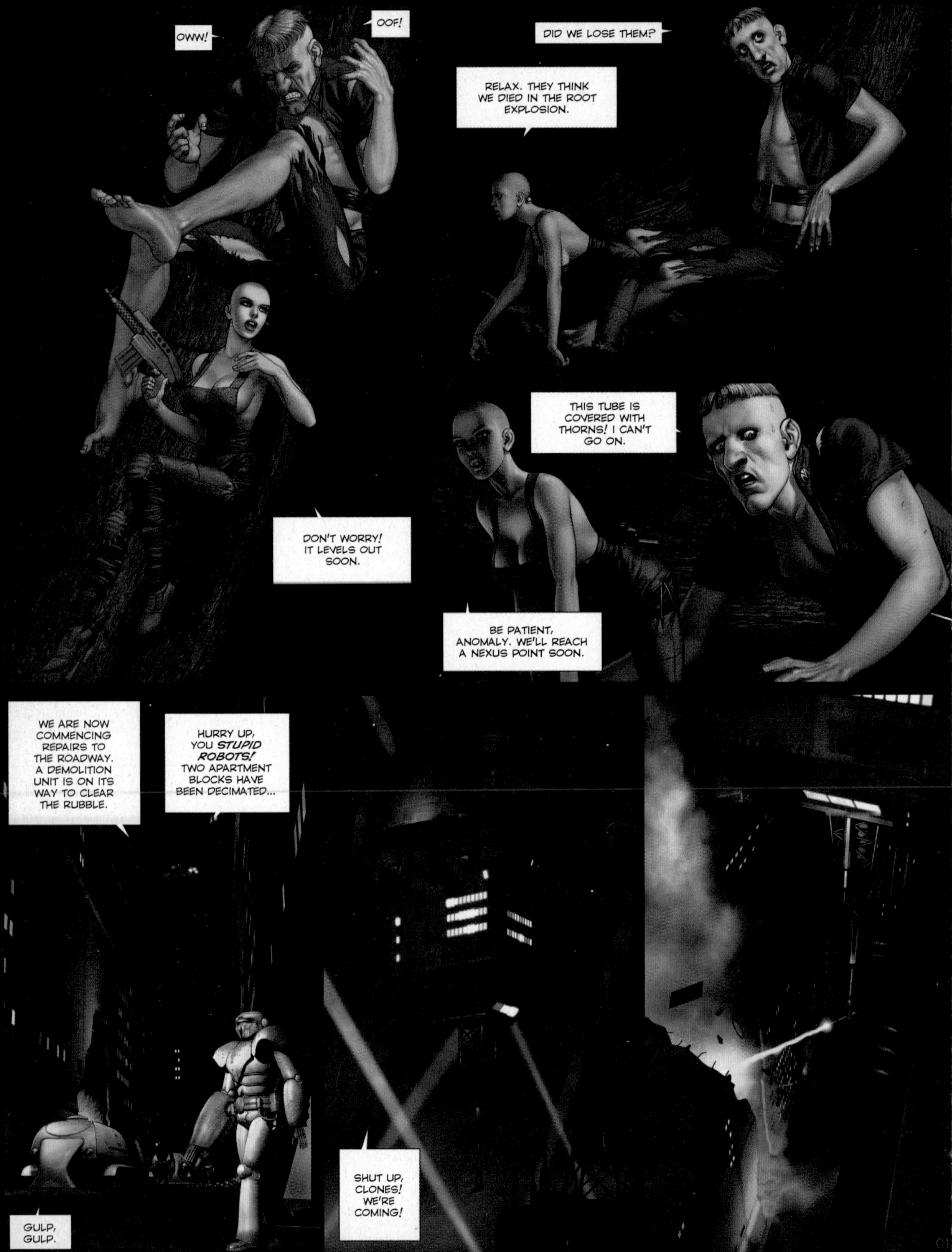
OWW!
OOF!
DON'T WORRY! IT LEVELS OUT SOON.
DID WE LOSE THEM?
RELAX. THEY THINK WE DIED IN THE ROOT EXPLOSION.
THIS TUBE IS COVERED WITH THORNS! I CAN'T GO ON.
BE PATIENT, ANOMALY. WE'LL REACH A NEXUS POINT SOON.
WE ARE NOW COMMENCING REPAIRS TO THE ROADWAY. A DEMOLITION UNIT IS ON ITS WAY TO CLEAR THE RUBBLE.
HURRY UP, YOU STUPID ROBOTS! TWO APARTMENT BLOCKS HAVE BEEN DECIMATED...
GULP, GULP.
SHUT UP, CLONES! WE'RE COMING!

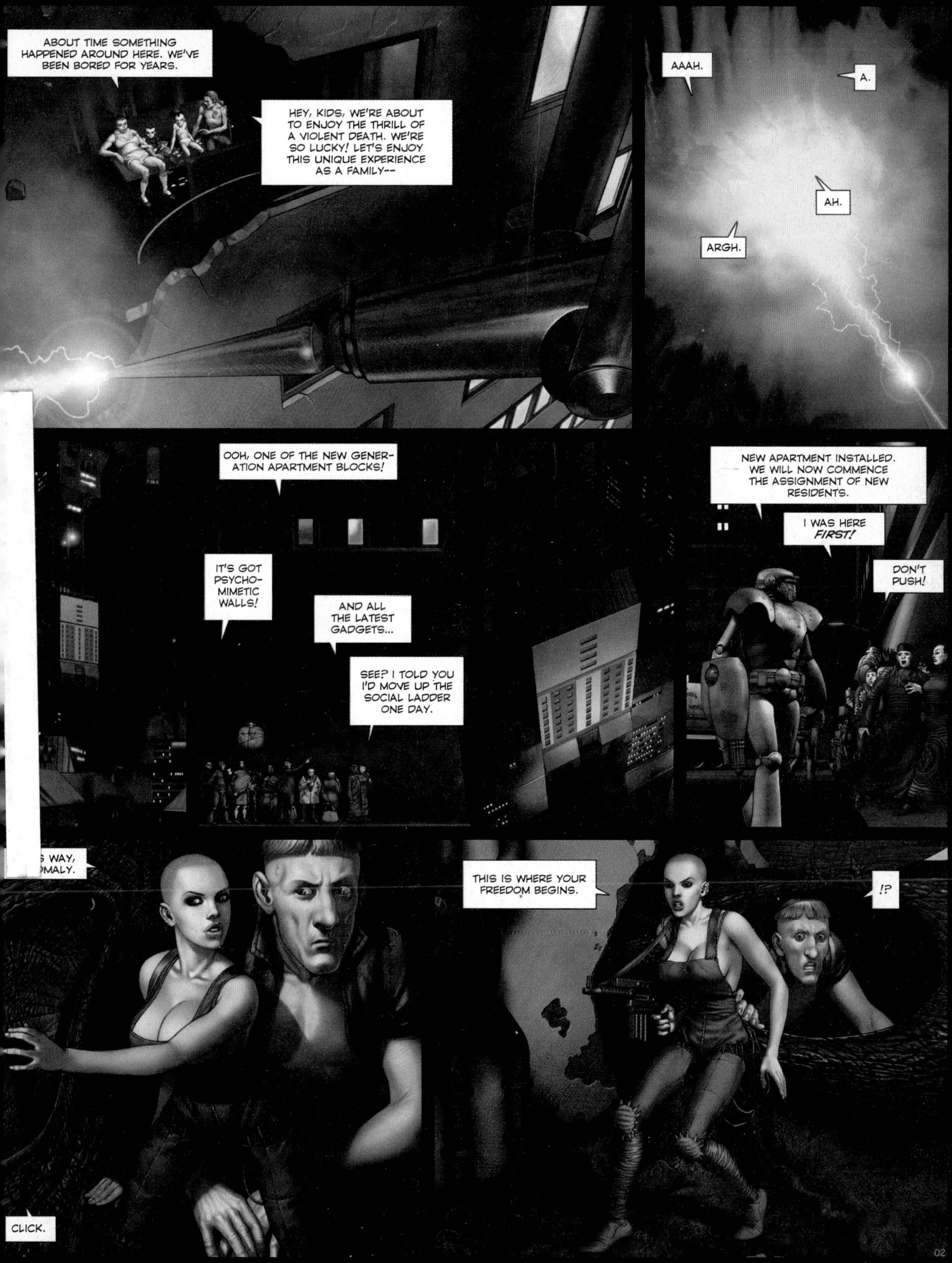

ABOUT TIME SOMETHING HAPPENED AROUND HERE. WE'VE BEEN BORED FOR YEARS.
HEY, KIDS, WE'RE ABOUT TO ENJOY THE THRILL OF A VIOLENT DEATH. WE'RE SO LUCKY! LET'S ENJOY THIS UNIQUE EXPERIENCE AS A FAMILY--
AAAH.
A.
AH.
ARGH.
OOH, ONE OF THE NEW GENERATION APARTMENT BLOCKS!
IT'S GOT PSYCHOMIMETIC WALLS!
AND ALL THE LATEST GADGETS...
SEE? I TOLD YOU I'D MOVE UP THE SOCIAL LADDER ONE DAY.
NEW APARTMENT INSTALLED. WE WILL NOW COMMENCE THE ASSIGNMENT OF NEW RESIDENTS.
I WAS HERE FIRST!
DON'T PUSH!
CLICK.
THIS IS WHERE YOUR FREEDOM BEGINS.
!?

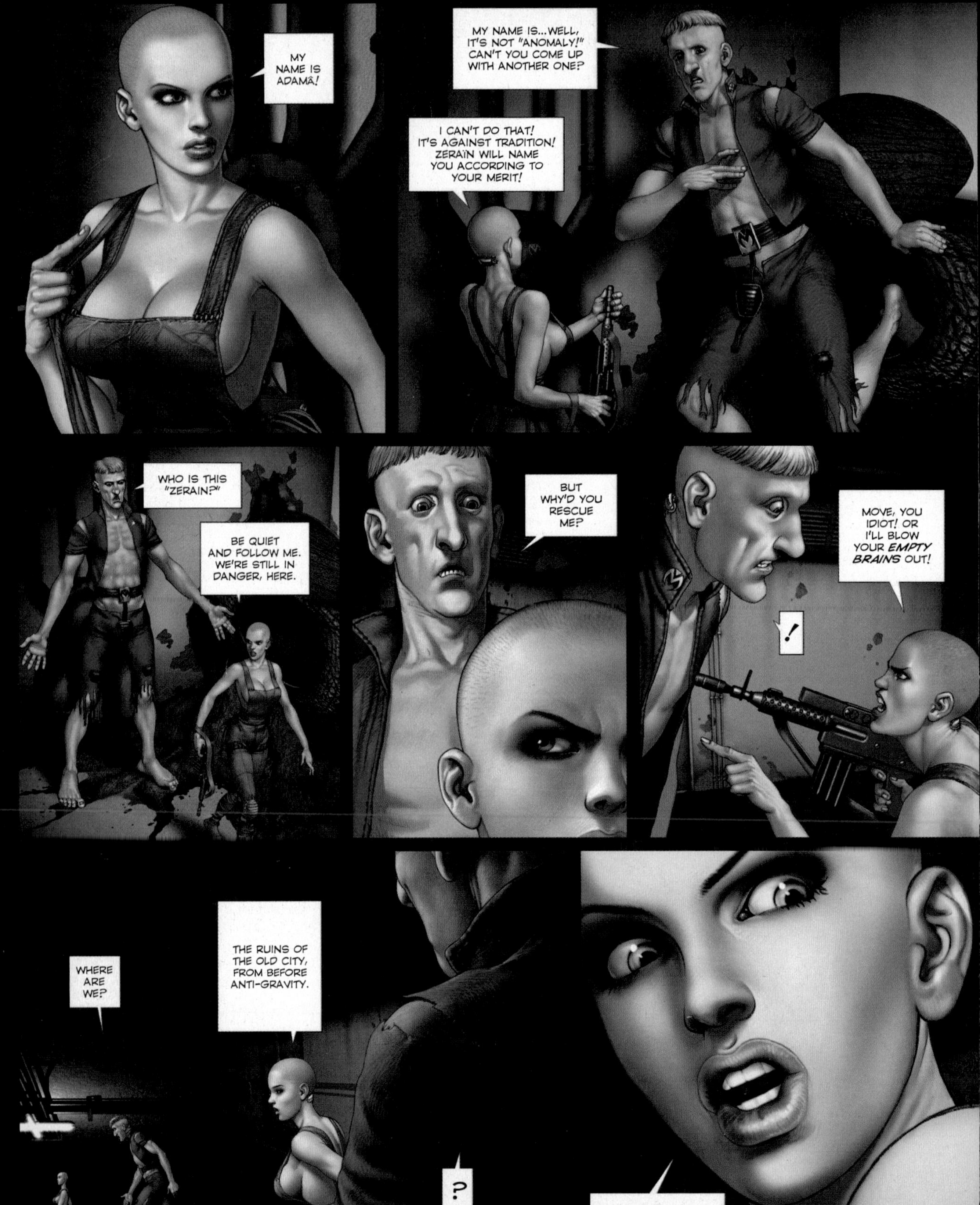
MY NAME IS ADAMÂ!
MY NAME IS...WELL, IT'S NOT "ANOMALY!" CAN'T YOU COME UP WITH ANOTHER ONE?
I CAN'T DO THAT! IT'S AGAINST TRADITION! ZERAÏN WILL NAME YOU ACCORDING TO YOUR MERIT!
WHO IS THIS "ZERAIN?"
BE QUIET AND FOLLOW ME. WE'RE STILL IN DANGER, HERE.
BUT WHY'D YOU RESCUE ME?
MOVE, YOU IDIOT! OR I'LL BLOW YOUR *EMPTY BRAINS* OUT!
!
WHERE ARE WE?
THE RUINS OF THE OLD CITY, FROM BEFORE ANTI-GRAVITY.
?
ANOMALY! WATCH OUT!!
03

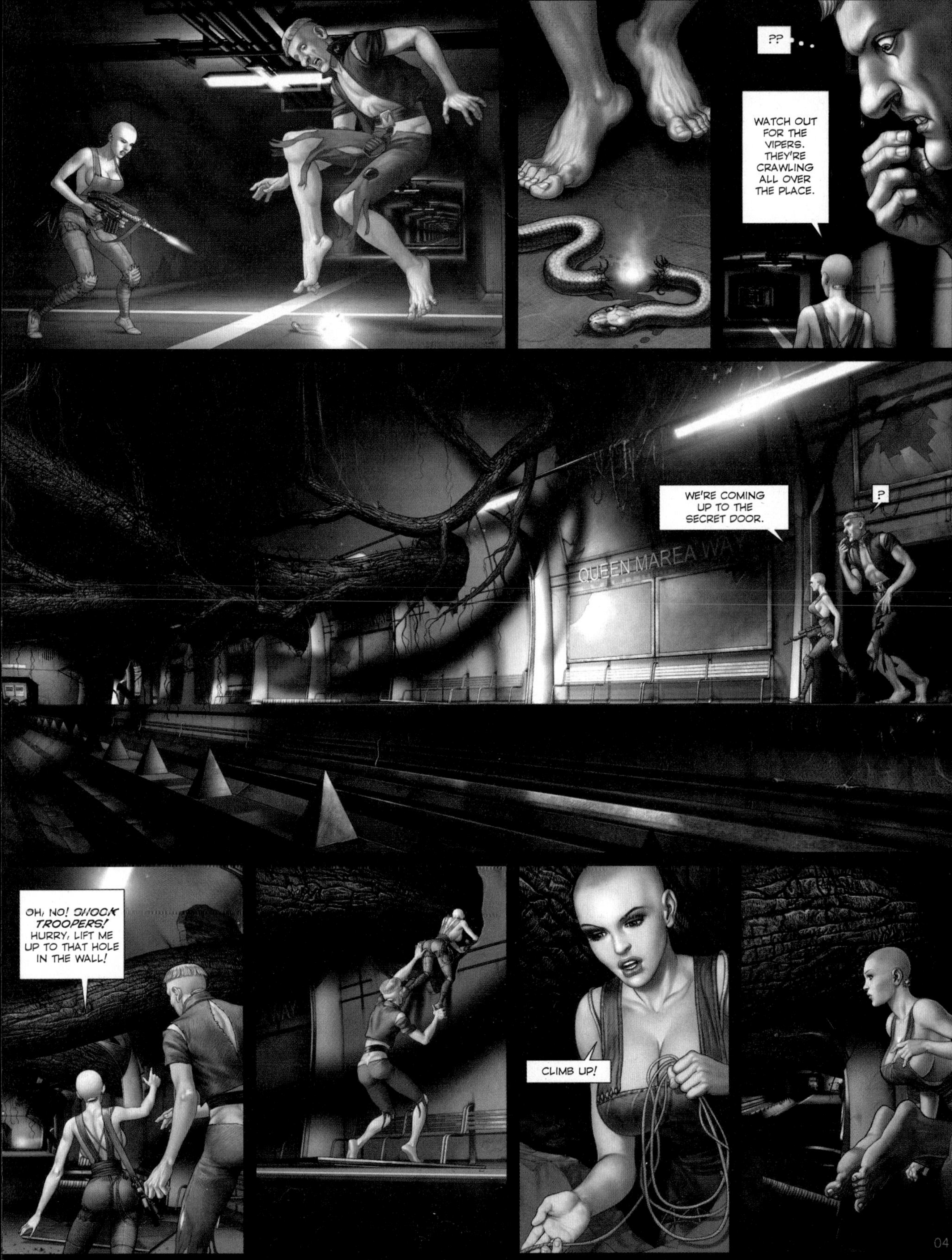

??...
WATCH OUT FOR THE VIPERS. THEY'RE CRAWLING ALL OVER THE PLACE.
WE'RE COMING UP TO THE SECRET DOOR.
?
QUEEN MAREA WAY
OH, NO! SHOCK TROOPERS! HURRY, LIFT ME UP TO THAT HOLE IN THE WALL!
CLIMB UP!

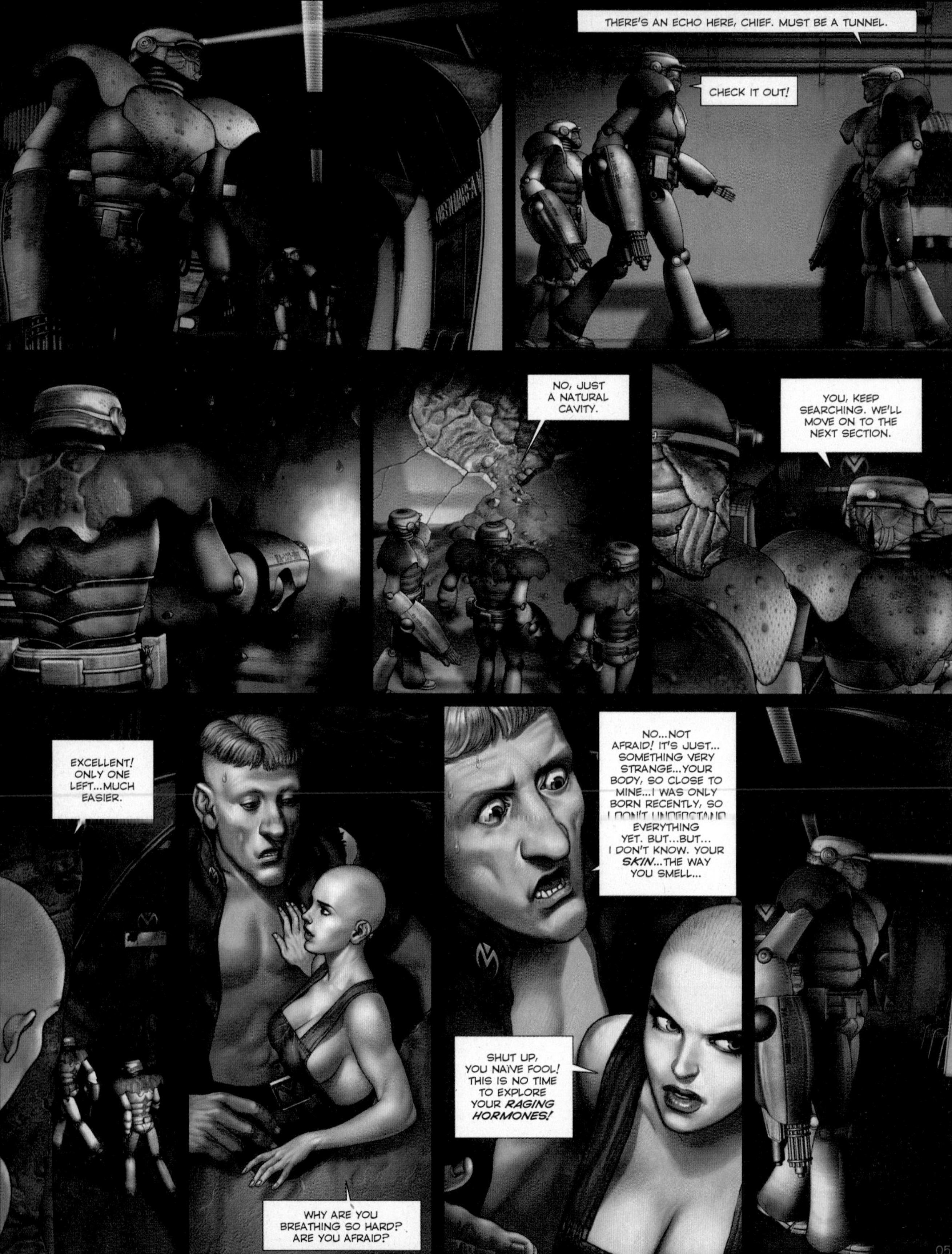
THERE'S AN ECHO HERE, CHIEF. MUST BE A TUNNEL.
CHECK IT OUT!
NO, JUST A NATURAL CAVITY.
YOU, KEEP SEARCHING. WE'LL MOVE ON TO THE NEXT SECTION.
EXCELLENT! ONLY ONE LEFT...MUCH EASIER.
WHY ARE YOU BREATHING SO HARD? ARE YOU AFRAID?
NO...NOT AFRAID! IT'S JUST... SOMETHING VERY STRANGE...YOUR BODY, SO CLOSE TO MINE...I WAS ONLY BORN RECENTLY, SO I DON'T UNDERSTAND EVERYTHING YET. BUT...BUT... I DON'T KNOW. YOUR *SKIN*...THE WAY YOU SMELL...
SHUT UP, YOU NAÏVE FOOL! THIS IS NO TIME TO EXPLORE YOUR *RAGING HORMONES!*

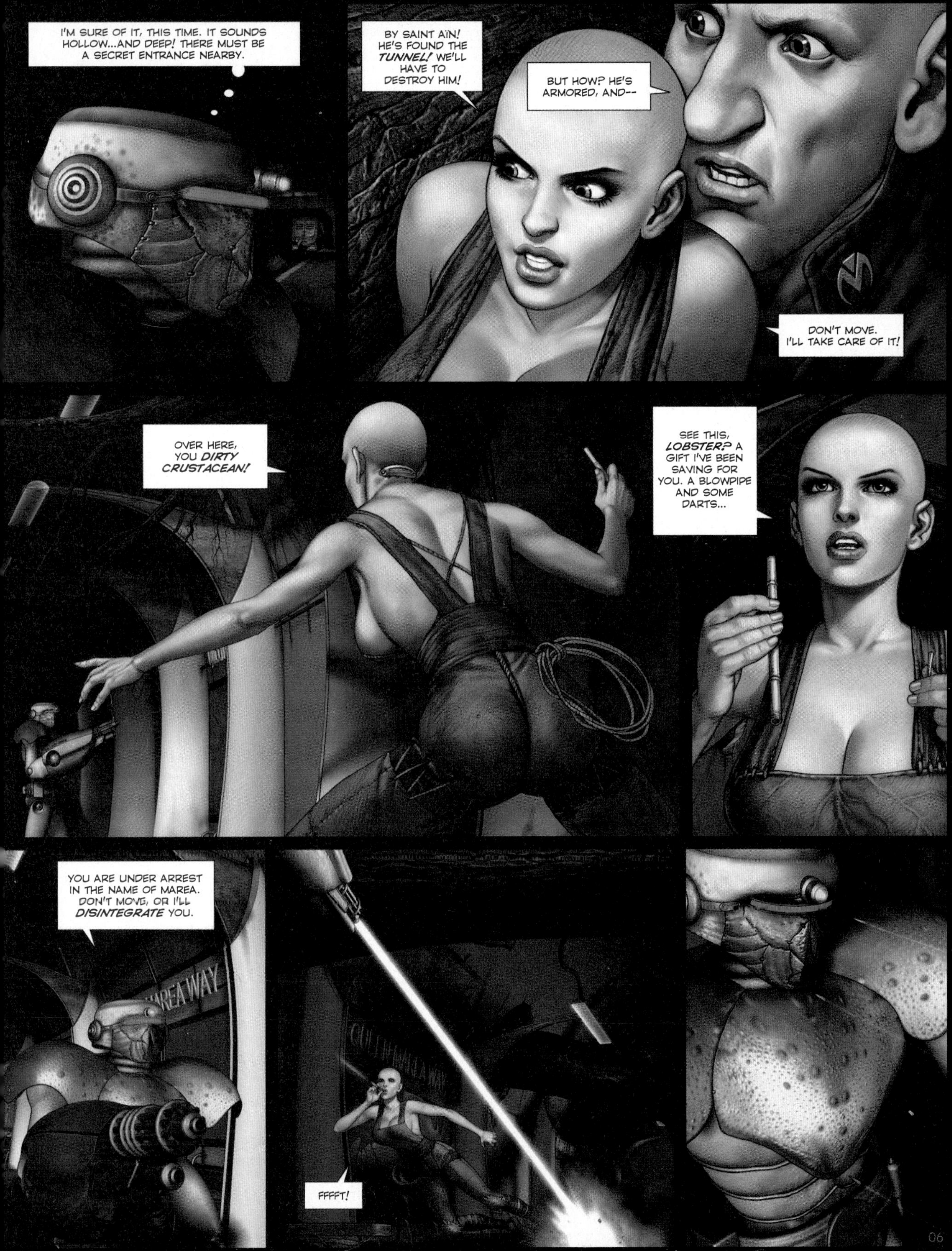
I'M SURE OF IT, THIS TIME. IT SOUNDS HOLLOW...AND DEEP! THERE MUST BE A SECRET ENTRANCE NEARBY.
BY SAINT AÏN! HE'S FOUND THE *TUNNEL!* WE'LL HAVE TO DESTROY HIM!
BUT HOW? HE'S ARMORED, AND--
DON'T MOVE. I'LL TAKE CARE OF IT!
OVER HERE, YOU *DIRTY CRUSTACEAN!*
SEE THIS, *LOBSTER?* A GIFT I'VE BEEN SAVING FOR YOU. A BLOWPIPE AND SOME DARTS...
YOU ARE UNDER ARREST IN THE NAME OF MAREA. DON'T MOVE, OR I'LL *DISINTEGRATE* YOU.
MAREA WAY
FFFFT!
06

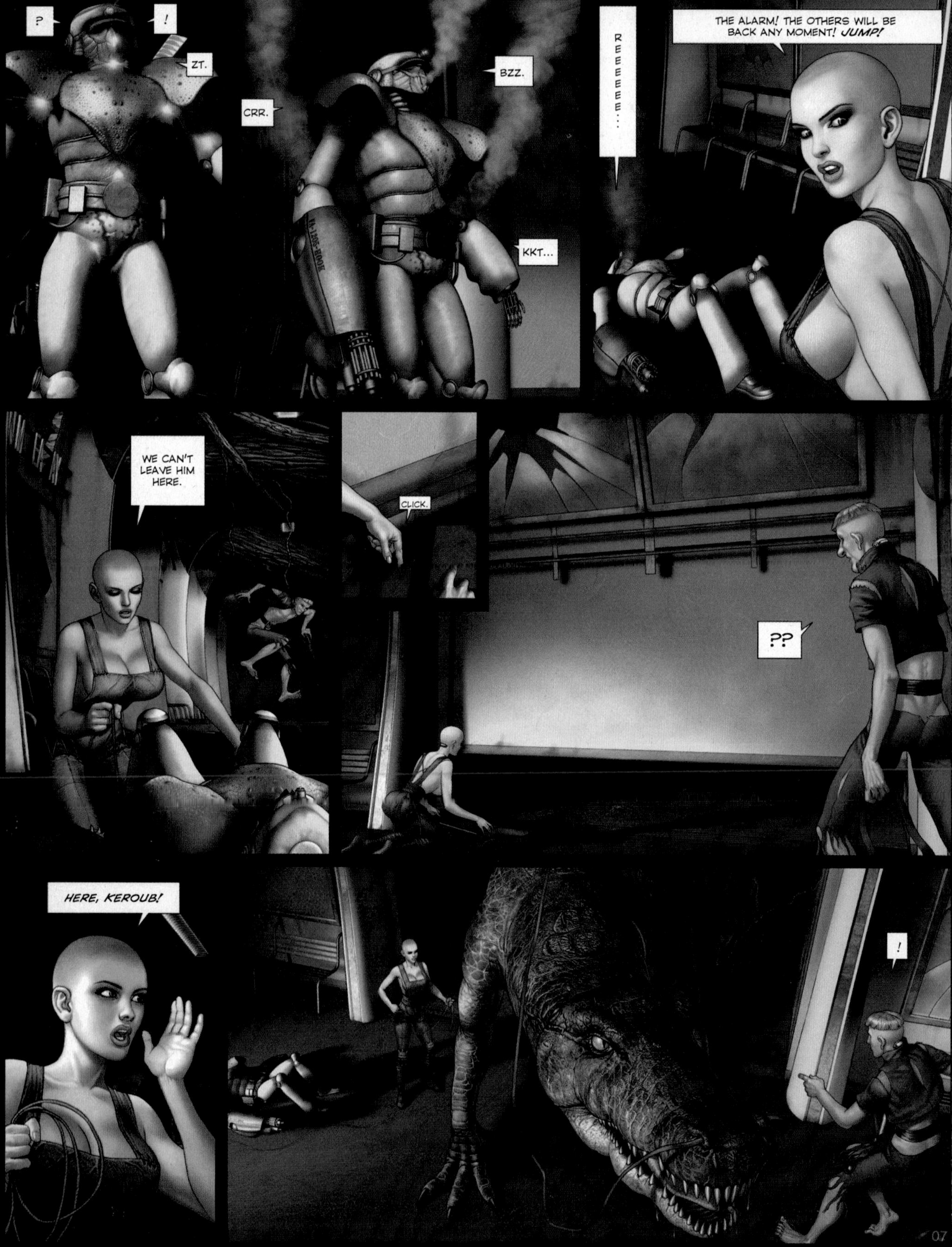
?
!
ZT.
CRR.
BZZ.
KKT...
REEEEEE...
THE ALARM! THE OTHERS WILL BE BACK ANY MOMENT! *JUMP!*
WE CAN'T LEAVE HIM HERE.
CLICK.
??
HERE, KEROUB!
!

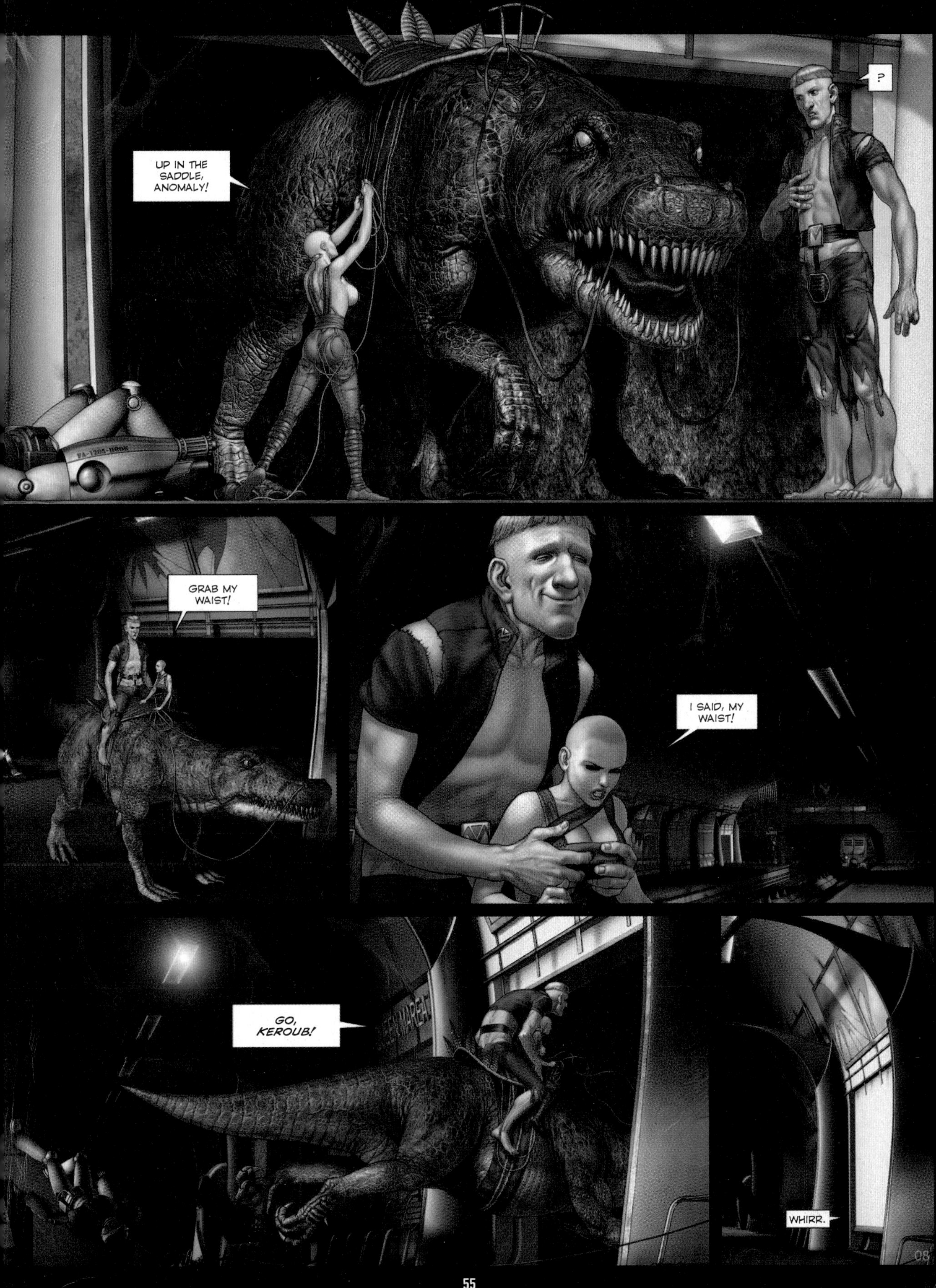
UP IN THE SADDLE, ANOMALY!
?
GRAB MY WAIST!
I SAID, MY WAIST!
GO, KEROUB!
WHIRR.

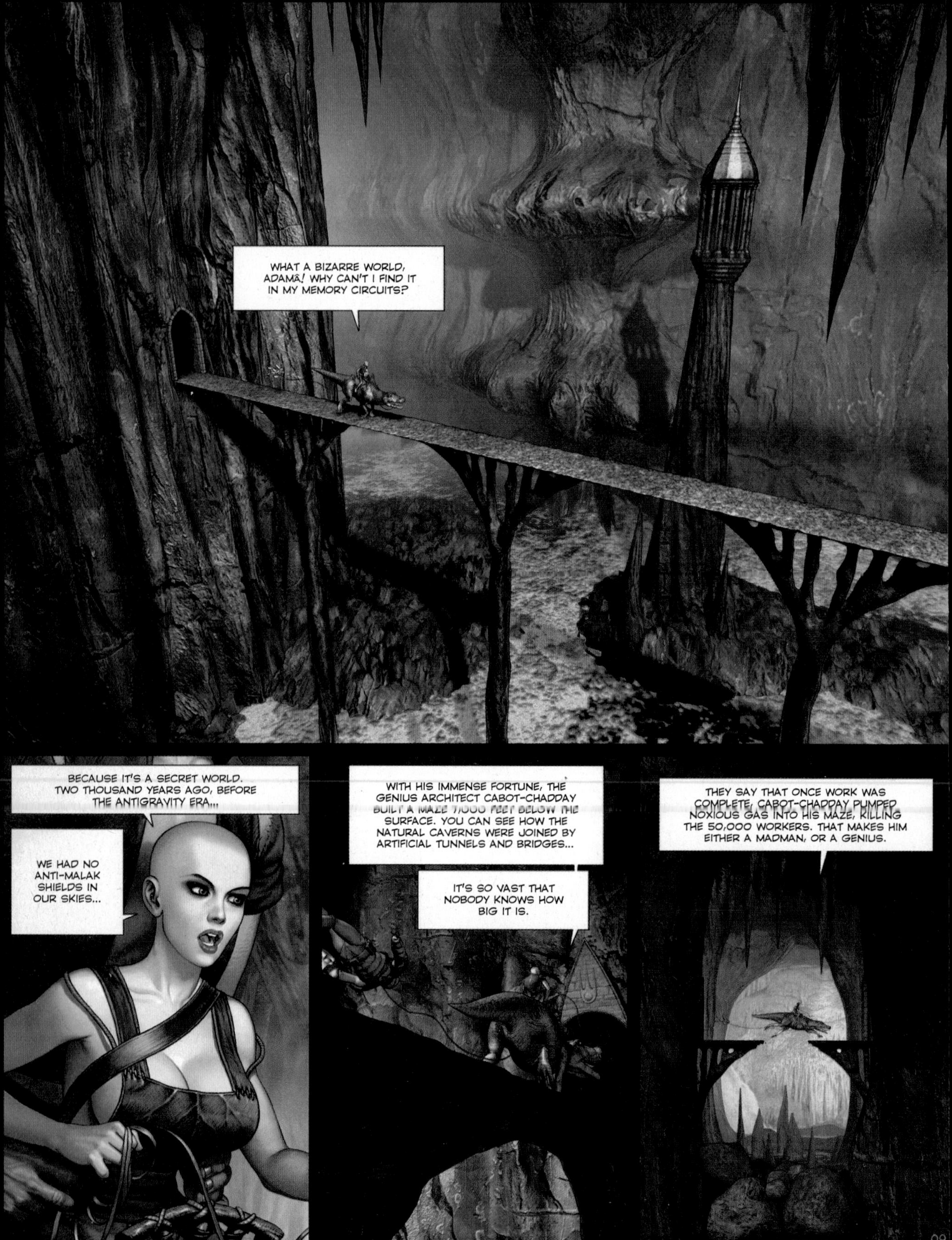
WHAT A BIZARRE WORLD, ADAMÂ! WHY CAN'T I FIND IT IN MY MEMORY CIRCUITS?
BECAUSE IT'S A SECRET WORLD. TWO THOUSAND YEARS AGO, BEFORE THE ANTIGRAVITY ERA...
WE HAD NO ANTI-MALAK SHIELDS IN OUR SKIES...
WITH HIS IMMENSE FORTUNE, THE GENIUS ARCHITECT CABOT-CHADDAY BUILT A MAZE 7,000 FEET BELOW THE SURFACE. YOU CAN SEE HOW THE NATURAL CAVERNS WERE JOINED BY ARTIFICIAL TUNNELS AND BRIDGES...
IT'S SO VAST THAT NOBODY KNOWS HOW BIG IT IS.
THEY SAY THAT ONCE WORK WAS COMPLETE, CABOT-CHADDAY PUMPED NOXIOUS GAS INTO HIS MAZE, KILLING THE 50,000 WORKERS. THAT MAKES HIM EITHER A MADMAN, OR A GENIUS.

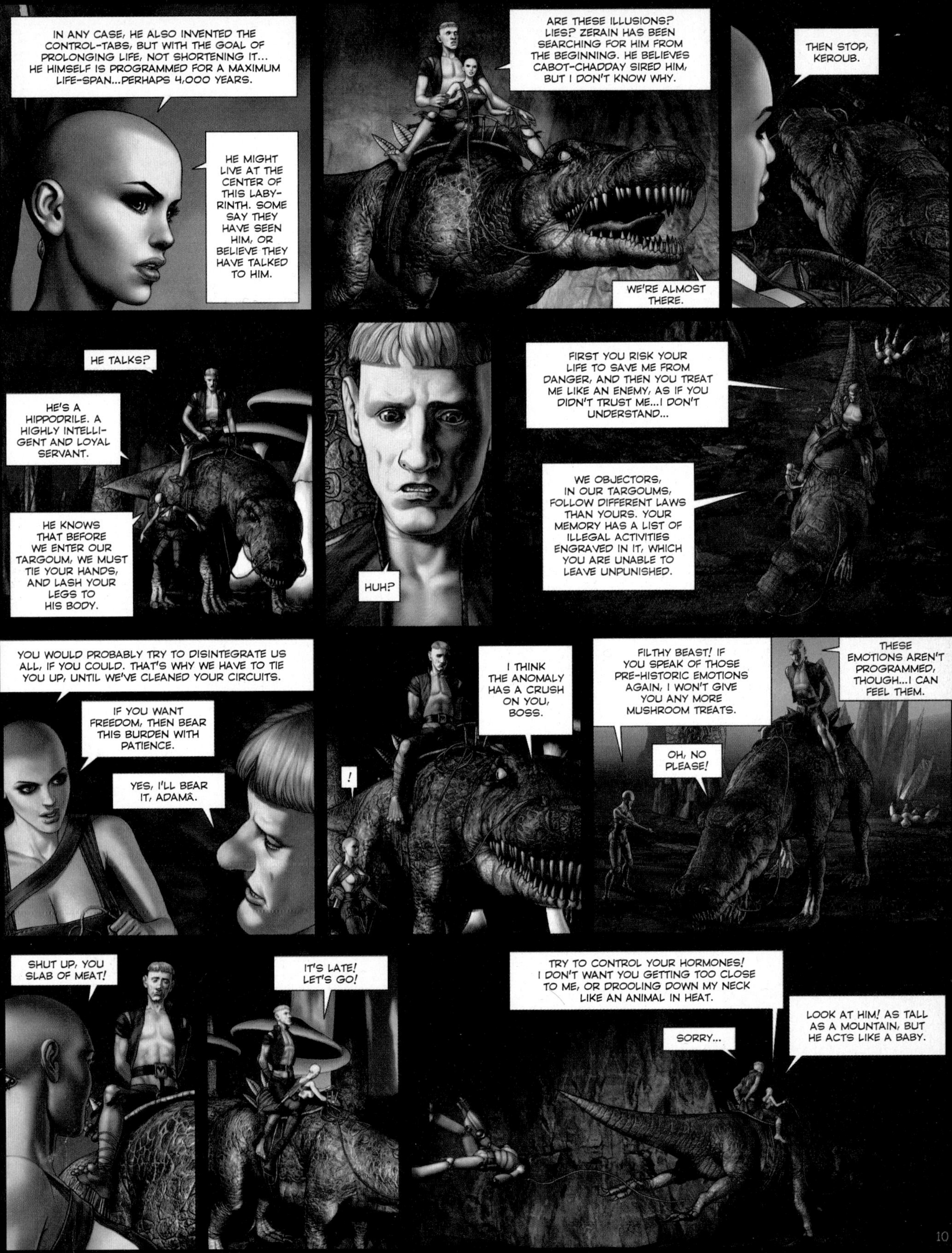

IN ANY CASE, HE ALSO INVENTED THE CONTROL-TABS, BUT WITH THE GOAL OF PROLONGING LIFE, NOT SHORTENING IT... HE HIMSELF IS PROGRAMMED FOR A MAXIMUM LIFE-SPAN...PERHAPS 4,000 YEARS.
HE MIGHT LIVE AT THE CENTER OF THIS LABY-RINTH. SOME SAY THEY HAVE SEEN HIM, OR BELIEVE THEY HAVE TALKED TO HIM.
ARE THESE ILLUSIONS? LIES? ZERAIN HAS BEEN SEARCHING FOR HIM FROM THE BEGINNING. HE BELIEVES CABOT-CHADDAY SIRED HIM, BUT I DON'T KNOW WHY.
WE'RE ALMOST THERE.
THEN STOP, KEROUB.
HE TALKS?
HE'S A HIPPODRILE. A HIGHLY INTELLI-GENT AND LOYAL SERVANT.
HE KNOWS THAT BEFORE WE ENTER OUR TARGOUM, WE MUST TIE YOUR HANDS, AND LASH YOUR LEGS TO HIS BODY.
HUH?
FIRST YOU RISK YOUR LIFE TO SAVE ME FROM DANGER, AND THEN YOU TREAT ME LIKE AN ENEMY, AS IF YOU DIDN'T TRUST ME...I DON'T UNDERSTAND...
WE OBJECTORS, IN OUR TARGOUMS, FOLLOW DIFFERENT LAWS THAN YOURS. YOUR MEMORY HAS A LIST OF ILLEGAL ACTIVITIES ENGRAVED IN IT, WHICH YOU ARE UNABLE TO LEAVE UNPUNISHED.
YOU WOULD PROBABLY TRY TO DISINTEGRATE US ALL, IF YOU COULD. THAT'S WHY WE HAVE TO TIE YOU UP, UNTIL WE'VE CLEANED YOUR CIRCUITS.
IF YOU WANT FREEDOM, THEN BEAR THIS BURDEN WITH PATIENCE.
YES, I'LL BEAR IT, ADAMÂ.
I THINK THE ANOMALY HAS A CRUSH ON YOU, BOSS.
!
FILTHY BEAST! IF YOU SPEAK OF THOSE PRE-HISTORIC EMOTIONS AGAIN, I WON'T GIVE YOU ANY MORE MUSHROOM TREATS.
OH, NO PLEASE!
THESE EMOTIONS AREN'T PROGRAMMED, THOUGH...I CAN FEEL THEM.
SHUT UP, YOU SLAB OF MEAT!
IT'S LATE! LET'S GO!
TRY TO CONTROL YOUR HORMONES! I DON'T WANT YOU GETTING TOO CLOSE TO ME, OR DROOLING DOWN MY NECK LIKE AN ANIMAL IN HEAT.
SORRY...
LOOK AT HIM! AS TALL AS A MOUNTAIN, BUT HE ACTS LIKE A BABY.

10

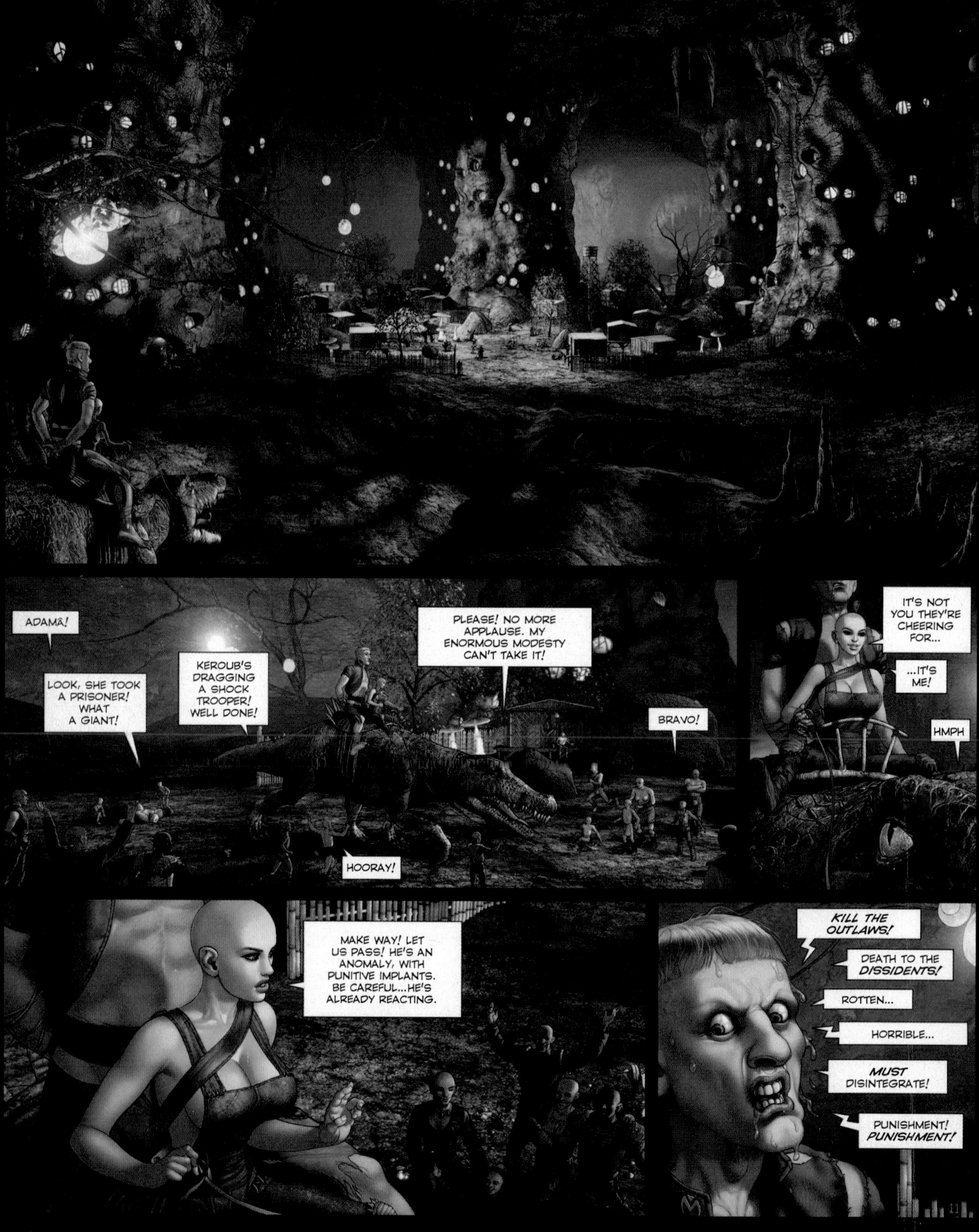

ADAMÂ!
LOOK, SHE TOOK A PRISONER! WHAT A GIANT!
KEROUB'S DRAGGING A SHOCK TROOPER! WELL DONE!
PLEASE! NO MORE APPLAUSE. MY ENORMOUS MODESTY CAN'T TAKE IT!
BRAVO!
HOORAY!
IT'S NOT YOU THEY'RE CHEERING FOR...
...IT'S ME!
HMPH
MAKE WAY! LET US PASS! HE'S AN ANOMALY, WITH PUNITIVE IMPLANTS. BE CAREFUL...HE'S ALREADY REACTING.
KILL THE OUTLAWS!
DEATH TO THE DISSIDENTS!
ROTTEN...
HORRIBLE...
MUST DISINTEGRATE!
PUNISHMENT! PUNISHMENT!

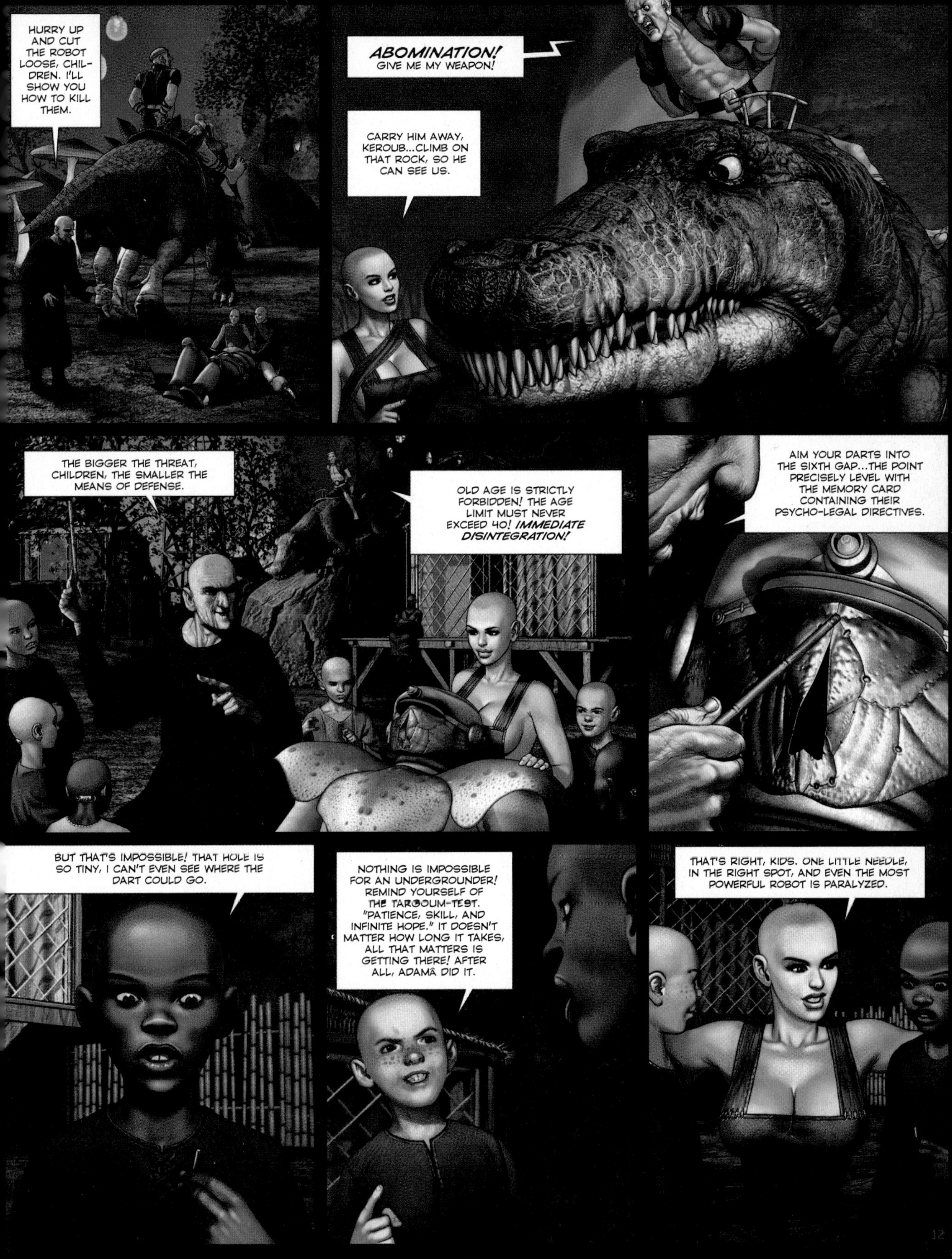

HURRY UP AND CUT THE ROBOT LOOSE, CHIL-DREN. I'LL SHOW YOU HOW TO KILL THEM.
ABOMINATION! GIVE ME MY WEAPON!
CARRY HIM AWAY, KEROUB...CLIMB ON THAT ROCK, SO HE CAN SEE US.
THE BIGGER THE THREAT, CHILDREN, THE SMALLER THE MEANS OF DEFENSE.
OLD AGE IS STRICTLY FORBIDDEN! THE AGE LIMIT MUST NEVER EXCEED 40! IMMEDIATE DISINTEGRATION!
AIM YOUR DARTS INTO THE SIXTH GAP...THE POINT PRECISELY LEVEL WITH THE MEMORY CARD CONTAINING THEIR PSYCHO-LEGAL DIRECTIVES.
BUT THAT'S IMPOSSIBLE! THAT HOLE IS SO TINY, I CAN'T EVEN SEE WHERE THE DART COULD GO.
NOTHING IS IMPOSSIBLE FOR AN UNDERGROUNDER! REMIND YOURSELF OF THE TARGOUM-TEST. "PATIENCE, SKILL, AND INFINITE HOPE." IT DOESN'T MATTER HOW LONG IT TAKES, ALL THAT MATTERS IS GETTING THERE! AFTER ALL, ADAMÂ DID IT.
THAT'S RIGHT, KIDS. ONE LITTLE NEEDLE, IN THE RIGHT SPOT, AND EVEN THE MOST POWERFUL ROBOT IS PARALYZED.

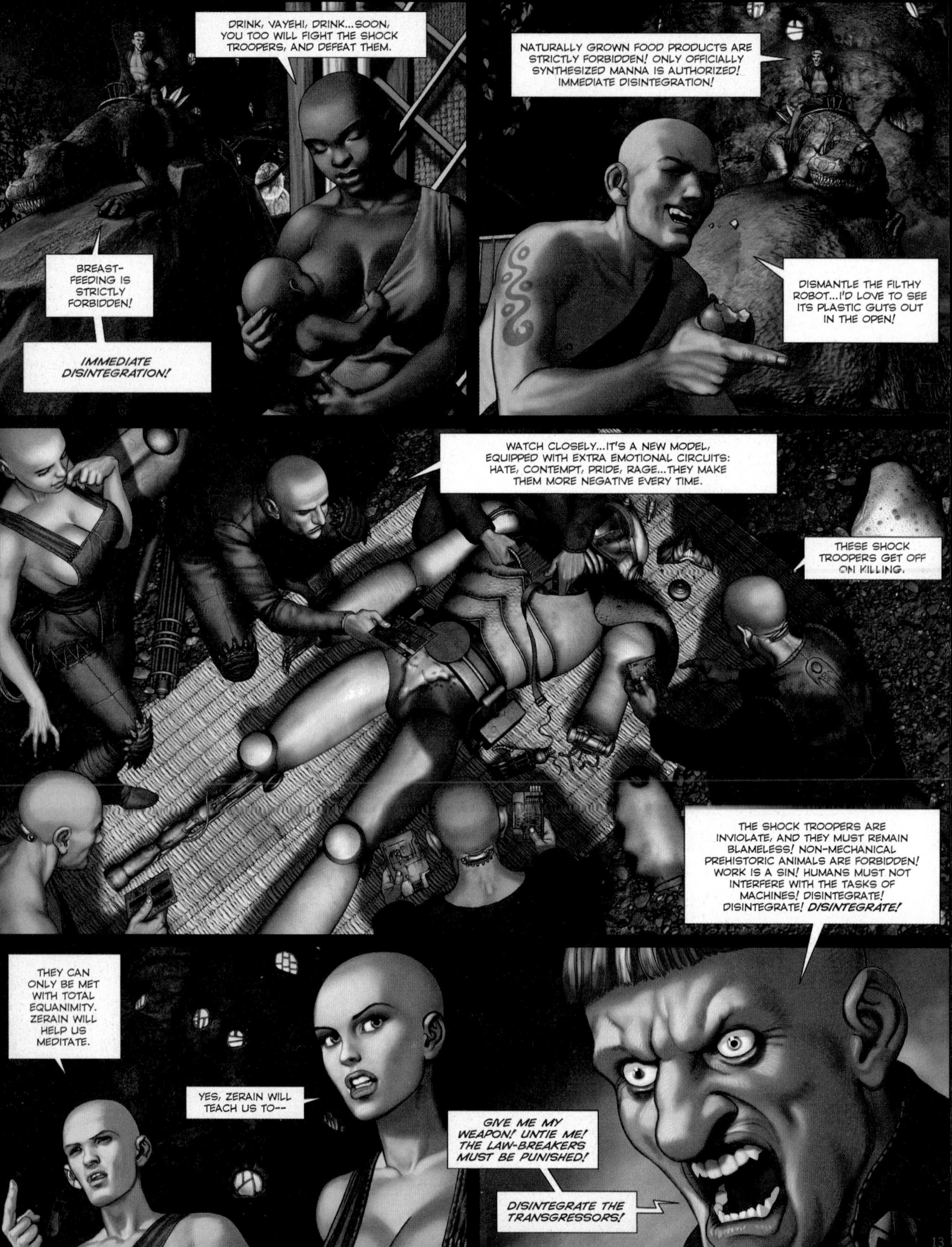
DRINK, VAYEHI, DRINK...SOON, YOU TOO WILL FIGHT THE SHOCK TROOPERS, AND DEFEAT THEM.
BREAST-FEEDING IS STRICTLY FORBIDDEN!
IMMEDIATE DISINTEGRATION!
NATURALLY GROWN FOOD PRODUCTS ARE STRICTLY FORBIDDEN! ONLY OFFICIALLY SYNTHESIZED MANNA IS AUTHORIZED! IMMEDIATE DISINTEGRATION!
DISMANTLE THE FILTHY ROBOT...I'D LOVE TO SEE ITS PLASTIC GUTS OUT IN THE OPEN!
WATCH CLOSELY...IT'S A NEW MODEL, EQUIPPED WITH EXTRA EMOTIONAL CIRCUITS: HATE, CONTEMPT, PRIDE, RAGE...THEY MAKE THEM MORE NEGATIVE EVERY TIME.
THESE SHOCK TROOPERS GET OFF ON KILLING.
THE SHOCK TROOPERS ARE INVIOLATE, AND THEY MUST REMAIN BLAMELESS! NON-MECHANICAL PREHISTORIC ANIMALS ARE FORBIDDEN! WORK IS A SIN! HUMANS MUST NOT INTERFERE WITH THE TASKS OF MACHINES! DISINTEGRATE! DISINTEGRATE! DISINTEGRATE!
THEY CAN ONLY BE MET WITH TOTAL EQUANIMITY. ZERAIN WILL HELP US MEDITATE.
YES, ZERAIN WILL TEACH US TO--
GIVE ME MY WEAPON! UNTIE ME! THE LAW-BREAKERS MUST BE PUNISHED!
DISINTEGRATE THE TRANSGRESSORS!

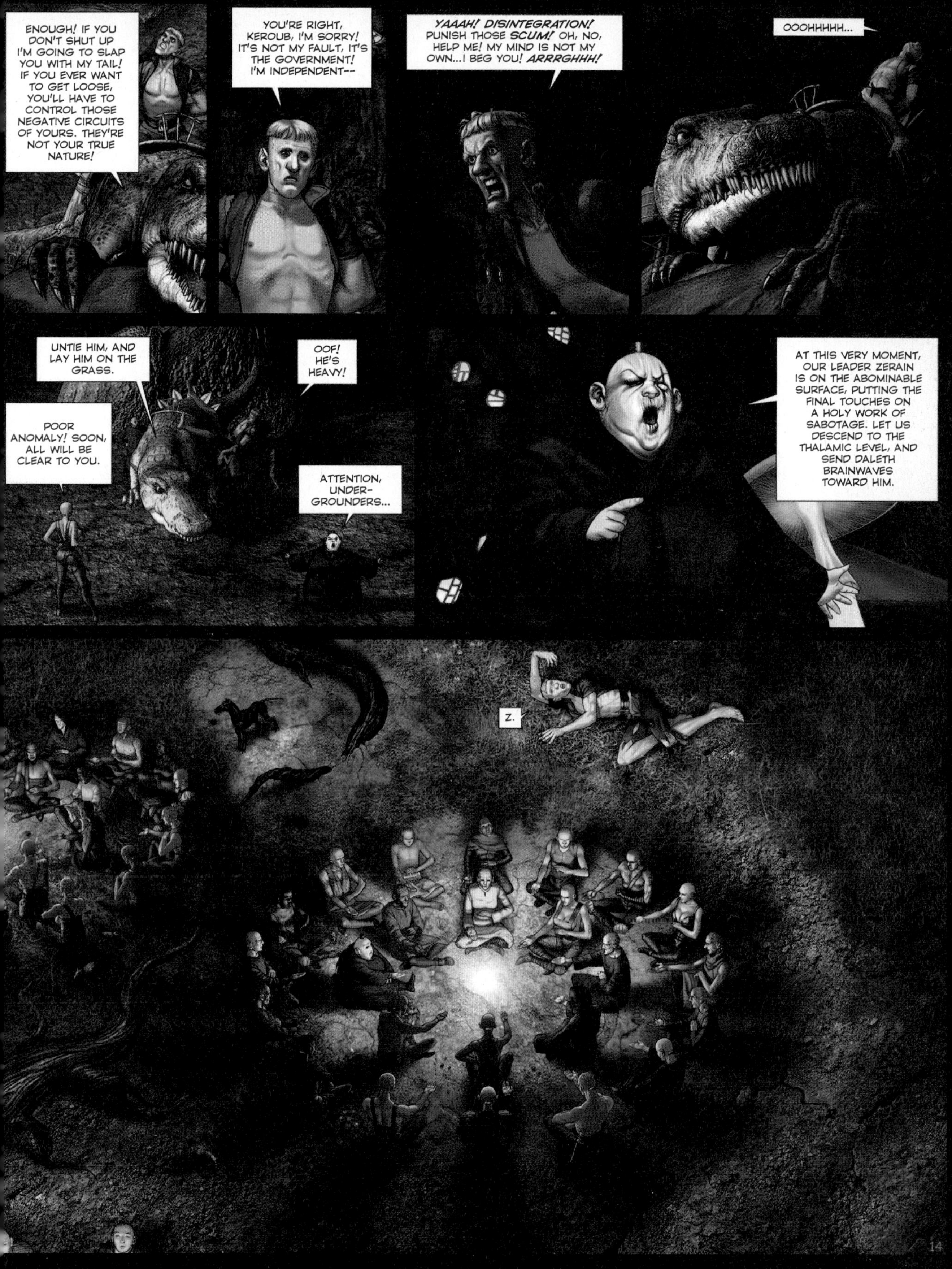
ENOUGH! IF YOU DON'T SHUT UP I'M GOING TO SLAP YOU WITH MY TAIL! IF YOU EVER WANT TO GET LOOSE, YOU'LL HAVE TO CONTROL THOSE NEGATIVE CIRCUITS OF YOURS. THEY'RE NOT YOUR TRUE NATURE!
YOU'RE RIGHT, KEROUB, I'M SORRY! IT'S NOT MY FAULT, IT'S THE GOVERNMENT! I'M INDEPENDENT--
YAAAH! DISINTEGRATION! PUNISH THOSE SCUM! OH, NO, HELP ME! MY MIND IS NOT MY OWN...I BEG YOU! ARRRGHHH!
OOOHHHHH...
UNTIE HIM, AND LAY HIM ON THE GRASS.
OOF! HE'S HEAVY!
POOR ANOMALY! SOON, ALL WILL BE CLEAR TO YOU.
ATTENTION, UNDER-GROUNDERS...
AT THIS VERY MOMENT, OUR LEADER ZERAIN IS ON THE ABOMINABLE SURFACE, PUTTING THE FINAL TOUCHES ON A HOLY WORK OF SABOTAGE. LET US DESCEND TO THE THALAMIC LEVEL, AND SEND DALETH BRAINWAVES TOWARD HIM.
Z.
14

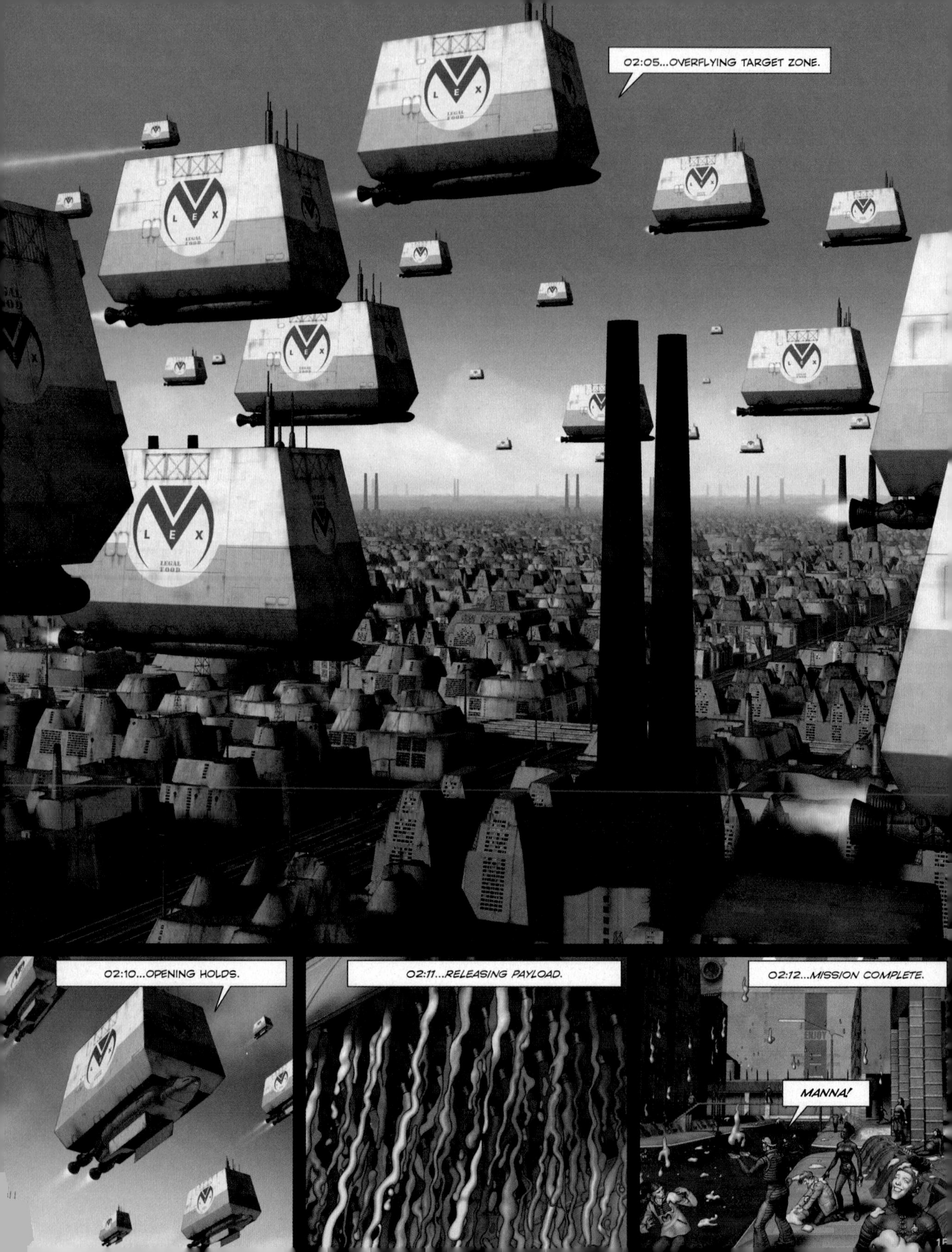
02:05...OVERFLYING TARGET ZONE.
02:10...OPENING HOLDS.
02:11...RELEASING PAYLOAD.
02:12...MISSION COMPLETE.
MANNA!

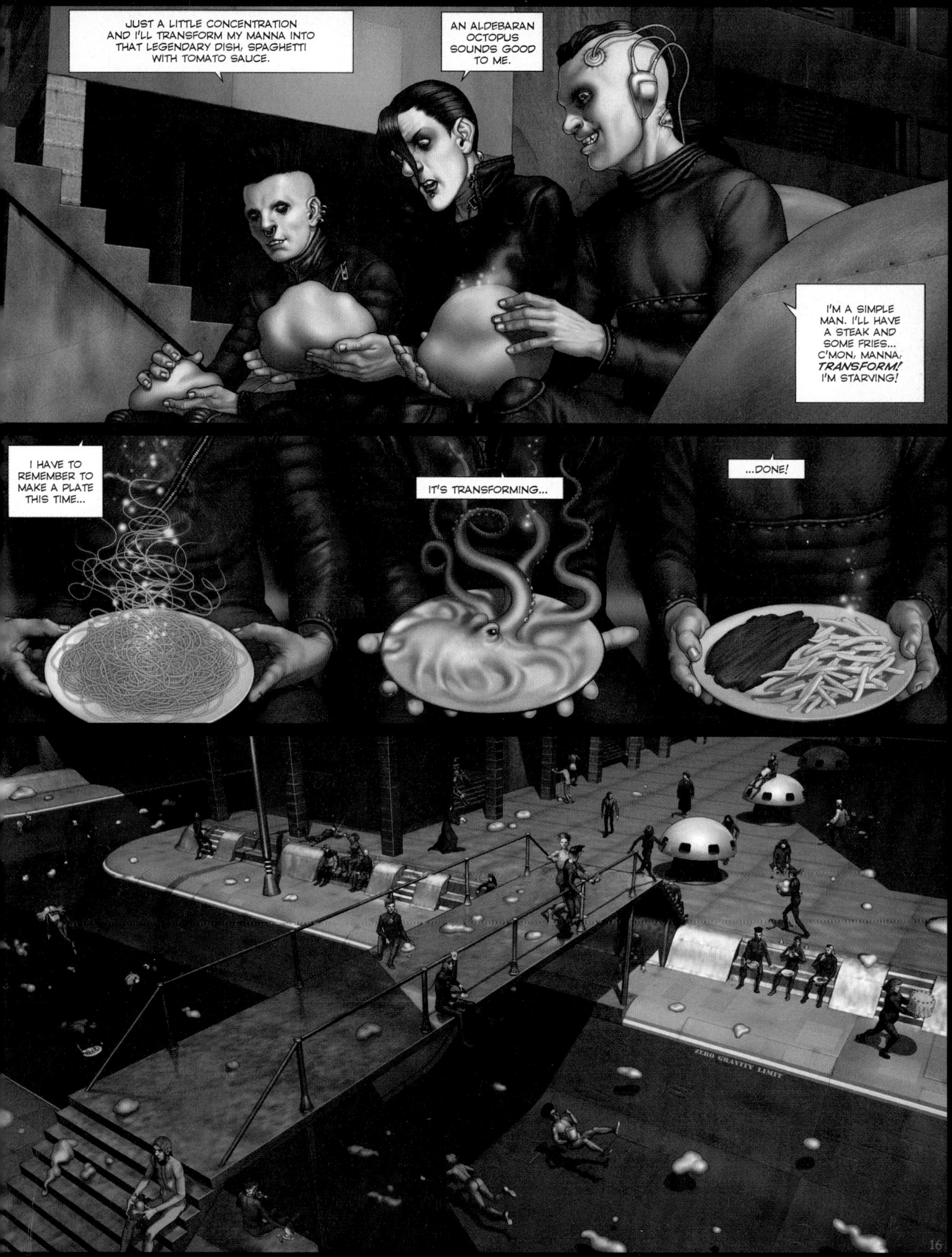
JUST A LITTLE CONCENTRATION AND I'LL TRANSFORM MY MANNA INTO THAT LEGENDARY DISH, SPAGHETTI WITH TOMATO SAUCE.
AN ALDEBARAN OCTOPUS SOUNDS GOOD TO ME.
I'M A SIMPLE MAN. I'LL HAVE A STEAK AND SOME FRIES... C'MON, MANNA, ***TRANSFORM!*** I'M STARVING!
I HAVE TO REMEMBER TO MAKE A PLATE THIS TIME...
IT'S TRANSFORMING...
...DONE!
ZERO GRAVITY LIMIT
16

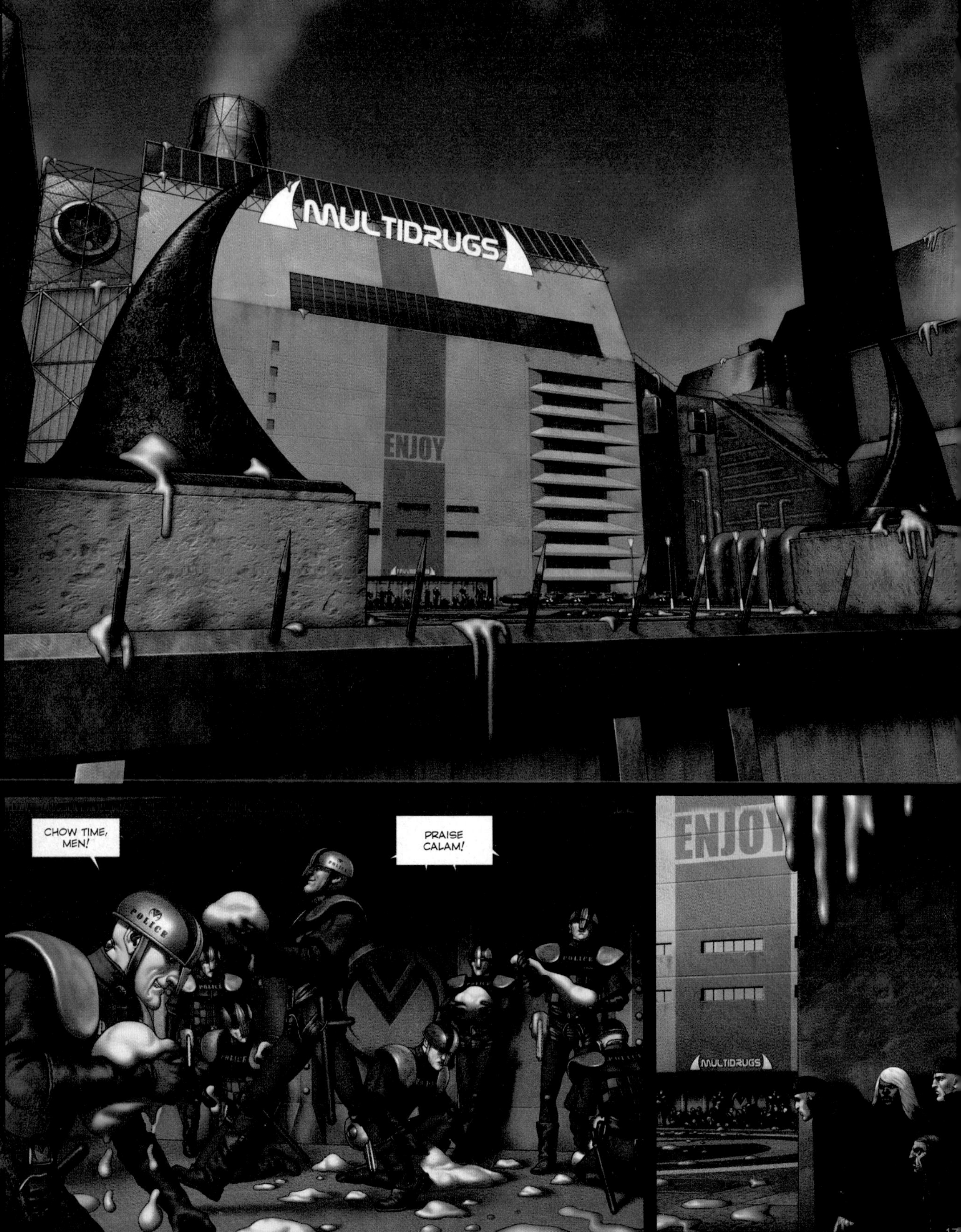
MULTIDRUGS
ENJOY
CHOW TIME, MEN!
PRAISE CALAM!
ENJOY
MULTIDRUGS

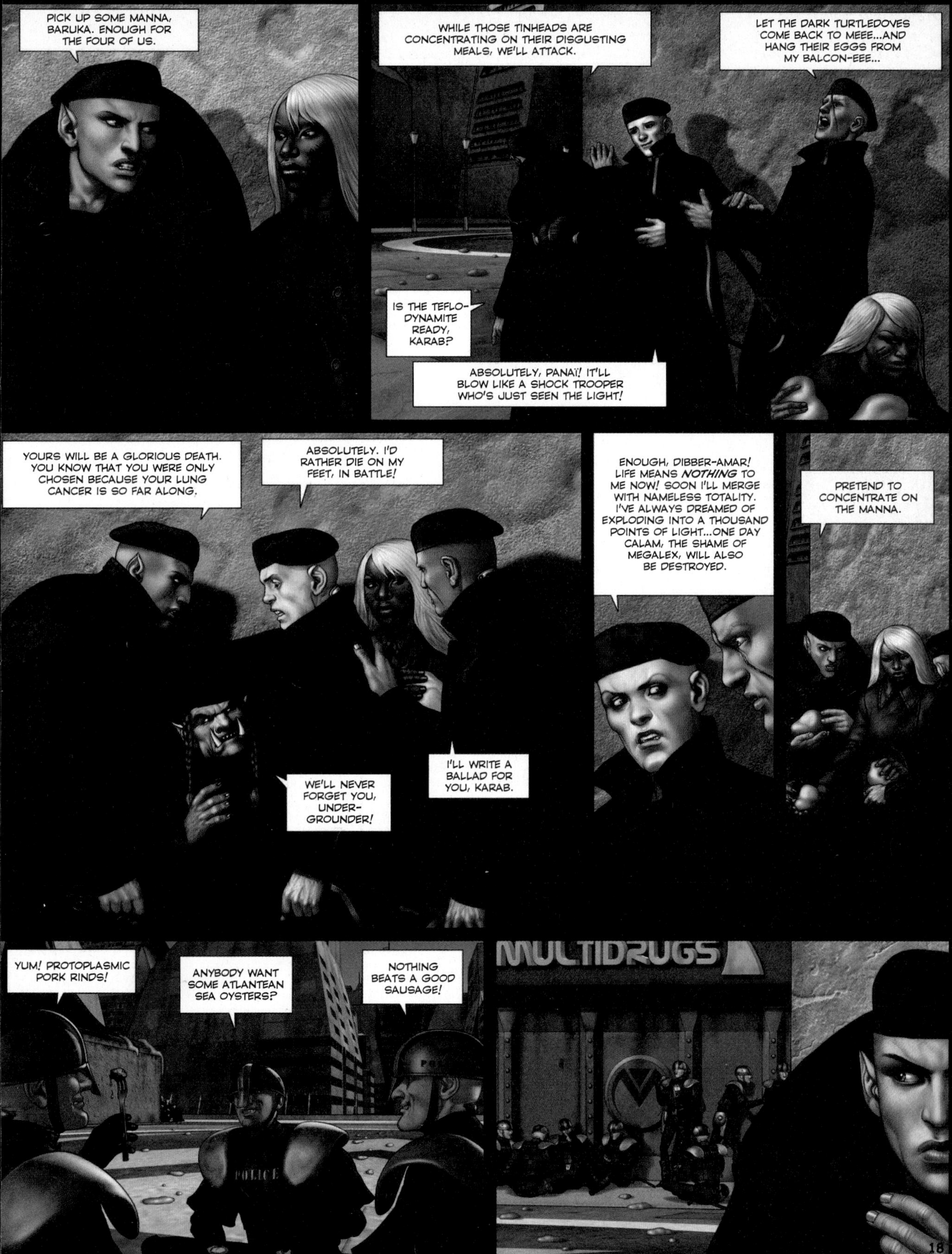

PICK UP SOME MANNA, BARUKA. ENOUGH FOR THE FOUR OF US.
WHILE THOSE TINHEADS ARE CONCENTRATING ON THEIR DISGUSTING MEALS, WE'LL ATTACK.
LET THE DARK TURTLEDOVES COME BACK TO MEEE...AND HANG THEIR EGGS FROM MY BALCON-EEE...
IS THE TEFLO-DYNAMITE READY, KARAB?
ABSOLUTELY, PANAÏ! IT'LL BLOW LIKE A SHOCK TROOPER WHO'S JUST SEEN THE LIGHT!
YOURS WILL BE A GLORIOUS DEATH. YOU KNOW THAT YOU WERE ONLY CHOSEN BECAUSE YOUR LUNG CANCER IS SO FAR ALONG.
ABSOLUTELY. I'D RATHER DIE ON MY FEET, IN BATTLE!
WE'LL NEVER FORGET YOU, UNDER-GROUNDER!
I'LL WRITE A BALLAD FOR YOU, KARAB.
ENOUGH, DIBBER-AMAR! LIFE MEANS ***NOTHING*** TO ME NOW! SOON I'LL MERGE WITH NAMELESS TOTALITY. I'VE ALWAYS DREAMED OF EXPLODING INTO A THOUSAND POINTS OF LIGHT...ONE DAY CALAM, THE SHAME OF MEGALEX, WILL ALSO BE DESTROYED.
PRETEND TO CONCENTRATE ON THE MANNA.
YUM! PROTOPLASMIC PORK RINDS!
ANYBODY WANT SOME ATLANTEAN SEA OYSTERS?
NOTHING BEATS A GOOD SAUSAGE!
POLICE
MULTIDRUGS
18

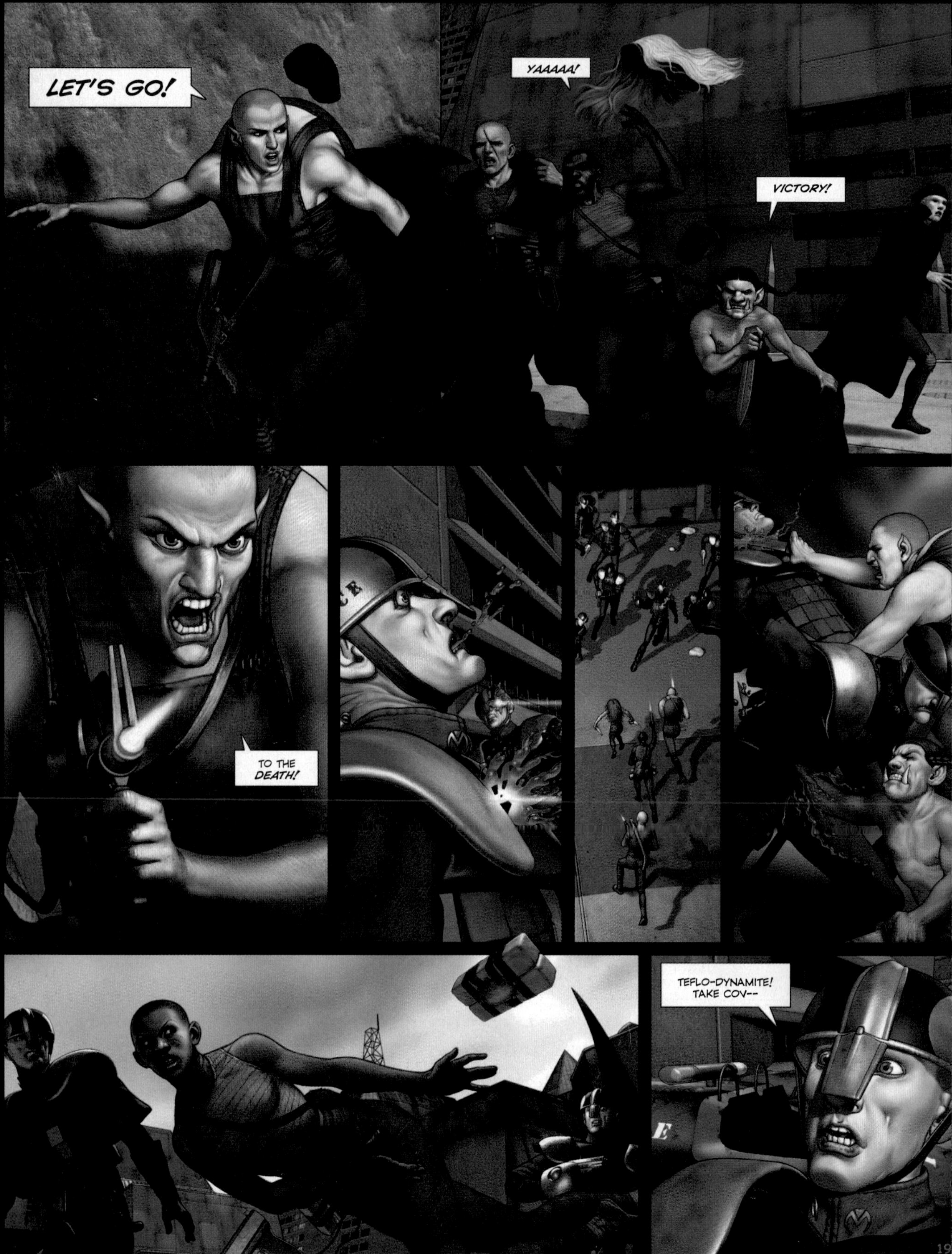
LET'S GO!
YAAAAA!
VICTORY!
TO THE DEATH!
TEFLO-DYNAMITE! TAKE COV--

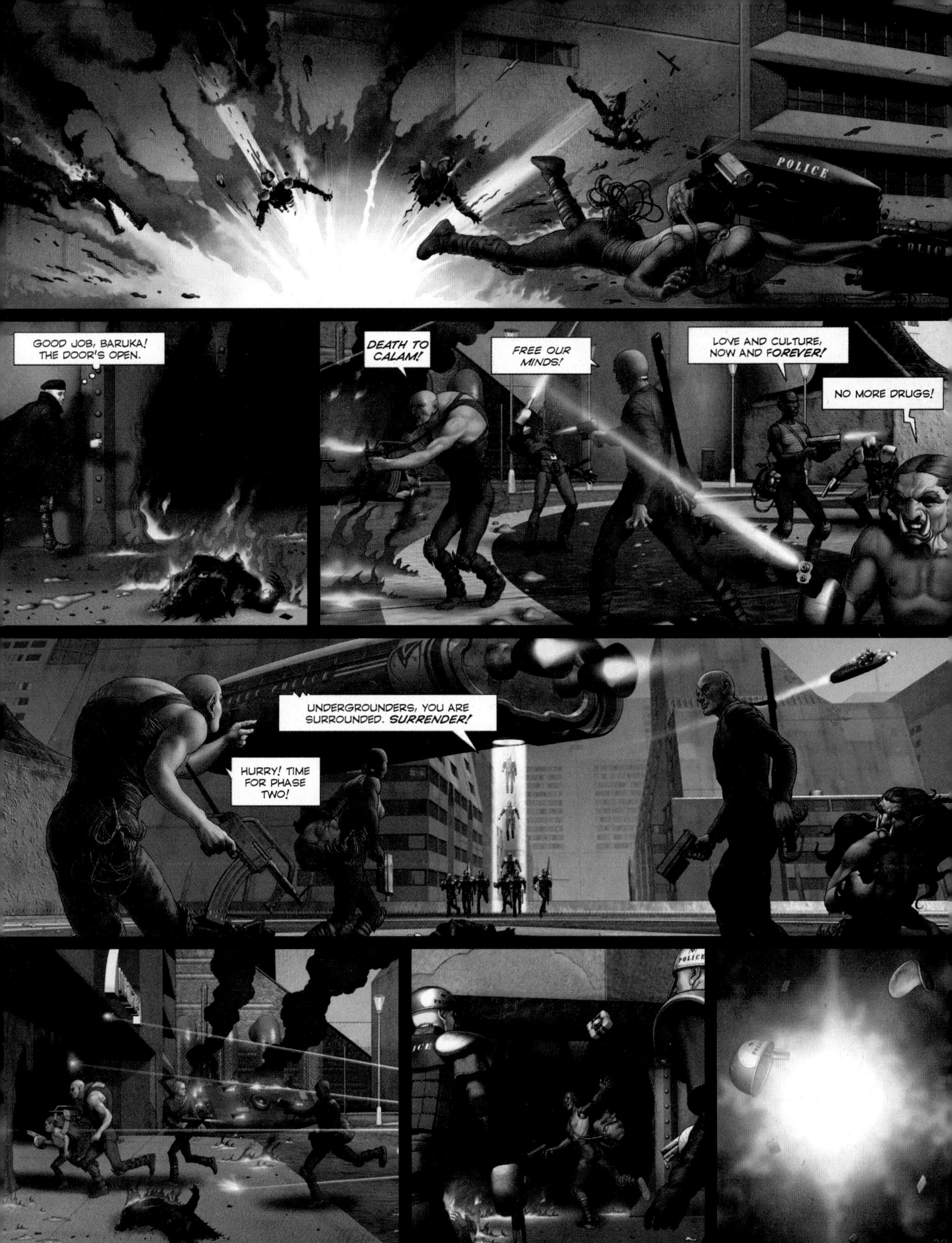
GOOD JOB, BARUKA! THE DOOR'S OPEN.
DEATH TO CALAM!
FREE OUR MINDS!
LOVE AND CULTURE, NOW AND FOREVER!
NO MORE DRUGS!
UNDERGROUNDERS, YOU ARE SURROUNDED. SURRENDER!
HURRY! TIME FOR PHASE TWO!
POLICE

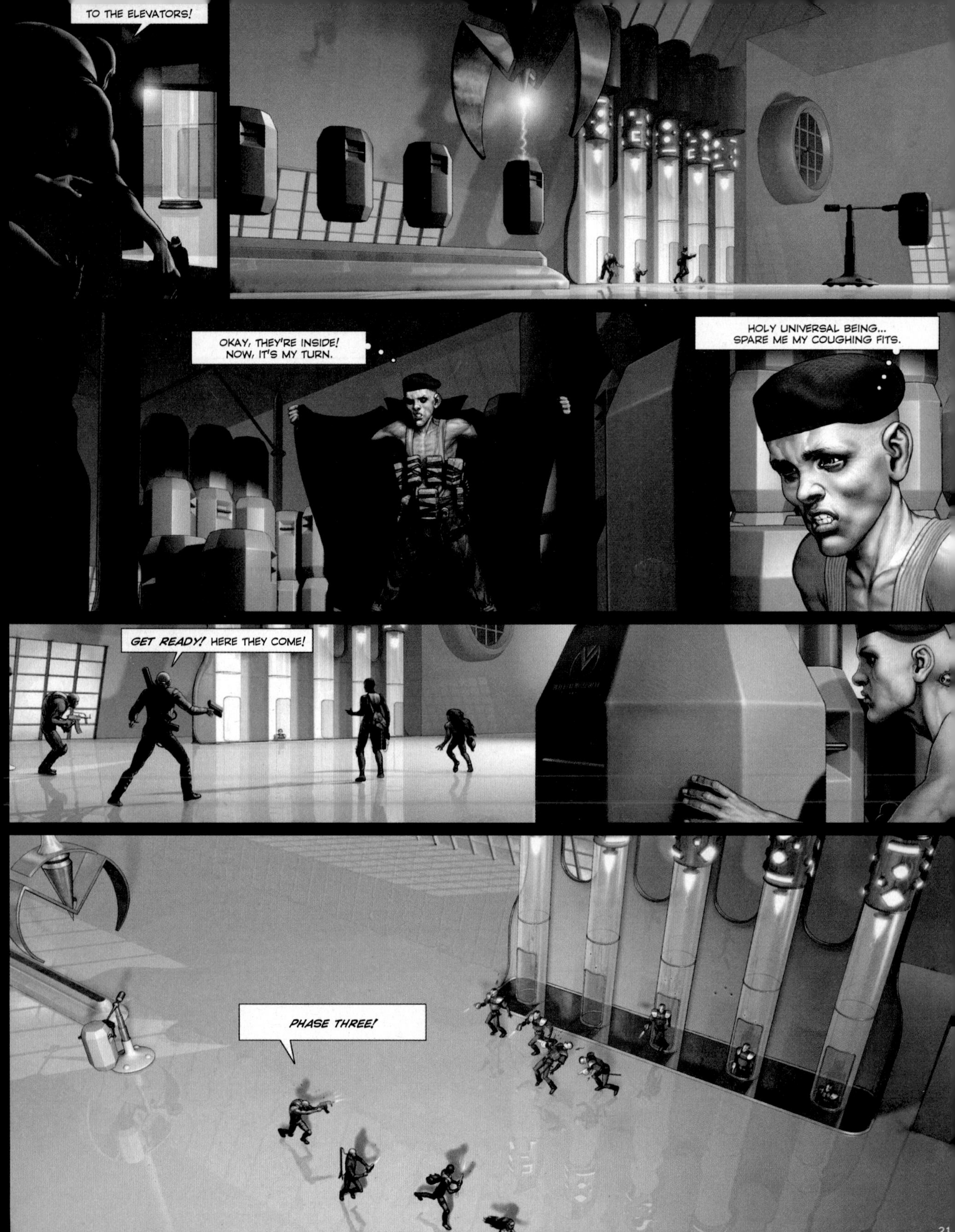
TO THE ELEVATORS!
OKAY, THEY'RE INSIDE! NOW, IT'S MY TURN.
HOLY UNIVERSAL BEING... SPARE ME MY COUGHING FITS.
GET READY! HERE THEY COME!
PHASE THREE!

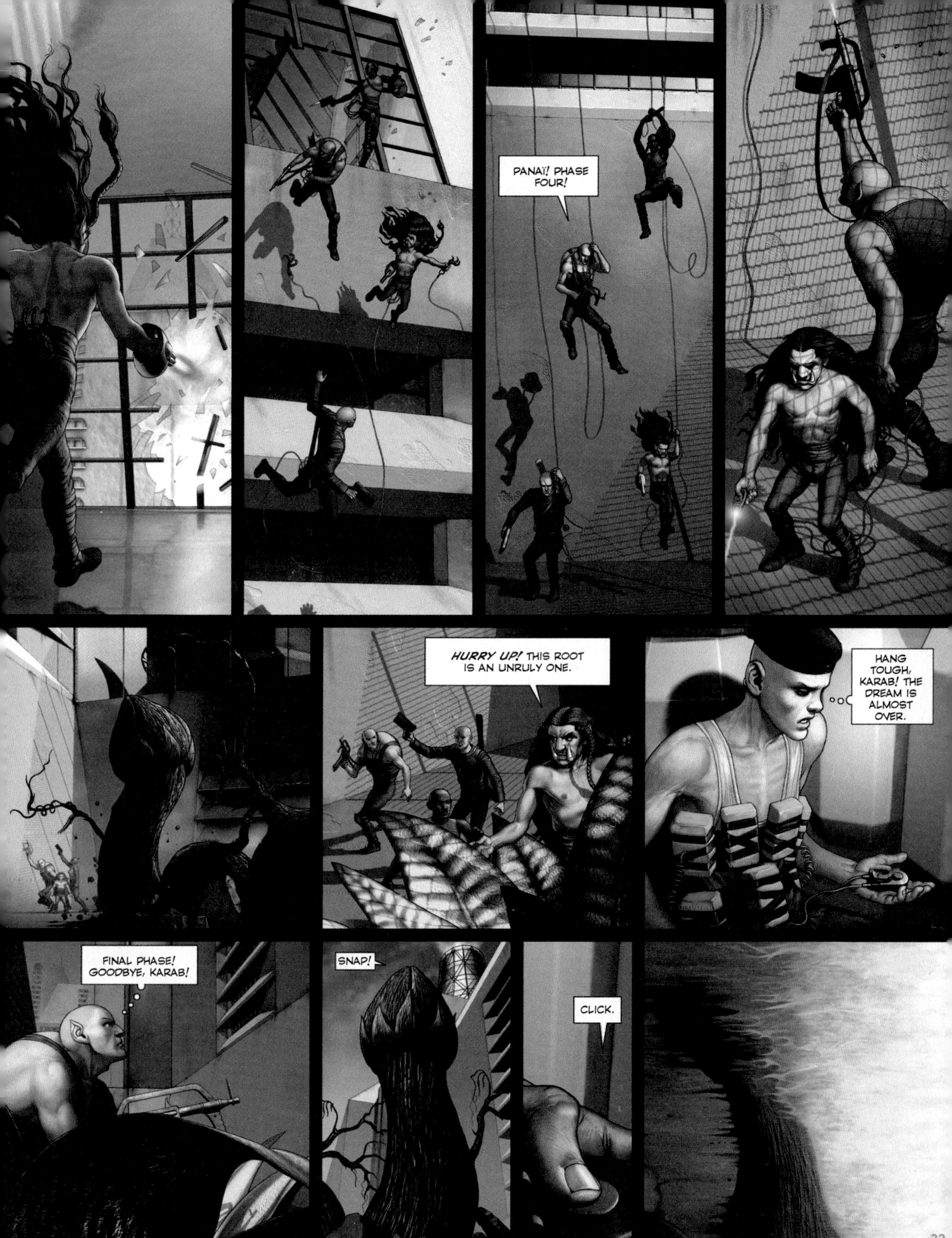

PANAÏ! PHASE FOUR!
HURRY UP! THIS ROOT IS AN UNRULY ONE.
HANG TOUGH, KARAB! THE DREAM IS ALMOST OVER.
FINAL PHASE! GOODBYE, KARAB!
SNAP!
CLICK.

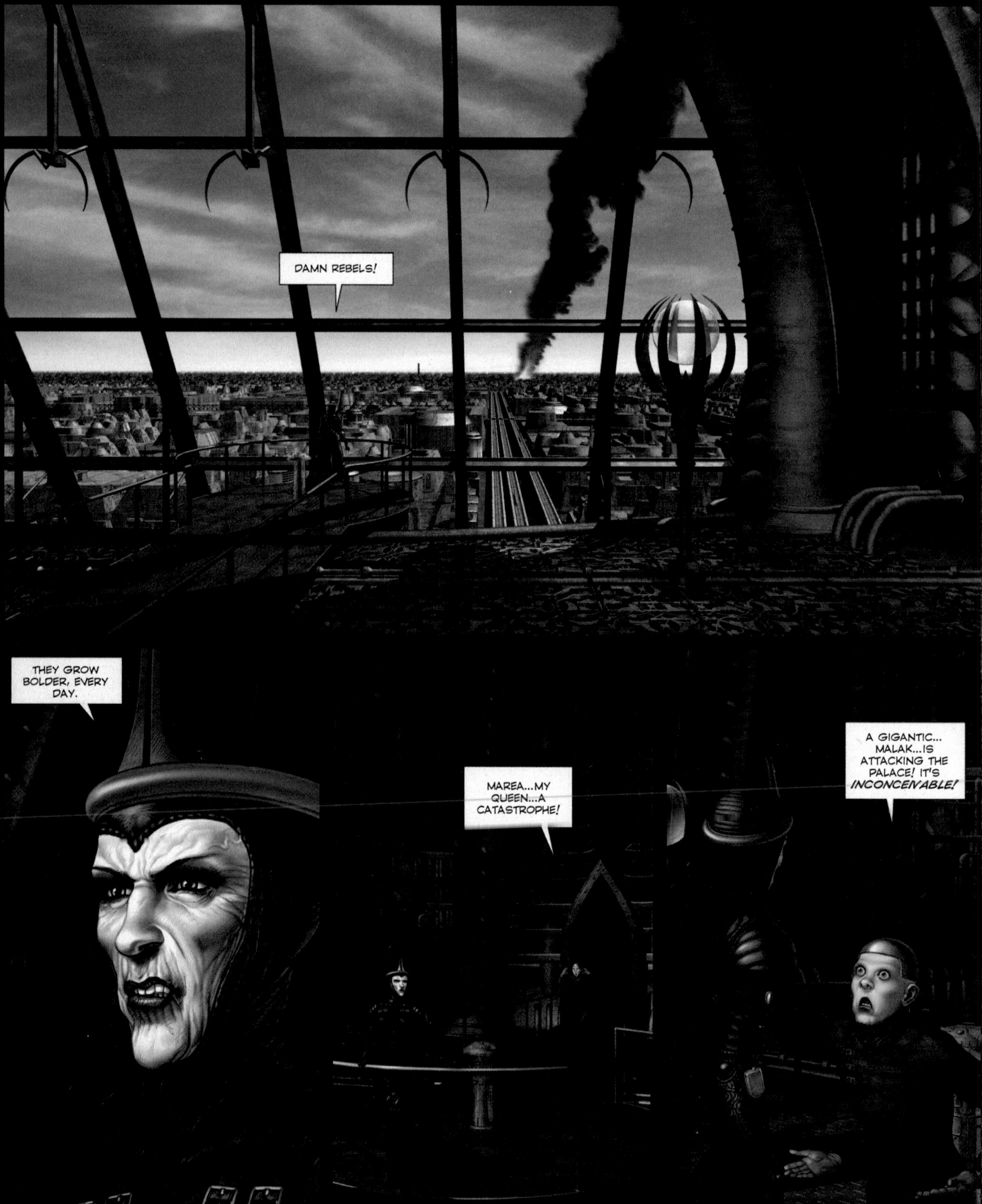
DAMN REBELS!
THEY GROW BOLDER, EVERY DAY.
MAREA...MY QUEEN...A CATASTROPHE!
A GIGANTIC... MALAK...IS ATTACKING THE PALACE! IT'S *INCONCEIVABLE!*
WHAT? A DIRECT ATTACK ON THE PALACE? BLACK ALERT!
23

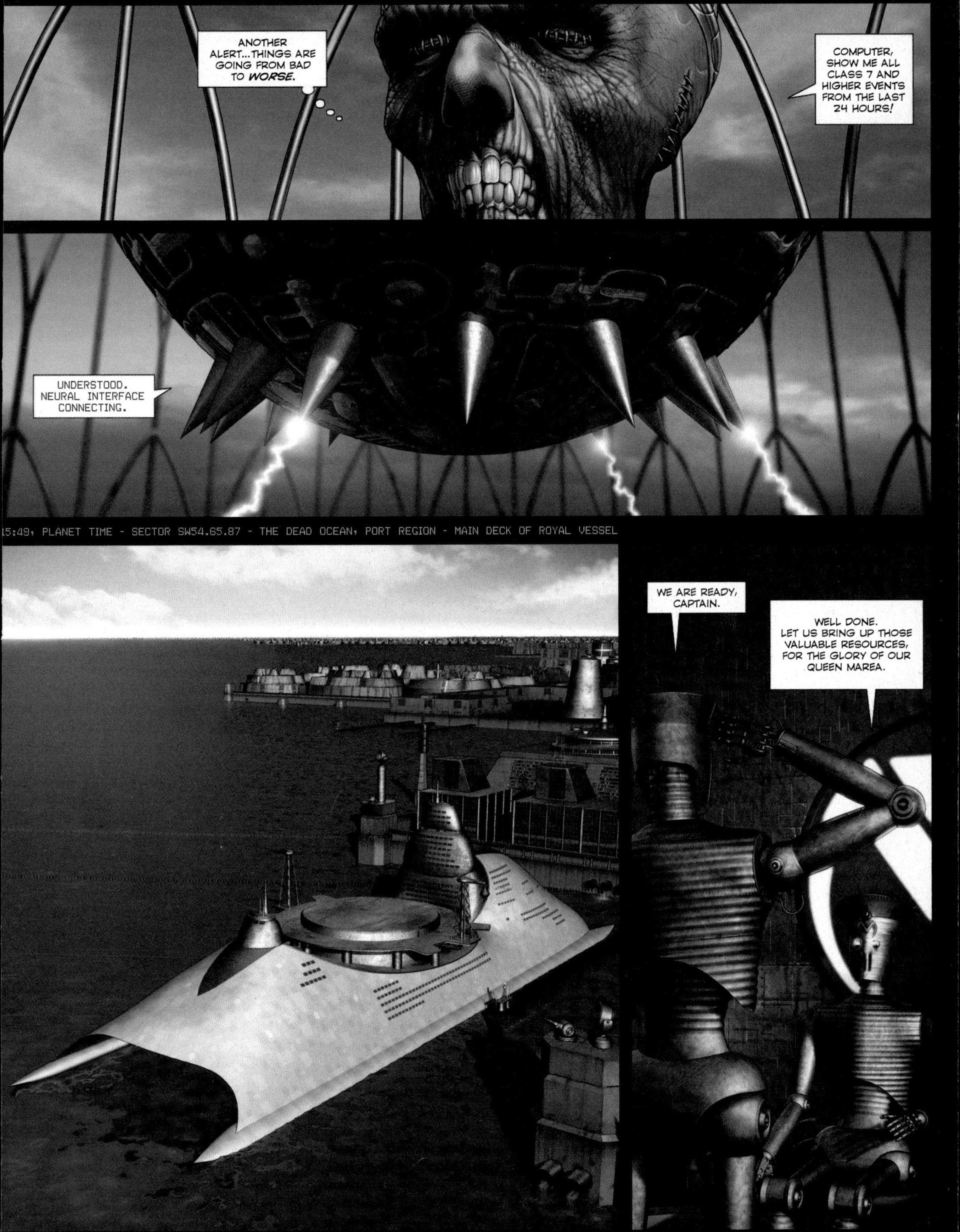
ANOTHER ALERT...THINGS ARE GOING FROM BAD TO WORSE.
COMPUTER, SHOW ME ALL CLASS 7 AND HIGHER EVENTS FROM THE LAST 24 HOURS!
UNDERSTOOD. NEURAL INTERFACE CONNECTING.
15:49, PLANET TIME - SECTOR SW54.65.87 - THE DEAD OCEAN, PORT REGION - MAIN DECK OF ROYAL VESSEL
WE ARE READY, CAPTAIN.
WELL DONE. LET US BRING UP THOSE VALUABLE RESOURCES, FOR THE GLORY OF OUR QUEEN MAREA.

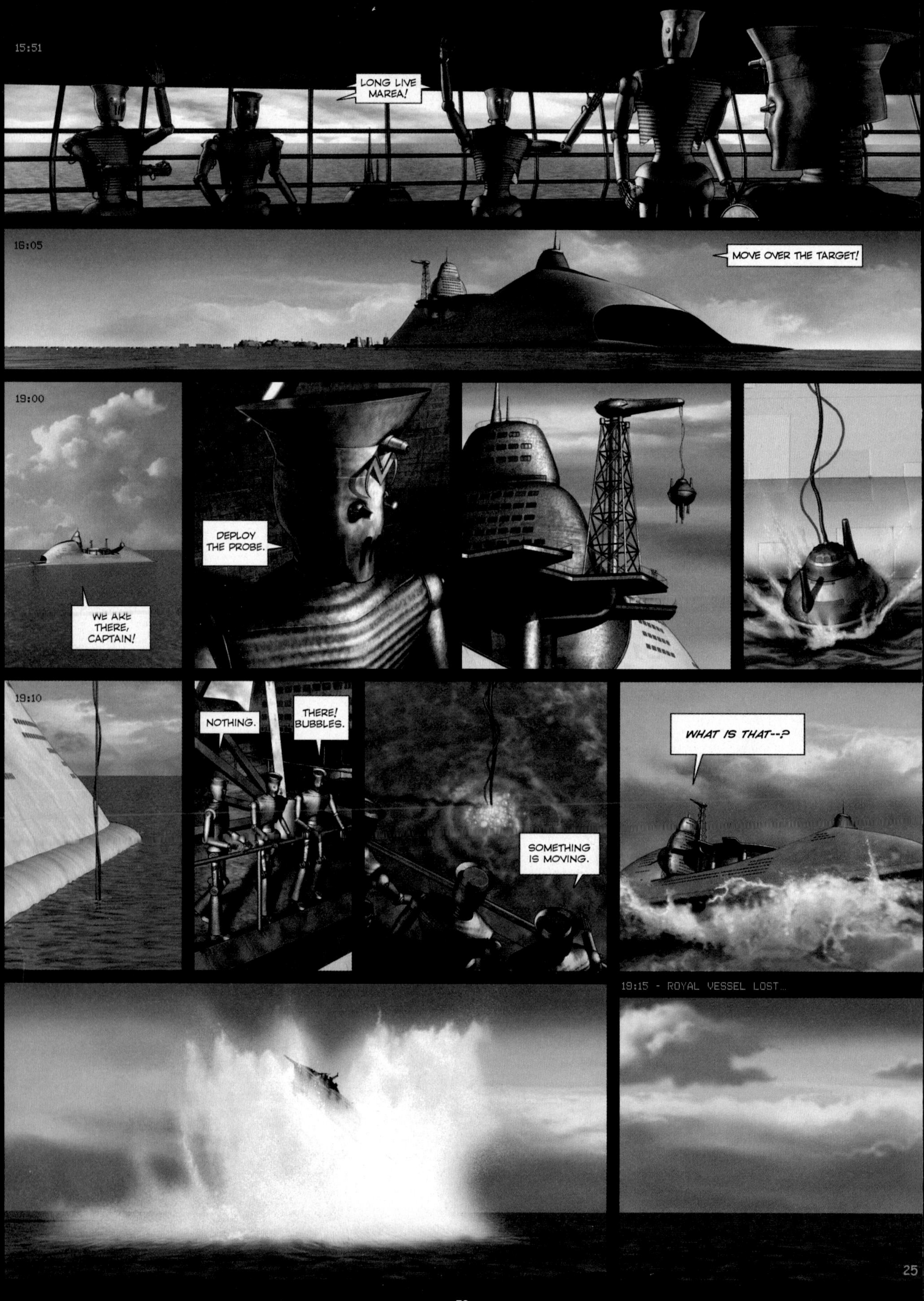
15:51
LONG LIVE MAREA!
16:05
MOVE OVER THE TARGET!
19:00
WE ARE THERE, CAPTAIN!
DEPLOY THE PROBE.
19:10
NOTHING.
THERE! BUBBLES.
SOMETHING IS MOVING.
WHAT IS THAT--?
19:15 - ROYAL VESSEL LOST...
25

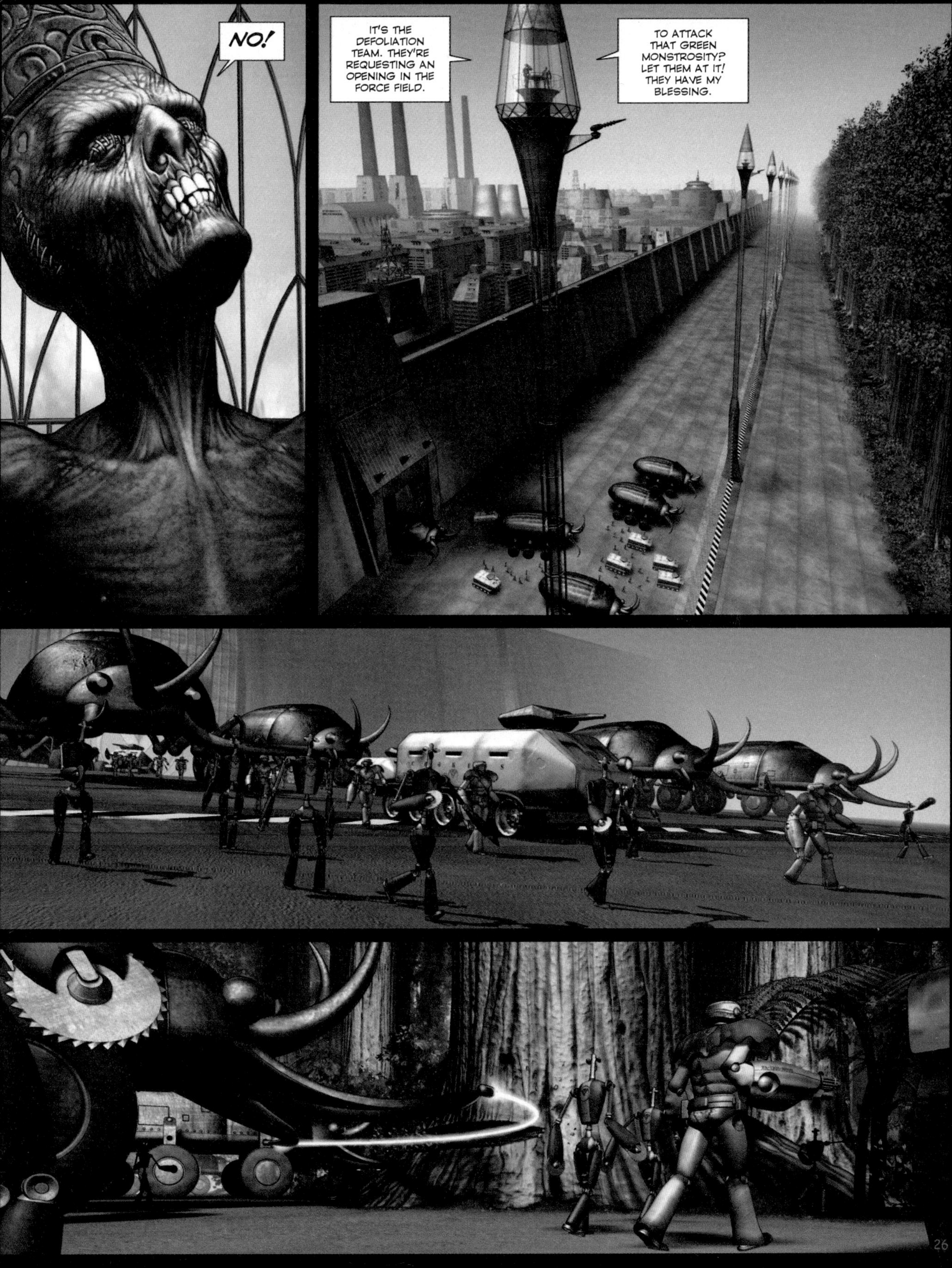
NO!
IT'S THE DEFOLIATION TEAM. THEY'RE REQUESTING AN OPENING IN THE FORCE FIELD.
TO ATTACK THAT GREEN MONSTROSITY? LET THEM AT IT! THEY HAVE MY BLESSING.
26

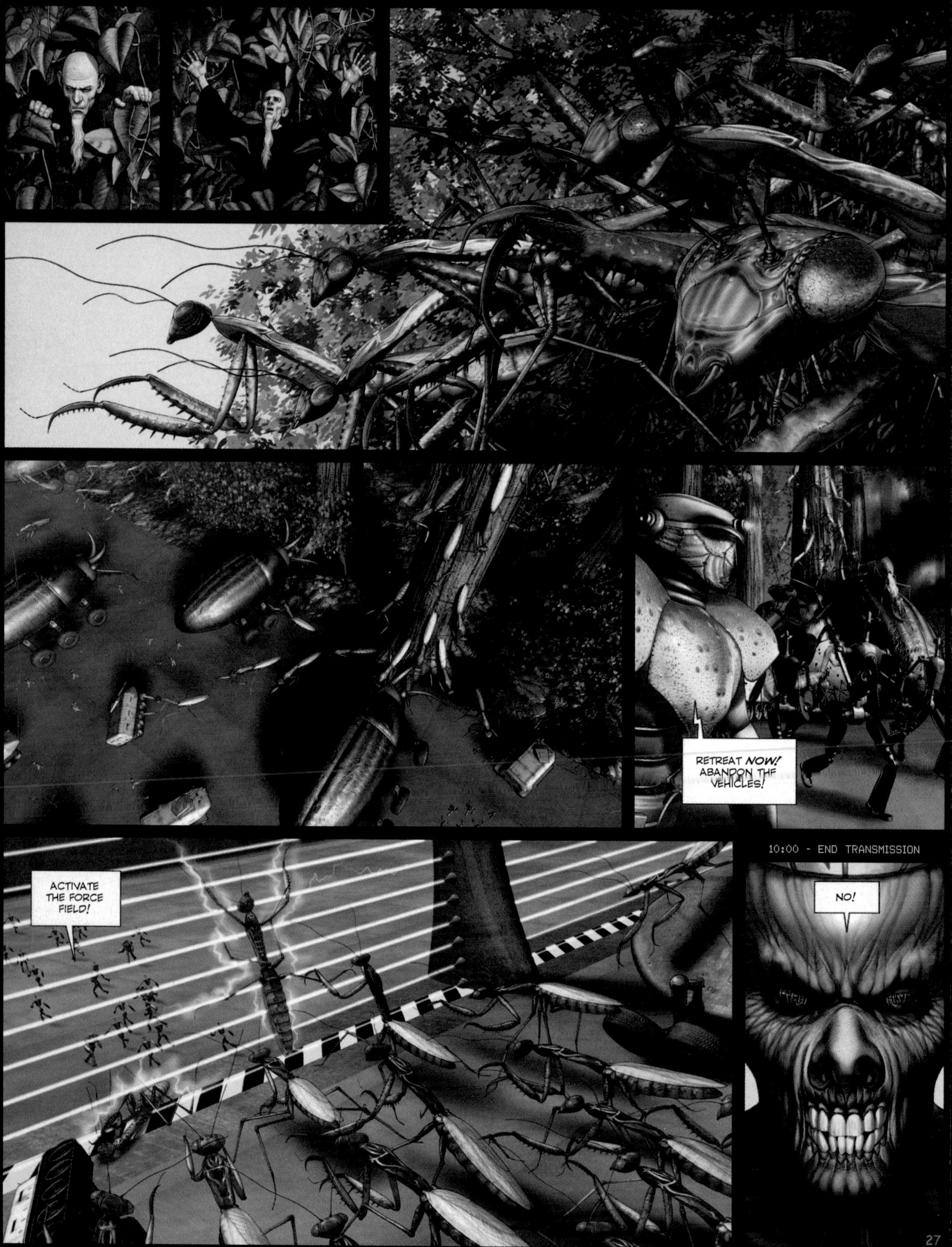
RETREAT NOW! ABANDON THF VEHICLES!
ACTIVATE THE FORCE FIELD!
10:00 - END TRANSMISSION
NO!

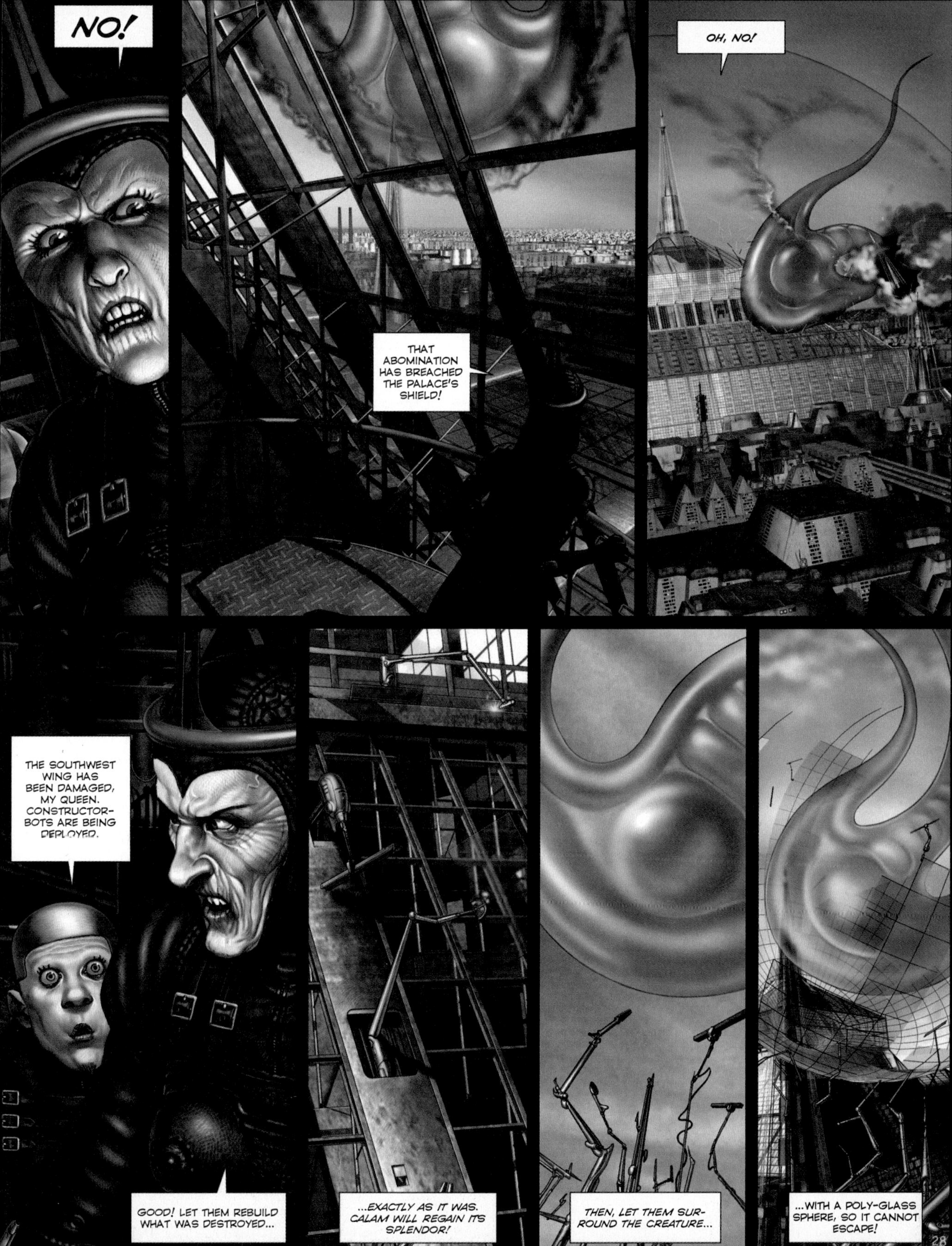
NO!
THAT ABOMINATION HAS BREACHED THE PALACE'S SHIELD!
OH, NO!
THE SOUTHWEST WING HAS BEEN DAMAGED, MY QUEEN. CONSTRUCTOR-BOTS ARE BEING DEPLOYED.
GOOD! LET THEM REBUILD WHAT WAS DESTROYED...
...EXACTLY AS IT WAS. CALAM WILL REGAIN ITS SPLENDOR!
THEN, LET THEM SURROUND THE CREATURE...
...WITH A POLY-GLASS SPHERE, SO IT CANNOT ESCAPE!

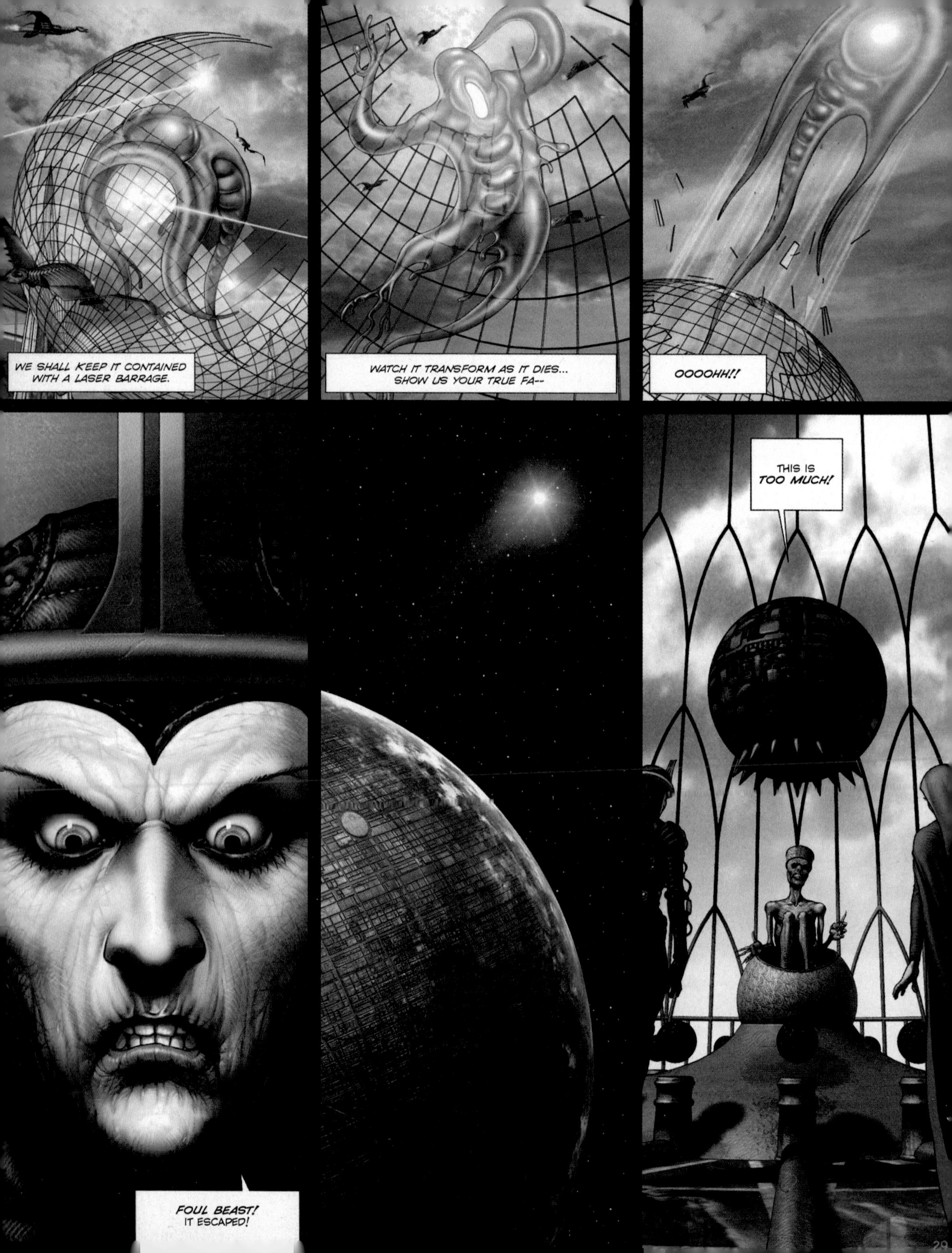
WE SHALL KEEP IT CONTAINED WITH A LASER BARRAGE.
WATCH IT TRANSFORM AS IT DIES... SHOW US YOUR TRUE FA--
OOOOHH!!
FOUL BEAST! IT ESCAPED!
THIS IS TOO MUCH!

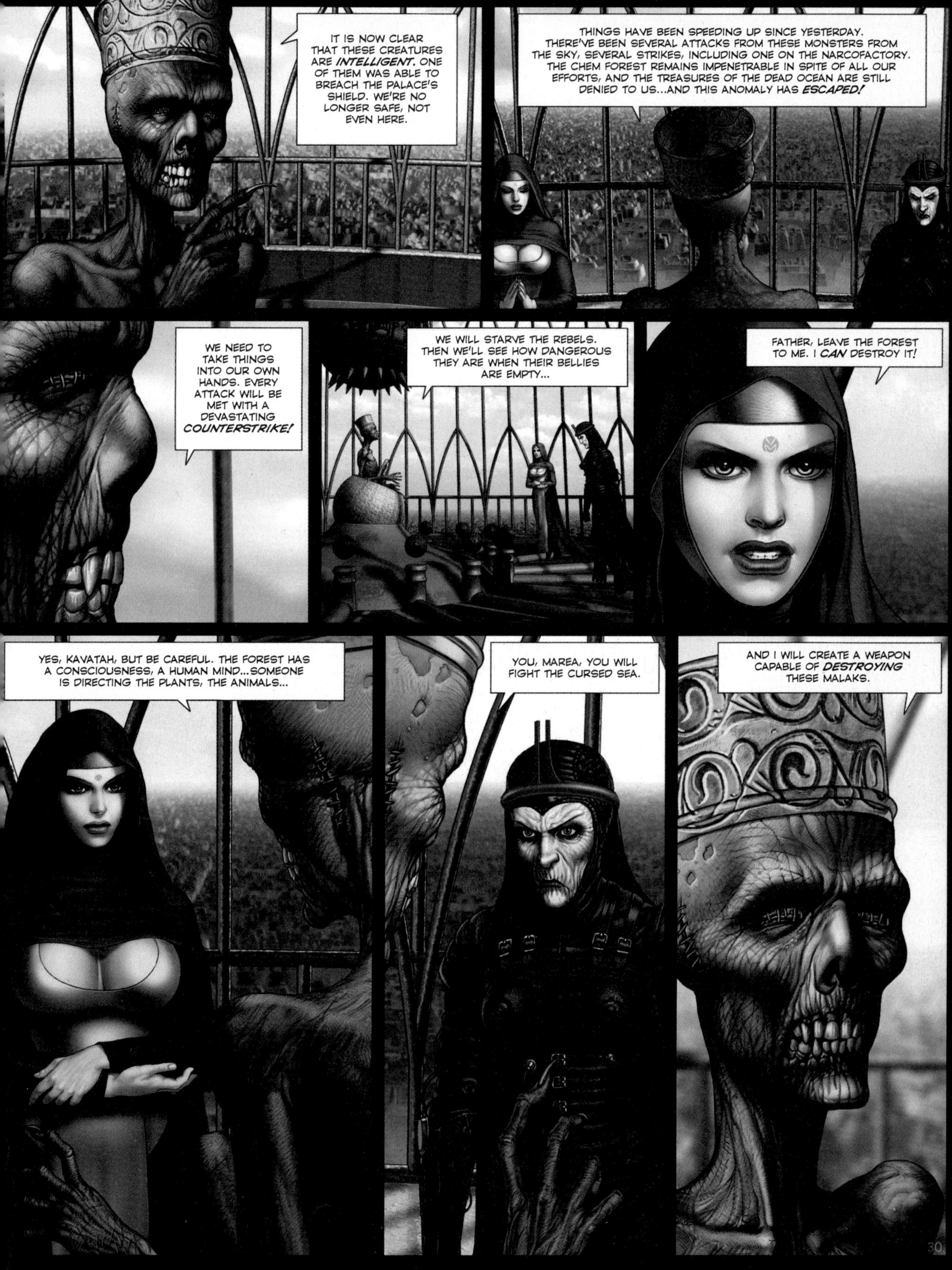
IT IS NOW CLEAR THAT THESE CREATURES ARE *INTELLIGENT*. ONE OF THEM WAS ABLE TO BREACH THE PALACE'S SHIELD. WE'RE NO LONGER SAFE, NOT EVEN HERE.
THINGS HAVE BEEN SPEEDING UP SINCE YESTERDAY. THERE'VE BEEN SEVERAL ATTACKS FROM THESE MONSTERS FROM THE SKY, SEVERAL STRIKES, INCLUDING ONE ON THE NARCOFACTORY. THE CHEM FOREST REMAINS IMPENETRABLE IN SPITE OF ALL OUR EFFORTS, AND THE TREASURES OF THE DEAD OCEAN ARE STILL DENIED TO US...AND THIS ANOMALY HAS *ESCAPED!*
WE NEED TO TAKE THINGS INTO OUR OWN HANDS. EVERY ATTACK WILL BE MET WITH A DEVASTATING *COUNTERSTRIKE!*
WE WILL STARVE THE REBELS. THEN WE'LL SEE HOW DANGEROUS THEY ARE WHEN THEIR BELLIES ARE EMPTY...
FATHER, LEAVE THE FOREST TO ME. I *CAN* DESTROY IT!
YES, KAVATAH, BUT BE CAREFUL. THE FOREST HAS A CONSCIOUSNESS, A HUMAN MIND...SOMEONE IS DIRECTING THE PLANTS, THE ANIMALS...
YOU, MAREA, YOU WILL FIGHT THE CURSED SEA.
AND I WILL CREATE A WEAPON CAPABLE OF *DESTROYING* THESE MALAKS.
30

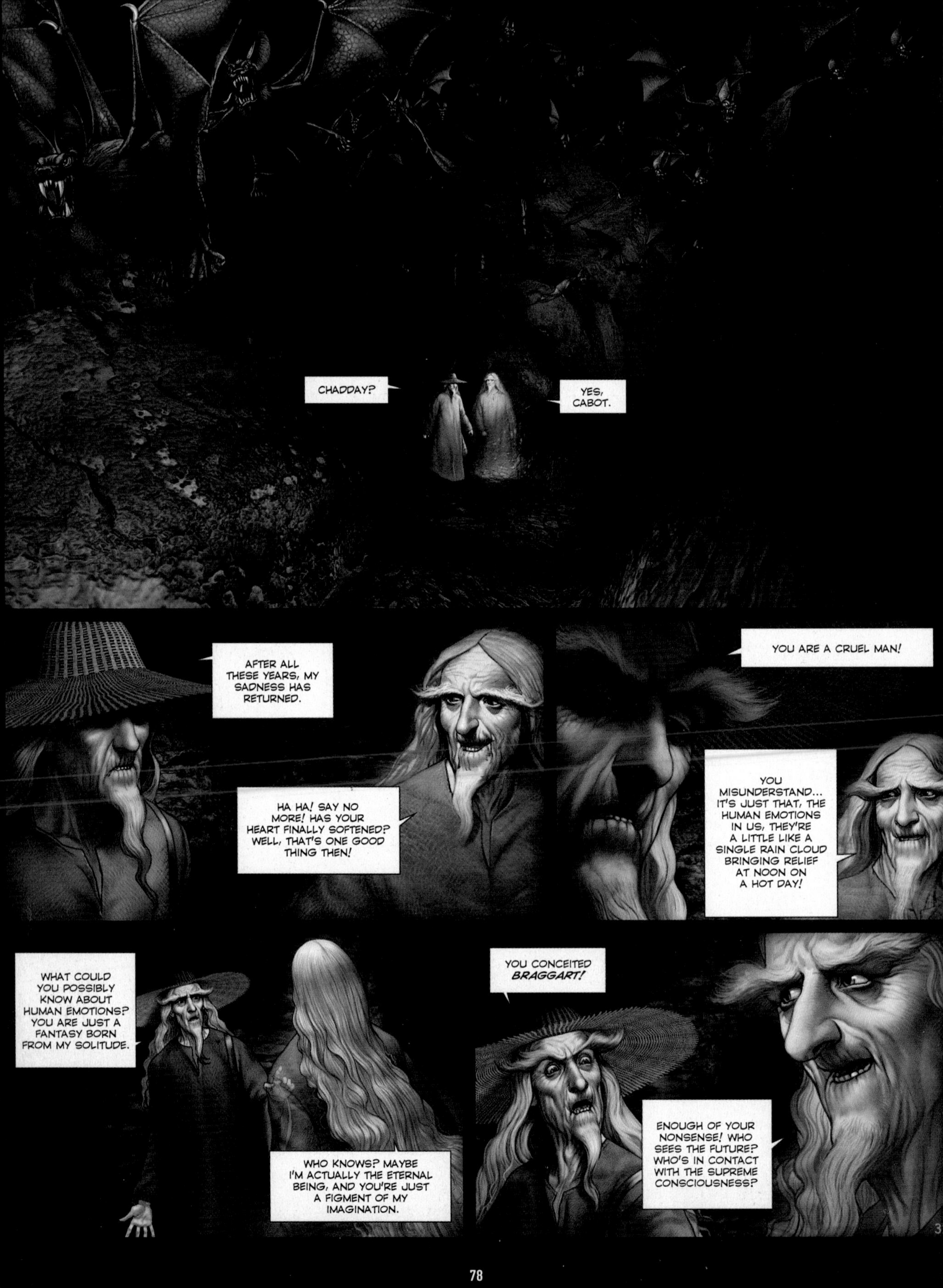
CHADDAY?
YES, CABOT.
AFTER ALL THESE YEARS, MY SADNESS HAS RETURNED.
HA HA! SAY NO MORE! HAS YOUR HEART FINALLY SOFTENED? WELL, THAT'S ONE GOOD THING THEN!
YOU ARE A CRUEL MAN!
YOU MISUNDERSTAND... IT'S JUST THAT, THE HUMAN EMOTIONS IN US, THEY'RE A LITTLE LIKE A SINGLE RAIN CLOUD BRINGING RELIEF AT NOON ON A HOT DAY!
WHAT COULD YOU POSSIBLY KNOW ABOUT HUMAN EMOTIONS? YOU ARE JUST A FANTASY BORN FROM MY SOLITUDE.
WHO KNOWS? MAYBE I'M ACTUALLY THE ETERNAL BEING, AND YOU'RE JUST A FIGMENT OF MY IMAGINATION.
YOU CONCEITED ***BRAGGART!***
ENOUGH OF YOUR NONSENSE! WHO SEES THE FUTURE? WHO'S IN CONTACT WITH THE SUPREME CONSCIOUSNESS?

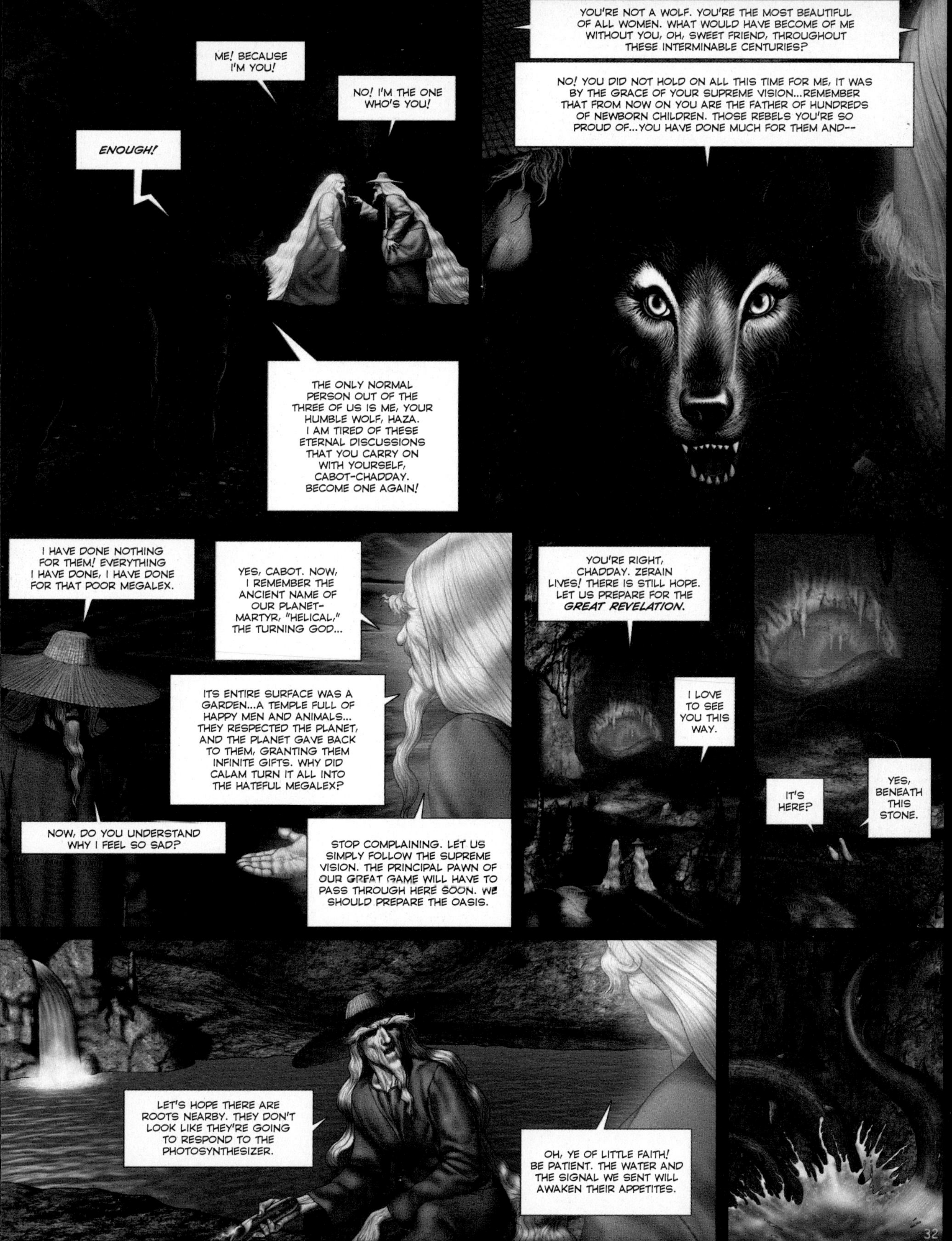
ME! BECAUSE I'M YOU!
NO! I'M THE ONE WHO'S YOU!
ENOUGH!
THE ONLY NORMAL PERSON OUT OF THE THREE OF US IS ME, YOUR HUMBLE WOLF, HAZA. I AM TIRED OF THESE ETERNAL DISCUSSIONS THAT YOU CARRY ON WITH YOURSELF, CABOT-CHADDAY. BECOME ONE AGAIN!
YOU'RE NOT A WOLF. YOU'RE THE MOST BEAUTIFUL OF ALL WOMEN. WHAT WOULD HAVE BECOME OF ME WITHOUT YOU, OH, SWEET FRIEND, THROUGHOUT THESE INTERMINABLE CENTURIES?
NO! YOU DID NOT HOLD ON ALL THIS TIME FOR ME, IT WAS BY THE GRACE OF YOUR SUPREME VISION...REMEMBER THAT FROM NOW ON YOU ARE THE FATHER OF HUNDREDS OF NEWBORN CHILDREN. THOSE REBELS YOU'RE SO PROUD OF...YOU HAVE DONE MUCH FOR THEM AND--
I HAVE DONE NOTHING FOR THEM! EVERYTHING I HAVE DONE, I HAVE DONE FOR THAT POOR MEGALEX.
YES, CABOT. NOW, I REMEMBER THE ANCIENT NAME OF OUR PLANET-MARTYR, "HELICAL," THE TURNING GOD...
ITS ENTIRE SURFACE WAS A GARDEN...A TEMPLE FULL OF HAPPY MEN AND ANIMALS... THEY RESPECTED THE PLANET, AND THE PLANET GAVE BACK TO THEM, GRANTING THEM INFINITE GIFTS. WHY DID CALAM TURN IT ALL INTO THE HATEFUL MEGALEX?
NOW, DO YOU UNDERSTAND WHY I FEEL SO SAD?
STOP COMPLAINING. LET US SIMPLY FOLLOW THE SUPREME VISION. THE PRINCIPAL PAWN OF OUR GREAT GAME WILL HAVE TO PASS THROUGH HERE SOON. WE SHOULD PREPARE THE OASIS.
YOU'RE RIGHT, CHADDAY. ZERAIN LIVES! THERE IS STILL HOPE. LET US PREPARE FOR THE GREAT REVELATION.
I LOVE TO SEE YOU THIS WAY.
IT'S HERE?
YES, BENEATH THIS STONE.
LET'S HOPE THERE ARE ROOTS NEARBY. THEY DON'T LOOK LIKE THEY'RE GOING TO RESPOND TO THE PHOTOSYNTHESIZER.
OH, YE OF LITTLE FAITH! BE PATIENT. THE WATER AND THE SIGNAL WE SENT WILL AWAKEN THEIR APPETITES.

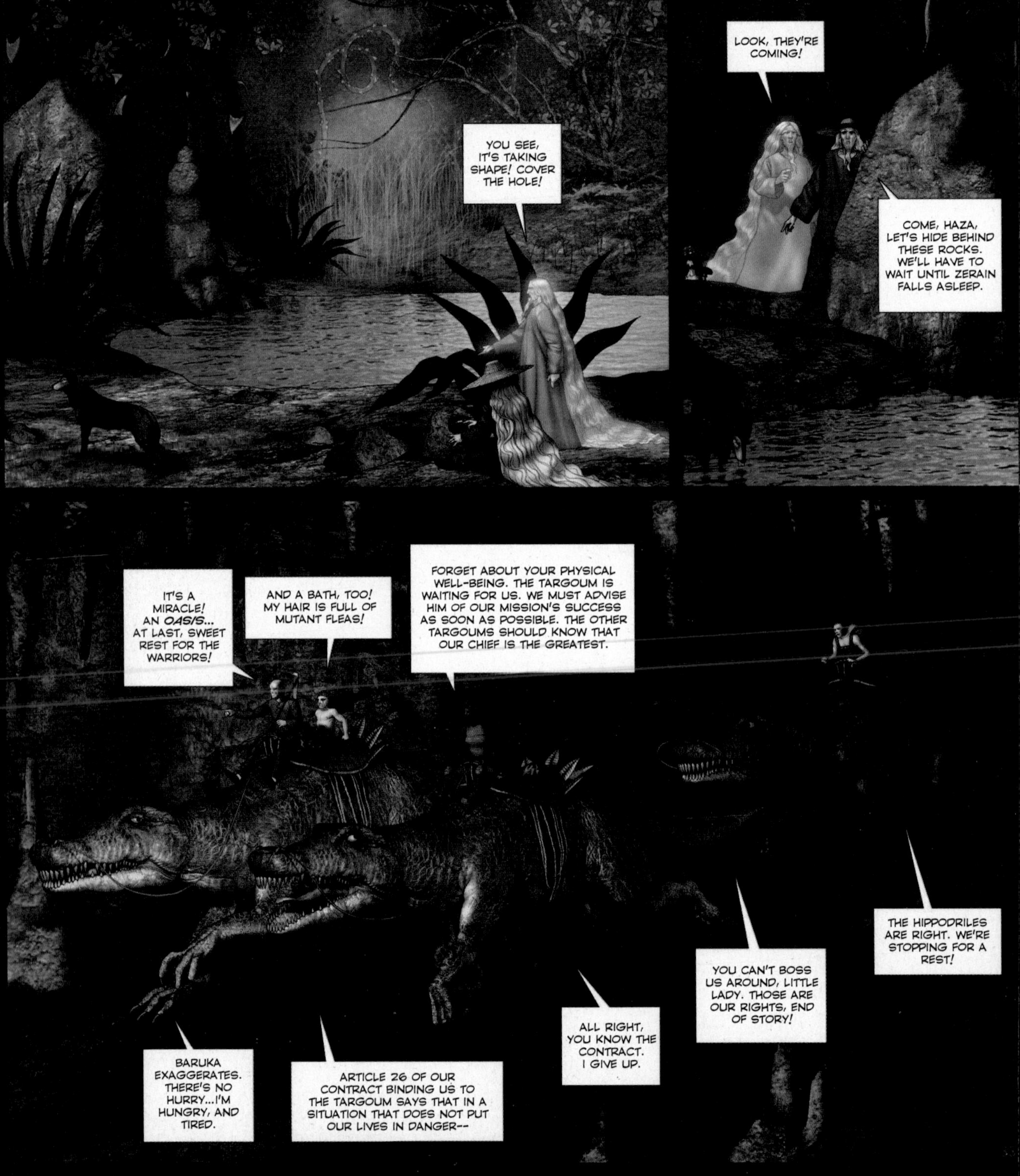

YOU SEE, IT'S TAKING SHAPE! COVER THE HOLE!
LOOK, THEY'RE COMING!
COME, HAZA, LET'S HIDE BEHIND THESE ROCKS. WE'LL HAVE TO WAIT UNTIL ZERAIN FALLS ASLEEP.
IT'S A MIRACLE! AN *OASIS*... AT LAST, SWEET REST FOR THE WARRIORS!
AND A BATH, TOO! MY HAIR IS FULL OF MUTANT FLEAS!
FORGET ABOUT YOUR PHYSICAL WELL-BEING. THE TARGOUM IS WAITING FOR US. WE MUST ADVISE HIM OF OUR MISSION'S SUCCESS AS SOON AS POSSIBLE. THE OTHER TARGOUMS SHOULD KNOW THAT OUR CHIEF IS THE GREATEST.
BARUKA EXAGGERATES. THERE'S NO HURRY...I'M HUNGRY, AND TIRED.
ARTICLE 26 OF OUR CONTRACT BINDING US TO THE TARGOUM SAYS THAT IN A SITUATION THAT DOES NOT PUT OUR LIVES IN DANGER--
ALL RIGHT, YOU KNOW THE CONTRACT. I GIVE UP.
YOU CAN'T BOSS US AROUND, LITTLE LADY. THOSE ARE OUR RIGHTS, END OF STORY!
THE HIPPODRILES ARE RIGHT. WE'RE STOPPING FOR A REST!

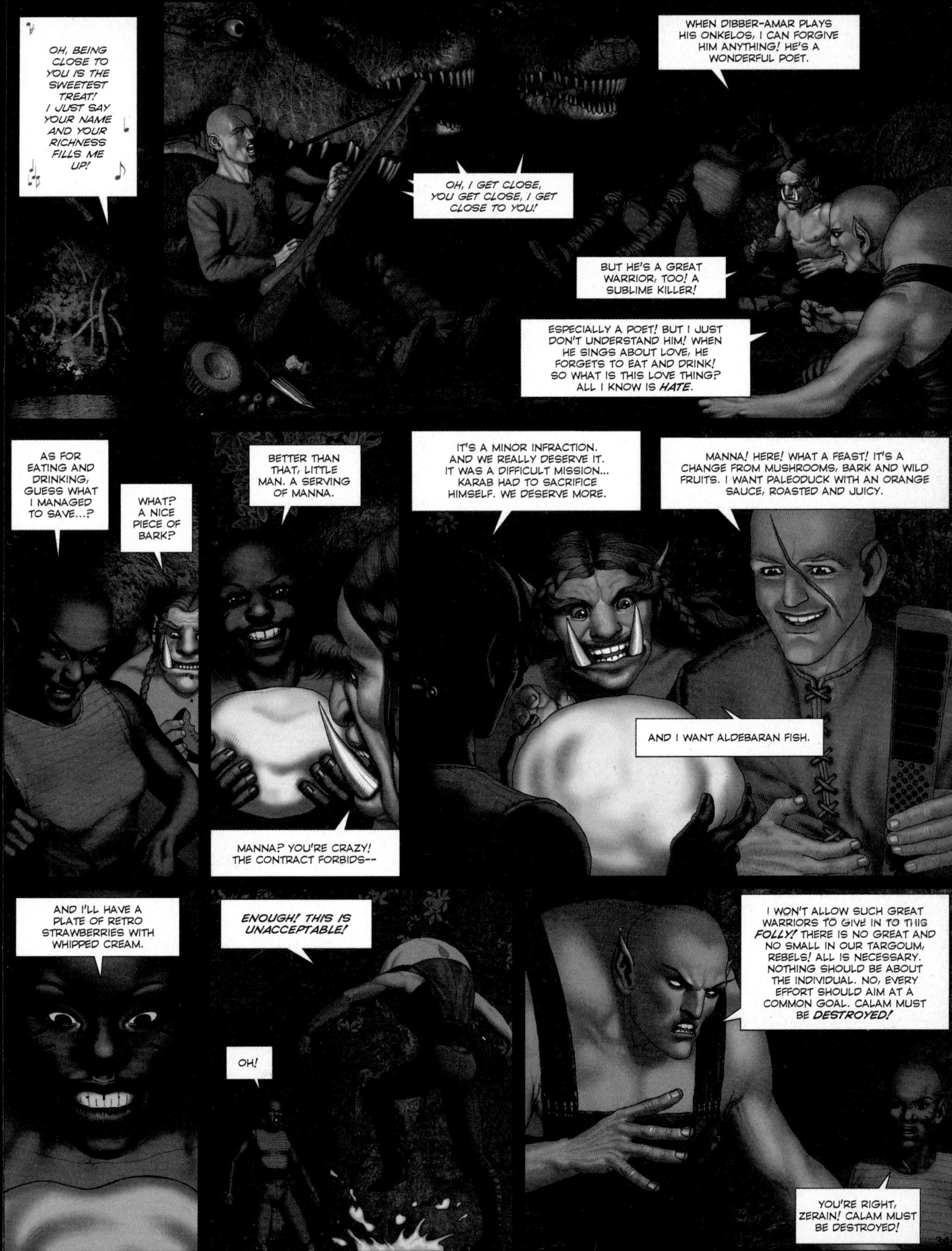
OH, BEING CLOSE TO YOU IS THE SWEETEST TREAT! I JUST SAY YOUR NAME AND YOUR RICHNESS FILLS ME UP!
OH, I GET CLOSE, YOU GET CLOSE, I GET CLOSE TO YOU!
WHEN DIBBER-AMAR PLAYS HIS ONKELOS, I CAN FORGIVE HIM ANYTHING! HE'S A WONDERFUL POET.
BUT HE'S A GREAT WARRIOR, TOO! A SUBLIME KILLER!
ESPECIALLY A POET! BUT I JUST DON'T UNDERSTAND HIM! WHEN HE SINGS ABOUT LOVE, HE FORGETS TO EAT AND DRINK! SO WHAT IS THIS LOVE THING? ALL I KNOW IS HATE.
AS FOR EATING AND DRINKING, GUESS WHAT I MANAGED TO SAVE...?
WHAT? A NICE PIECE OF BARK?
BETTER THAN THAT, LITTLE MAN. A SERVING OF MANNA.
MANNA? YOU'RE CRAZY! THE CONTRACT FORBIDS--
IT'S A MINOR INFRACTION. AND WE REALLY DESERVE IT. IT WAS A DIFFICULT MISSION... KARAB HAD TO SACRIFICE HIMSELF. WE DESERVE MORE.
MANNA! HERE! WHAT A FEAST! IT'S A CHANGE FROM MUSHROOMS, BARK AND WILD FRUITS. I WANT PALEODUCK WITH AN ORANGE SAUCE, ROASTED AND JUICY.
AND I WANT ALDEBARAN FISH.
AND I'LL HAVE A PLATE OF RETRO STRAWBERRIES WITH WHIPPED CREAM.
ENOUGH! THIS IS UNACCEPTABLE!
OH!
I WON'T ALLOW SUCH GREAT WARRIORS TO GIVE IN TO THIS FOLLY! THERE IS NO GREAT AND NO SMALL IN OUR TARGOUM, REBELS! ALL IS NECESSARY. NOTHING SHOULD BE ABOUT THE INDIVIDUAL. NO, EVERY EFFORT SHOULD AIM AT A COMMON GOAL. CALAM MUST BE DESTROYED!
YOU'RE RIGHT, ZERAIN! CALAM MUST BE DESTROYED!

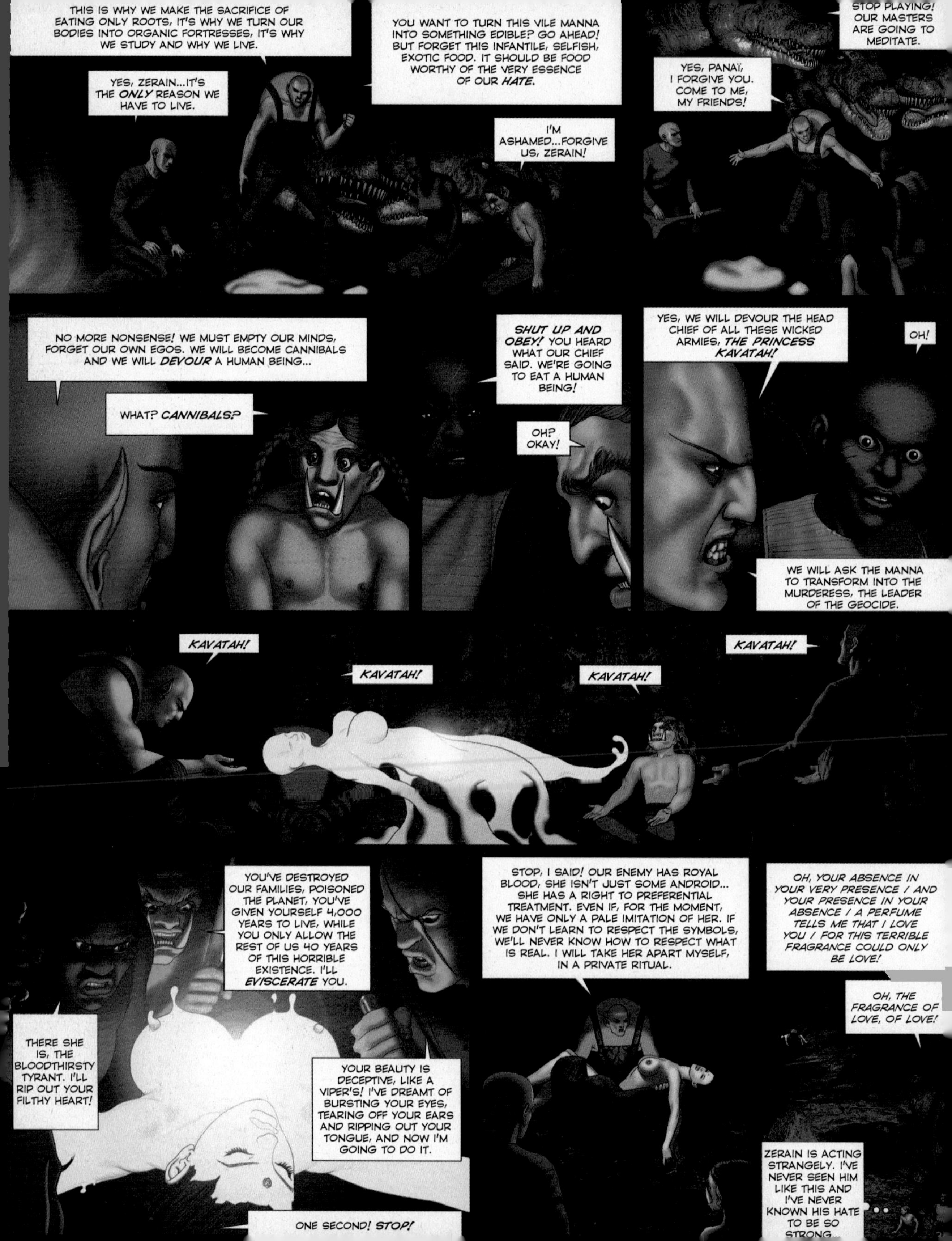

THIS IS WHY WE MAKE THE SACRIFICE OF EATING ONLY ROOTS, IT'S WHY WE TURN OUR BODIES INTO ORGANIC FORTRESSES, IT'S WHY WE STUDY AND WHY WE LIVE.
YES, ZERAIN...IT'S THE *ONLY* REASON WE HAVE TO LIVE.
YOU WANT TO TURN THIS VILE MANNA INTO SOMETHING EDIBLE? GO AHEAD! BUT FORGET THIS INFANTILE, SELFISH, EXOTIC FOOD. IT SHOULD BE FOOD WORTHY OF THE VERY ESSENCE OF OUR *HATE*.
I'M ASHAMED...FORGIVE US, ZERAIN!
STOP PLAYING! OUR MASTERS ARE GOING TO MEDITATE.
YES, PANAÏ, I FORGIVE YOU. COME TO ME, MY FRIENDS!
NO MORE NONSENSE! WE MUST EMPTY OUR MINDS, FORGET OUR OWN EGOS. WE WILL BECOME CANNIBALS AND WE WILL *DEVOUR* A HUMAN BEING...
WHAT? *CANNIBALS?*
SHUT UP AND OBEY! YOU HEARD WHAT OUR CHIEF SAID. WE'RE GOING TO EAT A HUMAN BEING!
OH? OKAY!
YES, WE WILL DEVOUR THE HEAD CHIEF OF ALL THESE WICKED ARMIES, *THE PRINCESS KAVATAH!*
OH!
WE WILL ASK THE MANNA TO TRANSFORM INTO THE MURDERESS, THE LEADER OF THE GEOCIDE.
KAVATAH!
KAVATAH!
KAVATAH!
KAVATAH!
YOU'VE DESTROYED OUR FAMILIES, POISONED THE PLANET, YOU'VE GIVEN YOURSELF 4,000 YEARS TO LIVE, WHILE YOU ONLY ALLOW THE REST OF US 40 YEARS OF THIS HORRIBLE EXISTENCE. I'LL *EVISCERATE* YOU.
THERE SHE IS, THE BLOODTHIRSTY TYRANT. I'LL RIP OUT YOUR FILTHY HEART!
YOUR BEAUTY IS DECEPTIVE, LIKE A VIPER'S! I'VE DREAMT OF BURSTING YOUR EYES, TEARING OFF YOUR EARS AND RIPPING OUT YOUR TONGUE, AND NOW I'M GOING TO DO IT.
ONE SECOND! *STOP!*
STOP, I SAID! OUR ENEMY HAS ROYAL BLOOD, SHE ISN'T JUST SOME ANDROID... SHE HAS A RIGHT TO PREFERENTIAL TREATMENT. EVEN IF, FOR THE MOMENT, WE HAVE ONLY A PALE IMITATION OF HER. IF WE DON'T LEARN TO RESPECT THE SYMBOLS, WE'LL NEVER KNOW HOW TO RESPECT WHAT IS REAL. I WILL TAKE HER APART MYSELF, IN A PRIVATE RITUAL.
OH, YOUR ABSENCE IN YOUR VERY PRESENCE / AND YOUR PRESENCE IN YOUR ABSENCE / A PERFUME TELLS ME THAT I LOVE YOU / FOR THIS TERRIBLE FRAGRANCE COULD ONLY BE LOVE!
OH, THE FRAGRANCE OF LOVE, OF LOVE!
ZERAIN IS ACTING STRANGELY. I'VE NEVER SEEN HIM LIKE THIS AND I'VE NEVER KNOWN HIS HATE TO BE SO STRONG...

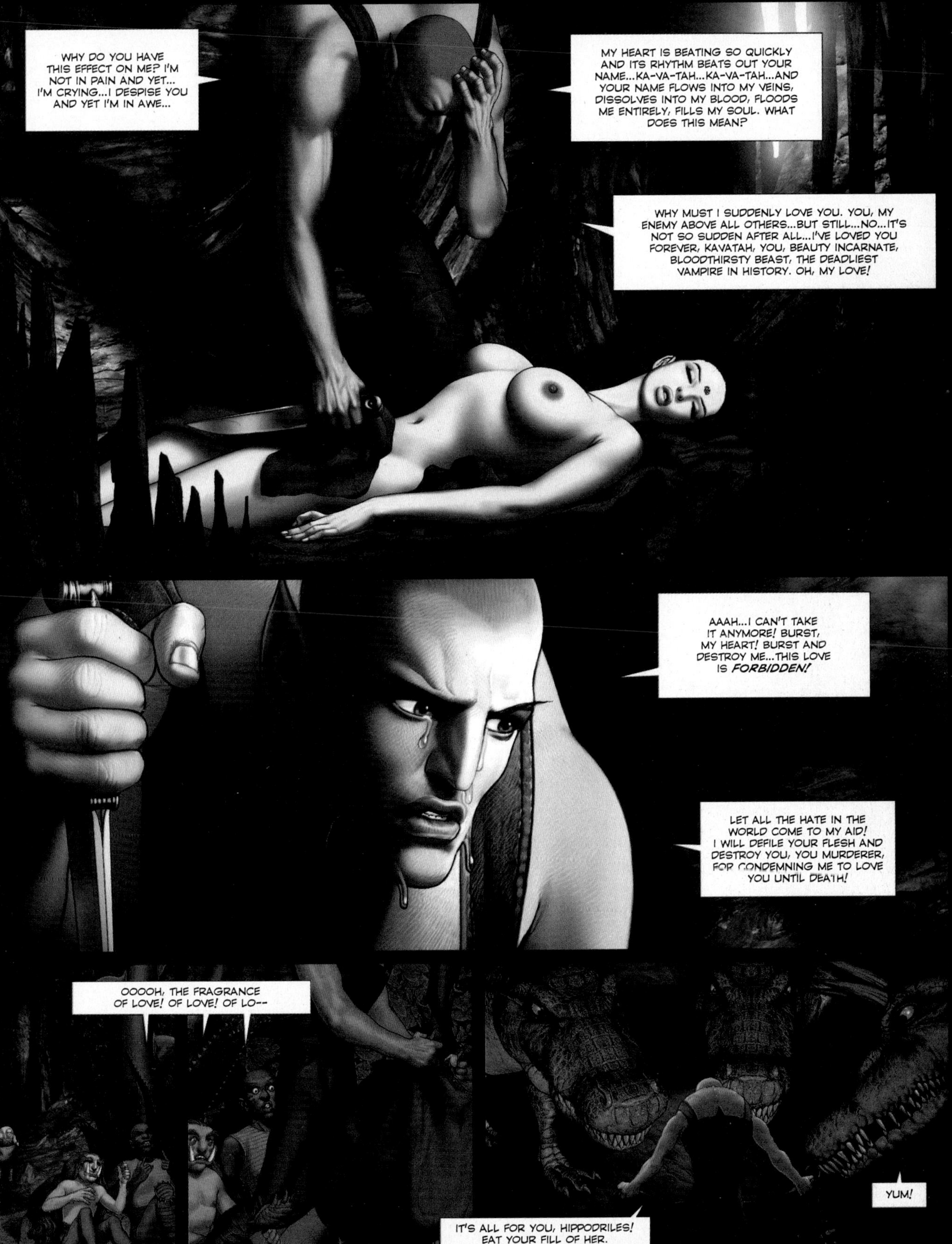
WHY DO YOU HAVE THIS EFFECT ON ME? I'M NOT IN PAIN AND YET... I'M CRYING...I DESPISE YOU AND YET I'M IN AWE...
MY HEART IS BEATING SO QUICKLY AND ITS RHYTHM BEATS OUT YOUR NAME...KA-VA-TAH...KA-VA-TAH...AND YOUR NAME FLOWS INTO MY VEINS, DISSOLVES INTO MY BLOOD, FLOODS ME ENTIRELY, FILLS MY SOUL. WHAT DOES THIS MEAN?
WHY MUST I SUDDENLY LOVE YOU. YOU, MY ENEMY ABOVE ALL OTHERS...BUT STILL...NO...IT'S NOT SO SUDDEN AFTER ALL...I'VE LOVED YOU FOREVER, KAVATAH, YOU, BEAUTY INCARNATE, BLOODTHIRSTY BEAST, THE DEADLIEST VAMPIRE IN HISTORY. OH, MY LOVE!
AAAH...I CAN'T TAKE IT ANYMORE! BURST, MY HEART! BURST AND DESTROY ME...THIS LOVE IS *FORBIDDEN!*
LET ALL THE HATE IN THE WORLD COME TO MY AID! I WILL DEFILE YOUR FLESH AND DESTROY YOU, YOU MURDERER, FOR CONDEMNING ME TO LOVE YOU UNTIL DEATH!
OOOOH, THE FRAGRANCE OF LOVE! OF LOVE! OF LO--
YUM!
IT'S ALL FOR YOU, HIPPODRILES! EAT YOUR FILL OF HER. ***DEATH TO CALAM!***

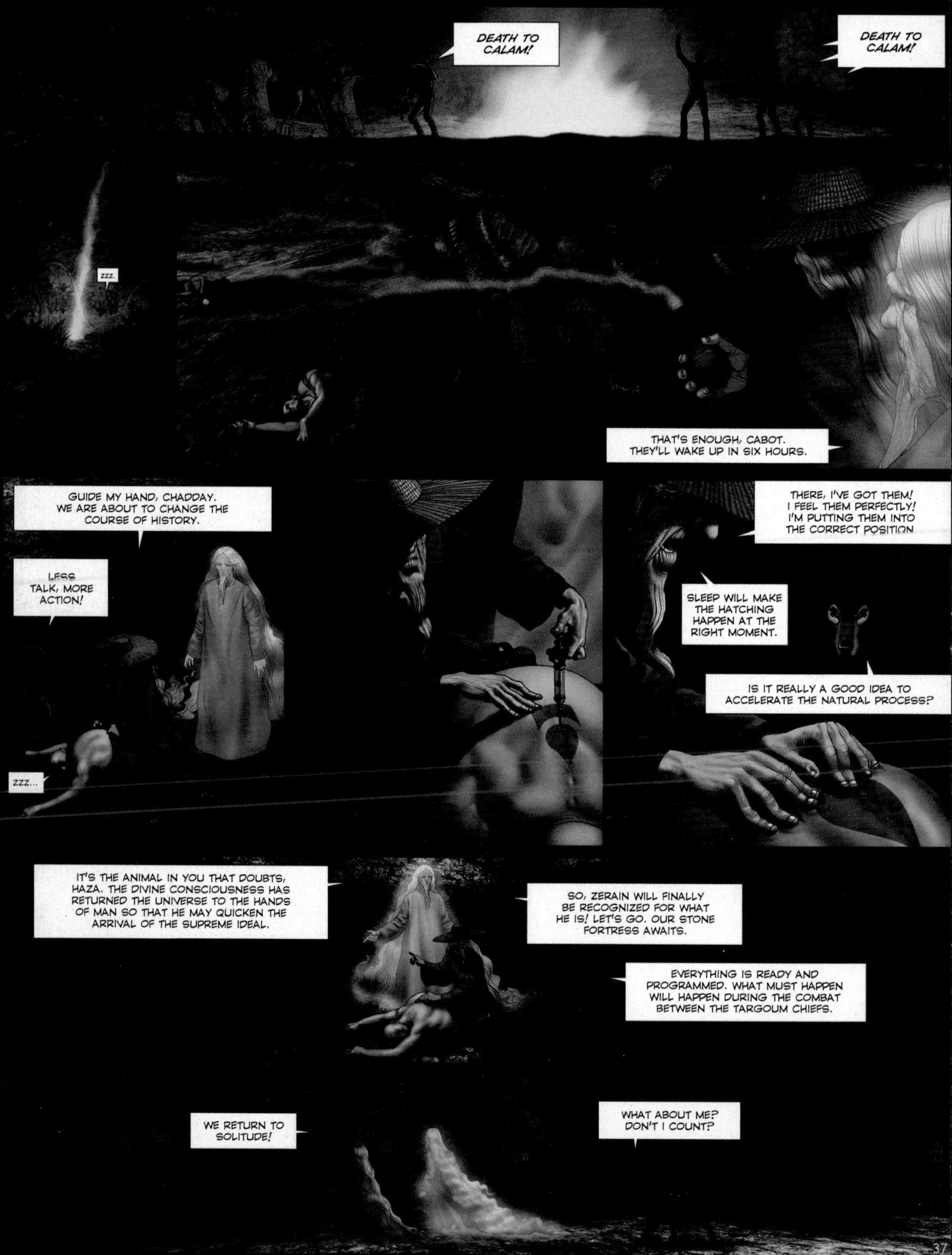
DEATH TO CALAM!
DEATH TO CALAM!
ZZZ.
THAT'S ENOUGH, CABOT. THEY'LL WAKE UP IN SIX HOURS.
GUIDE MY HAND, CHADDAY. WE ARE ABOUT TO CHANGE THE COURSE OF HISTORY.
LESS TALK, MORE ACTION!
ZZZ...
THERE, I'VE GOT THEM! I FEEL THEM PERFECTLY! I'M PUTTING THEM INTO THE CORRECT POSITION
SLEEP WILL MAKE THE HATCHING HAPPEN AT THE RIGHT MOMENT.
IS IT REALLY A GOOD IDEA TO ACCELERATE THE NATURAL PROCESS?
IT'S THE ANIMAL IN YOU THAT DOUBTS, HAZA. THE DIVINE CONSCIOUSNESS HAS RETURNED THE UNIVERSE TO THE HANDS OF MAN SO THAT HE MAY QUICKEN THE ARRIVAL OF THE SUPREME IDEAL.
SO, ZERAIN WILL FINALLY BE RECOGNIZED FOR WHAT HE IS! LET'S GO. OUR STONE FORTRESS AWAITS.
EVERYTHING IS READY AND PROGRAMMED. WHAT MUST HAPPEN WILL HAPPEN DURING THE COMBAT BETWEEN THE TARGOUM CHIEFS.
WE RETURN TO SOLITUDE!
WHAT ABOUT ME? DON'T I COUNT?

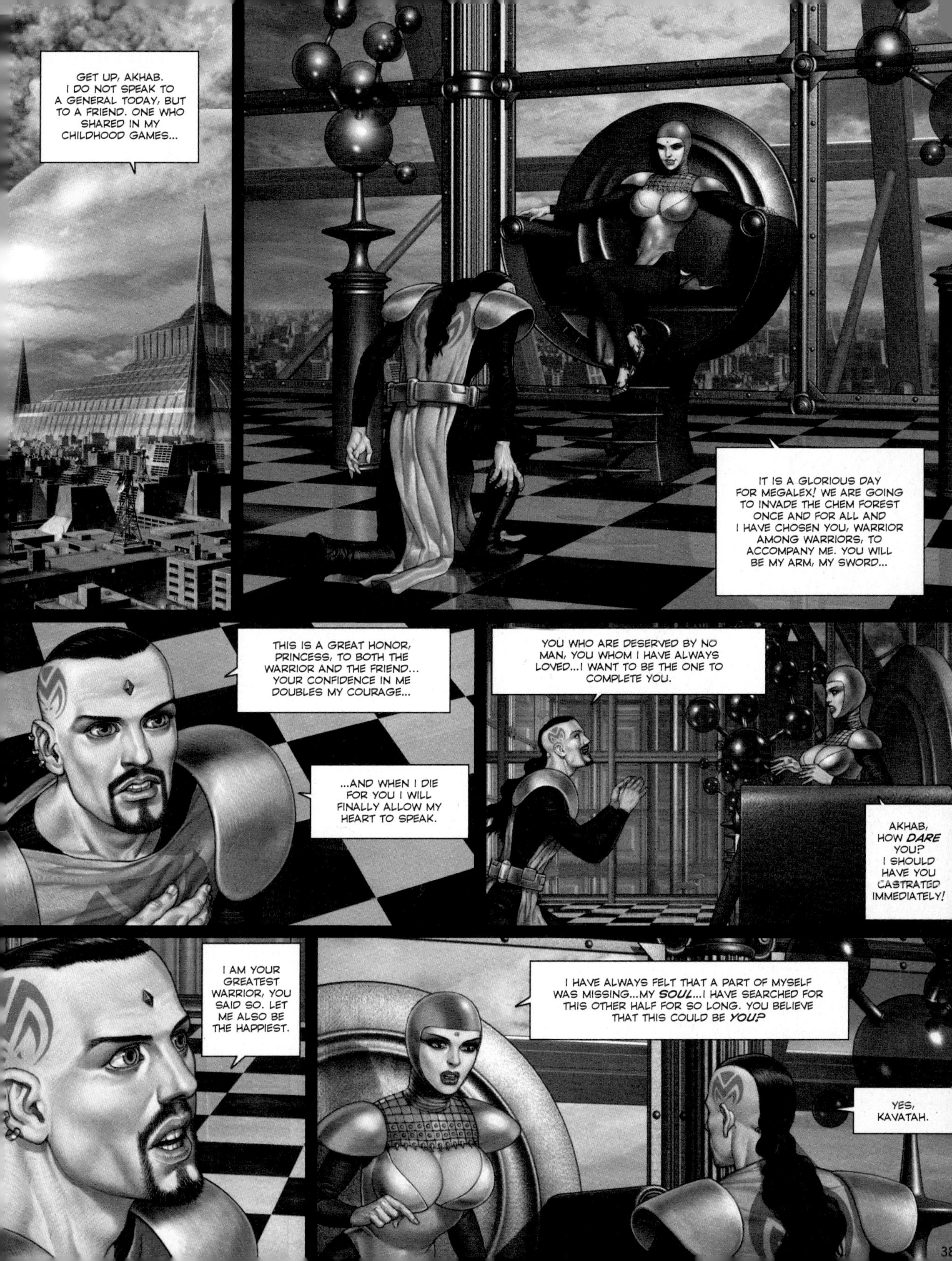
GET UP, AKHAB. I DO NOT SPEAK TO A GENERAL TODAY, BUT TO A FRIEND. ONE WHO SHARED IN MY CHILDHOOD GAMES...
IT IS A GLORIOUS DAY FOR MEGALEX! WE ARE GOING TO INVADE THE CHEM FOREST ONCE AND FOR ALL AND I HAVE CHOSEN YOU, WARRIOR AMONG WARRIORS, TO ACCOMPANY ME. YOU WILL BE MY ARM, MY SWORD...
THIS IS A GREAT HONOR, PRINCESS, TO BOTH THE WARRIOR AND THE FRIEND... YOUR CONFIDENCE IN ME DOUBLES MY COURAGE...
...AND WHEN I DIE FOR YOU I WILL FINALLY ALLOW MY HEART TO SPEAK.
YOU WHO ARE DESERVED BY NO MAN, YOU WHOM I HAVE ALWAYS LOVED...I WANT TO BE THE ONE TO COMPLETE YOU.
AKHAB, HOW DARE YOU? I SHOULD HAVE YOU CASTRATED IMMEDIATELY!
I AM YOUR GREATEST WARRIOR, YOU SAID SO. LET ME ALSO BE THE HAPPIEST.
I HAVE ALWAYS FELT THAT A PART OF MYSELF WAS MISSING...MY SOUL...I HAVE SEARCHED FOR THIS OTHER HALF FOR SO LONG. YOU BELIEVE THAT THIS COULD BE YOU?
YES, KAVATAH.

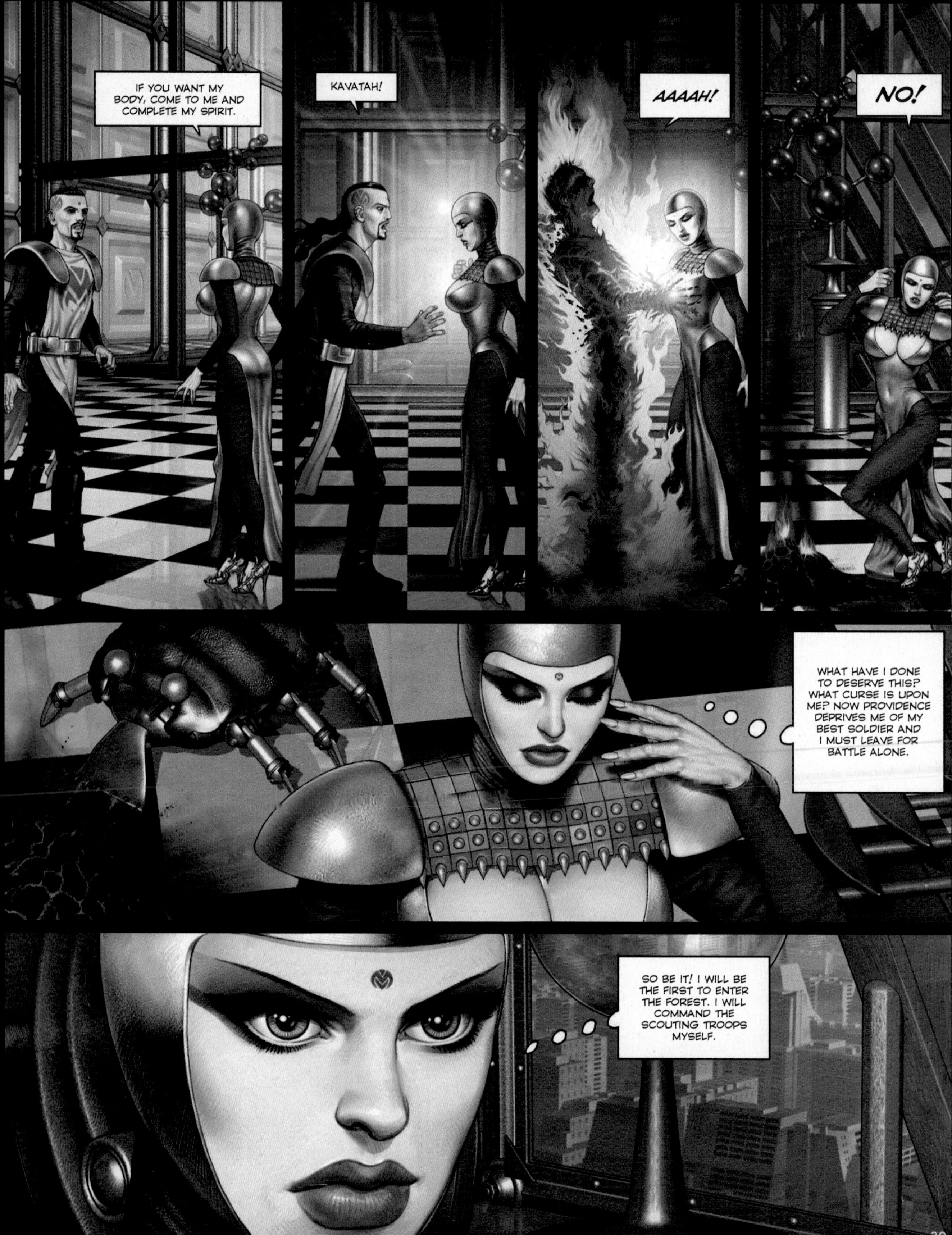
IF YOU WANT MY BODY, COME TO ME AND COMPLETE MY SPIRIT.
KAVATAH!
AAAAH!
NO!
WHAT HAVE I DONE TO DESERVE THIS? WHAT CURSE IS UPON ME? NOW PROVIDENCE DEPRIVES ME OF MY BEST SOLDIER AND I MUST LEAVE FOR BATTLE ALONE.
SO BE IT! I WILL BE THE FIRST TO ENTER THE FOREST. I WILL COMMAND THE SCOUTING TROOPS MYSELF.

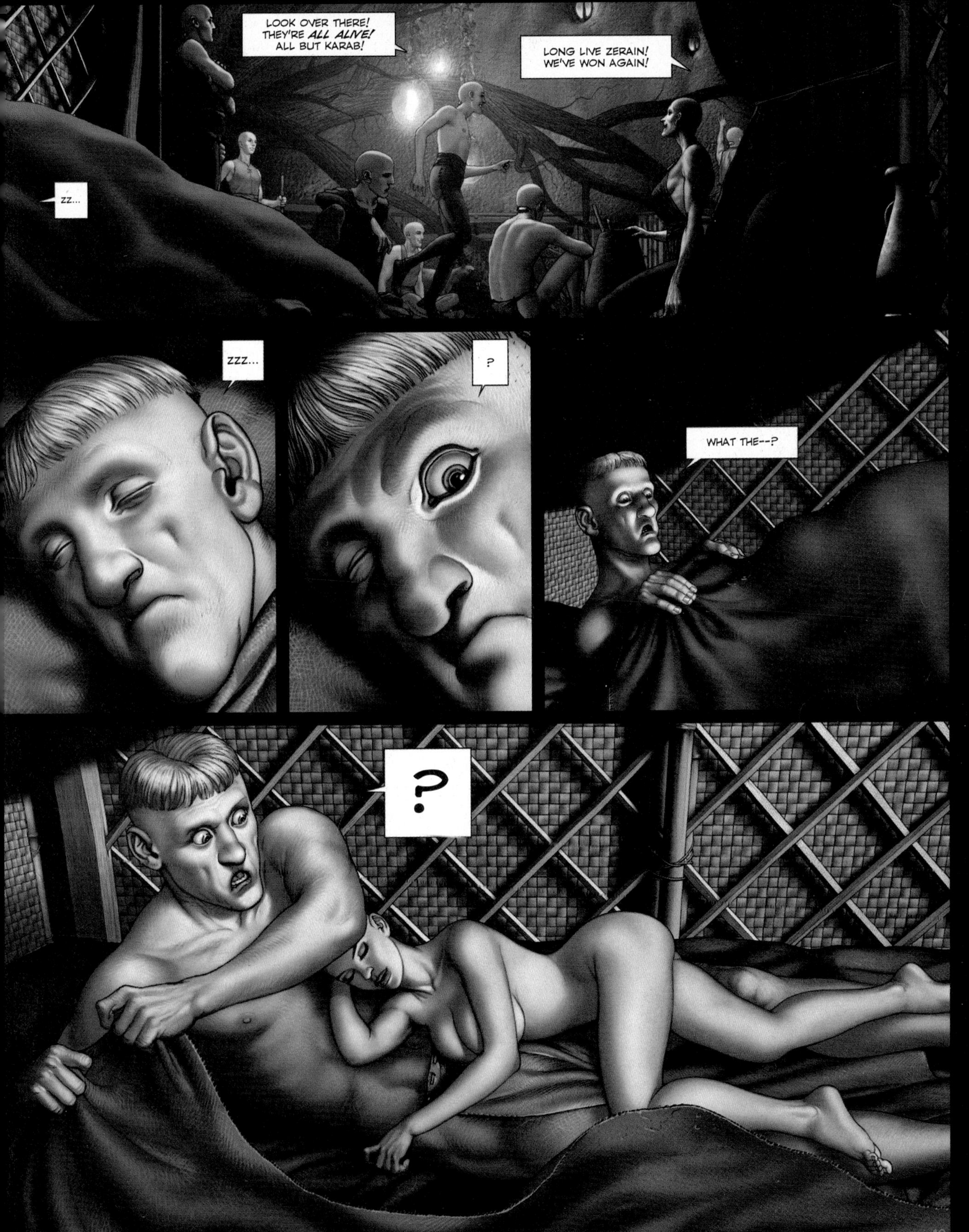
LOOK OVER THERE! THEY'RE ALL ALIVE! ALL BUT KARAB!
LONG LIVE ZERAIN! WE'VE WON AGAIN!
ZZ...
ZZZ...
?
WHAT THE--?
?

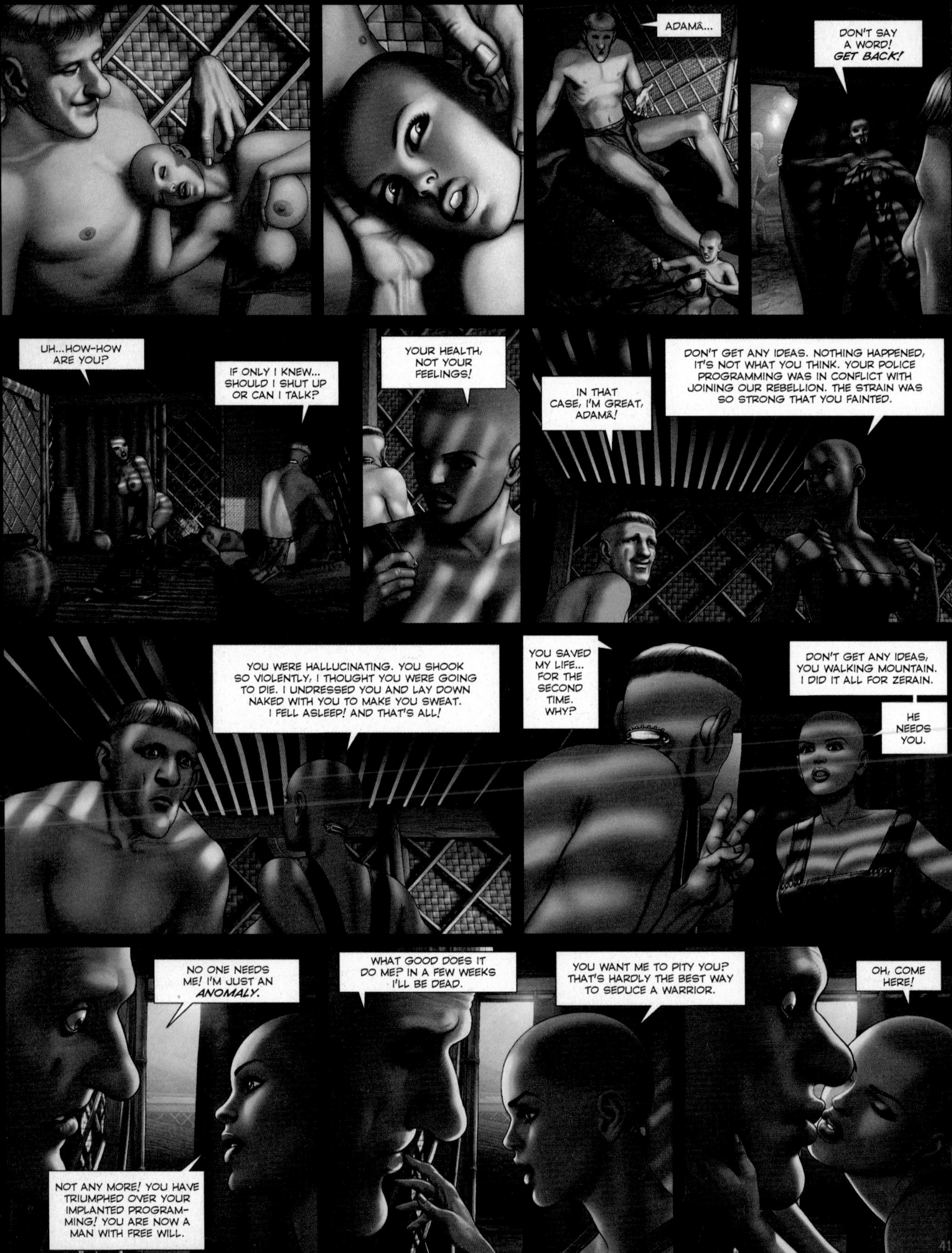
ADAMÂ...
DON'T SAY A WORD! GET BACK!
UH...HOW-HOW ARE YOU?
IF ONLY I KNEW... SHOULD I SHUT UP OR CAN I TALK?
YOUR HEALTH, NOT YOUR FEELINGS!
IN THAT CASE, I'M GREAT, ADAMÂ!
DON'T GET ANY IDEAS. NOTHING HAPPENED, IT'S NOT WHAT YOU THINK. YOUR POLICE PROGRAMMING WAS IN CONFLICT WITH JOINING OUR REBELLION. THE STRAIN WAS SO STRONG THAT YOU FAINTED.
YOU WERE HALLUCINATING. YOU SHOOK SO VIOLENTLY, I THOUGHT YOU WERE GOING TO DIE. I UNDRESSED YOU AND LAY DOWN NAKED WITH YOU TO MAKE YOU SWEAT. I FELL ASLEEP! AND THAT'S ALL!
YOU SAVED MY LIFE... FOR THE SECOND TIME. WHY?
DON'T GET ANY IDEAS, YOU WALKING MOUNTAIN. I DID IT ALL FOR ZERAIN.
HE NEEDS YOU.
NO ONE NEEDS ME! I'M JUST AN ANOMALY.
NOT ANY MORE! YOU HAVE TRIUMPHED OVER YOUR IMPLANTED PROGRAMMING! YOU ARE NOW A MAN WITH FREE WILL.
WHAT GOOD DOES IT DO ME? IN A FEW WEEKS I'LL BE DEAD.
YOU WANT ME TO PITY YOU? THAT'S HARDLY THE BEST WAY TO SEDUCE A WARRIOR.
OH, COME HERE!

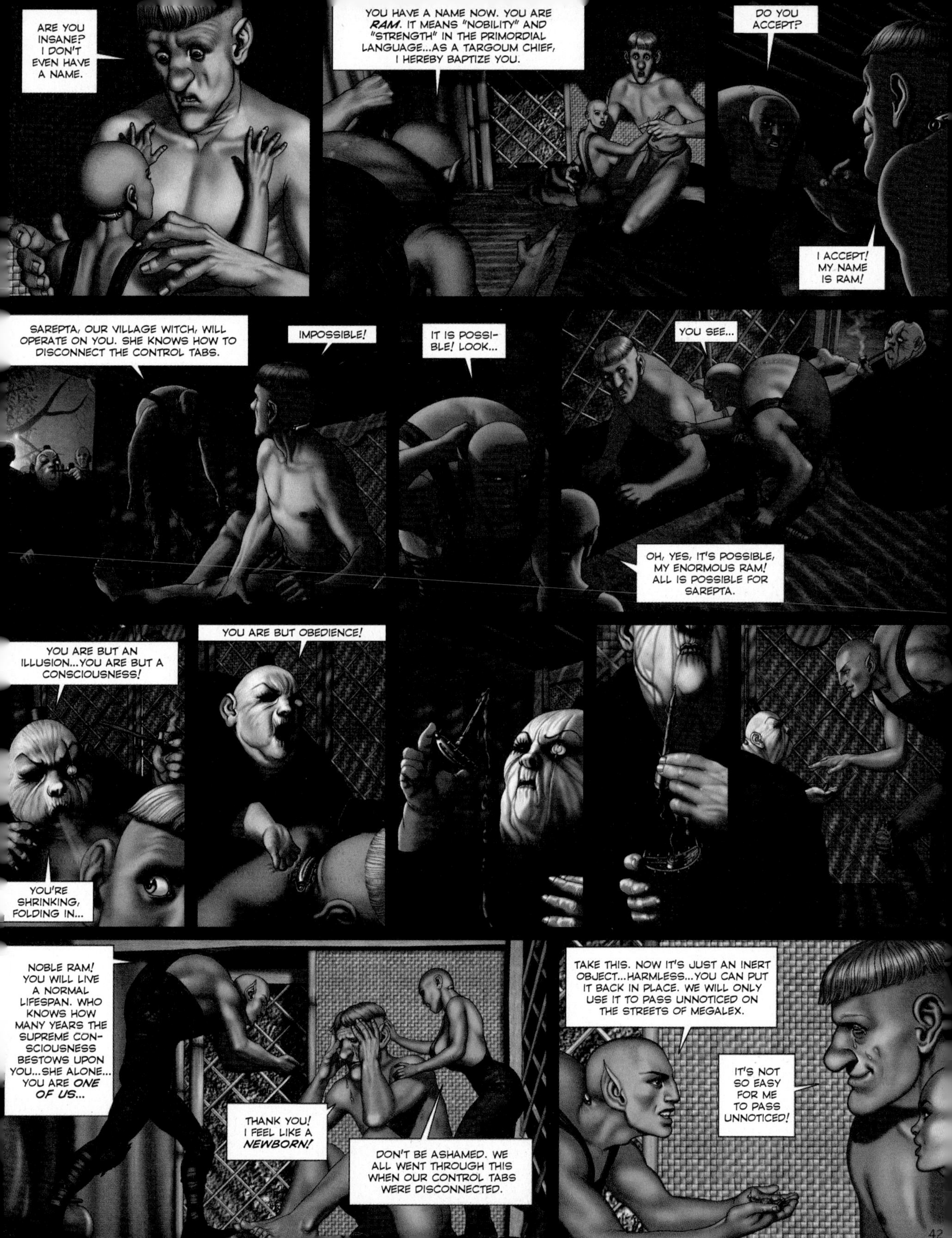
ARE YOU INSANE? I DON'T EVEN HAVE A NAME.
YOU HAVE A NAME NOW. YOU ARE RAM. IT MEANS "NOBILITY" AND "STRENGTH" IN THE PRIMORDIAL LANGUAGE...AS A TARGOUM CHIEF, I HEREBY BAPTIZE YOU.
DO YOU ACCEPT?
I ACCEPT! MY NAME IS RAM!
SAREPTA, OUR VILLAGE WITCH, WILL OPERATE ON YOU. SHE KNOWS HOW TO DISCONNECT THE CONTROL TABS.
IMPOSSIBLE!
IT IS POSSIBLE! LOOK...
YOU SEE...
OH, YES, IT'S POSSIBLE, MY ENORMOUS RAM! ALL IS POSSIBLE FOR SAREPTA.
YOU ARE BUT AN ILLUSION...YOU ARE BUT A CONSCIOUSNESS!
YOU'RE SHRINKING, FOLDING IN...
YOU ARE BUT OBEDIENCE!
NOBLE RAM! YOU WILL LIVE A NORMAL LIFESPAN. WHO KNOWS HOW MANY YEARS THE SUPREME CONSCIOUSNESS BESTOWS UPON YOU...SHE ALONE... YOU ARE ONE OF US...
THANK YOU! I FEEL LIKE A NEWBORN!
DON'T BE ASHAMED. WE ALL WENT THROUGH THIS WHEN OUR CONTROL TABS WERE DISCONNECTED.
TAKE THIS. NOW IT'S JUST AN INERT OBJECT...HARMLESS...YOU CAN PUT IT BACK IN PLACE. WE WILL ONLY USE IT TO PASS UNNOTICED ON THE STREETS OF MEGALEX.
IT'S NOT SO EASY FOR ME TO PASS UNNOTICED!

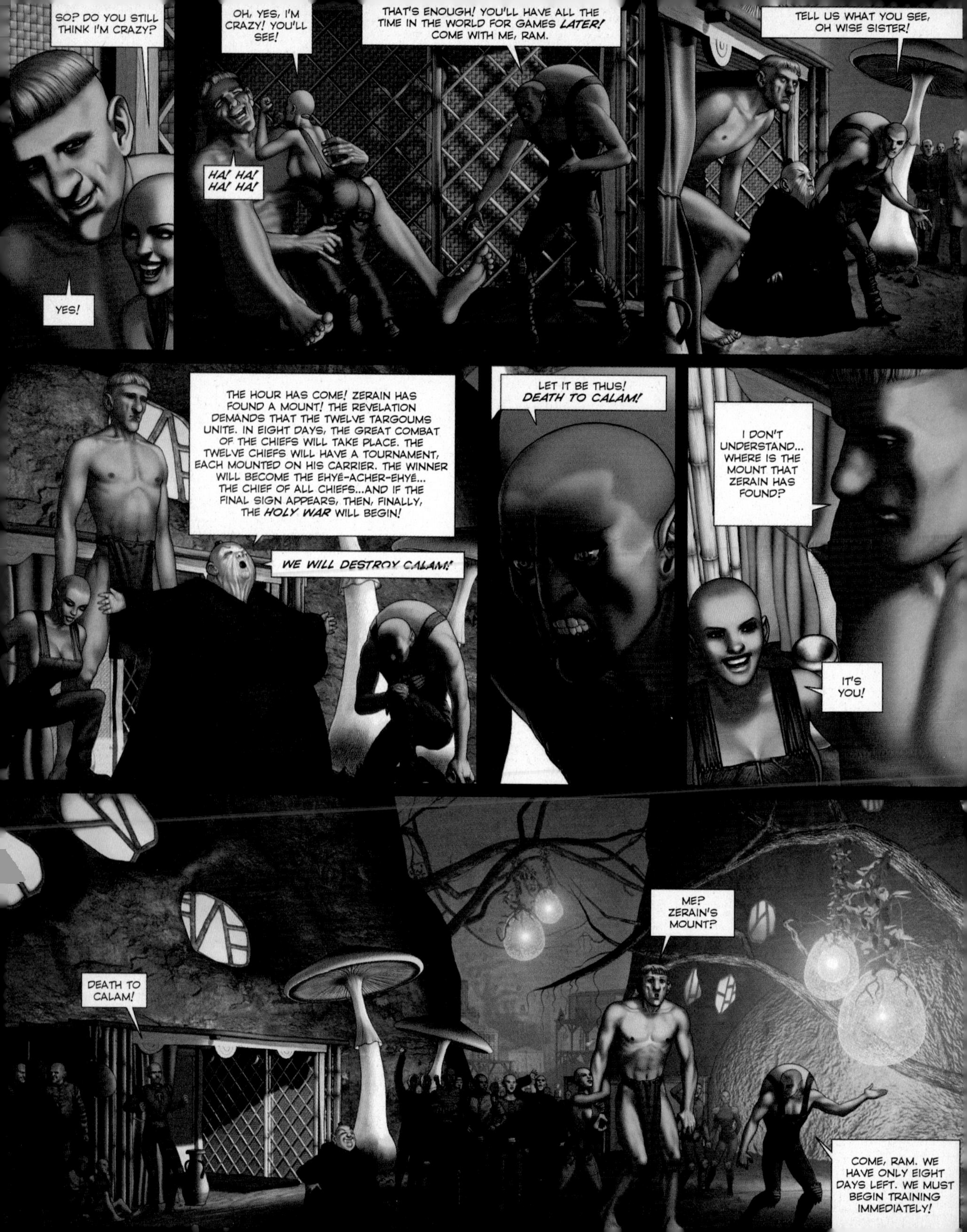
SO? DO YOU STILL THINK I'M CRAZY?
YES!
OH, YES, I'M CRAZY! YOU'LL SEE!
HA! HA! HA! HA!
THAT'S ENOUGH! YOU'LL HAVE ALL THE TIME IN THE WORLD FOR GAMES LATER! COME WITH ME, RAM.
TELL US WHAT YOU SEE, OH WISE SISTER!
THE HOUR HAS COME! ZERAIN HAS FOUND A MOUNT! THE REVELATION DEMANDS THAT THE TWELVE TARGOUMS UNITE. IN EIGHT DAYS, THE GREAT COMBAT OF THE CHIEFS WILL TAKE PLACE. THE TWELVE CHIEFS WILL HAVE A TOURNAMENT, EACH MOUNTED ON HIS CARRIER. THE WINNER WILL BECOME THE EHYÉ-ACHER-EHYÉ... THE CHIEF OF ALL CHIEFS...AND IF THE FINAL SIGN APPEARS, THEN, FINALLY, THE HOLY WAR WILL BEGIN!
WE WILL DESTROY CALAM!
LET IT BE THUS! DEATH TO CALAM!
I DON'T UNDERSTAND... WHERE IS THE MOUNT THAT ZERAIN HAS FOUND?
IT'S YOU!
DEATH TO CALAM!
ME? ZERAIN'S MOUNT?
COME, RAM. WE HAVE ONLY EIGHT DAYS LEFT. WE MUST BEGIN TRAINING IMMEDIATELY!

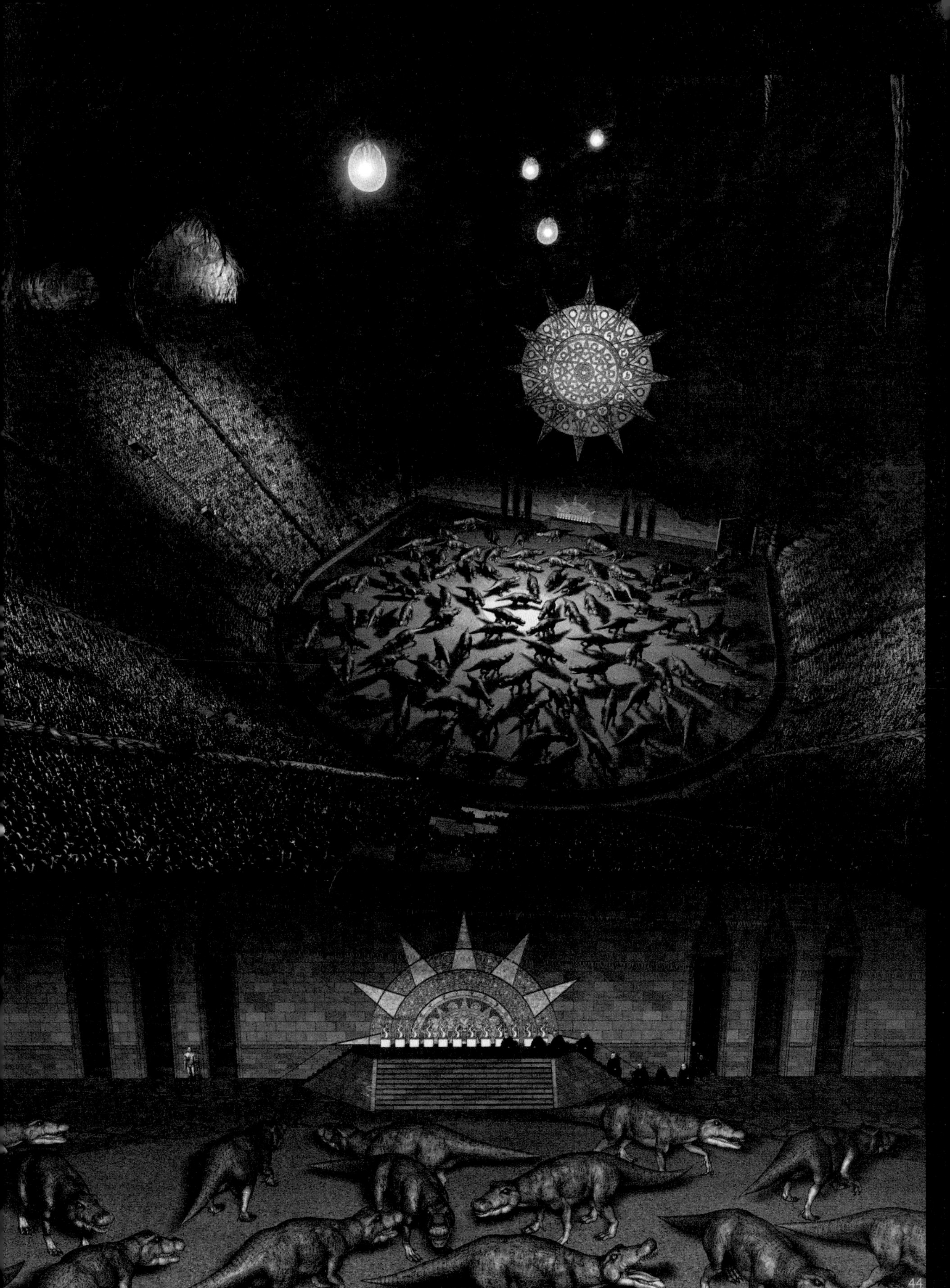

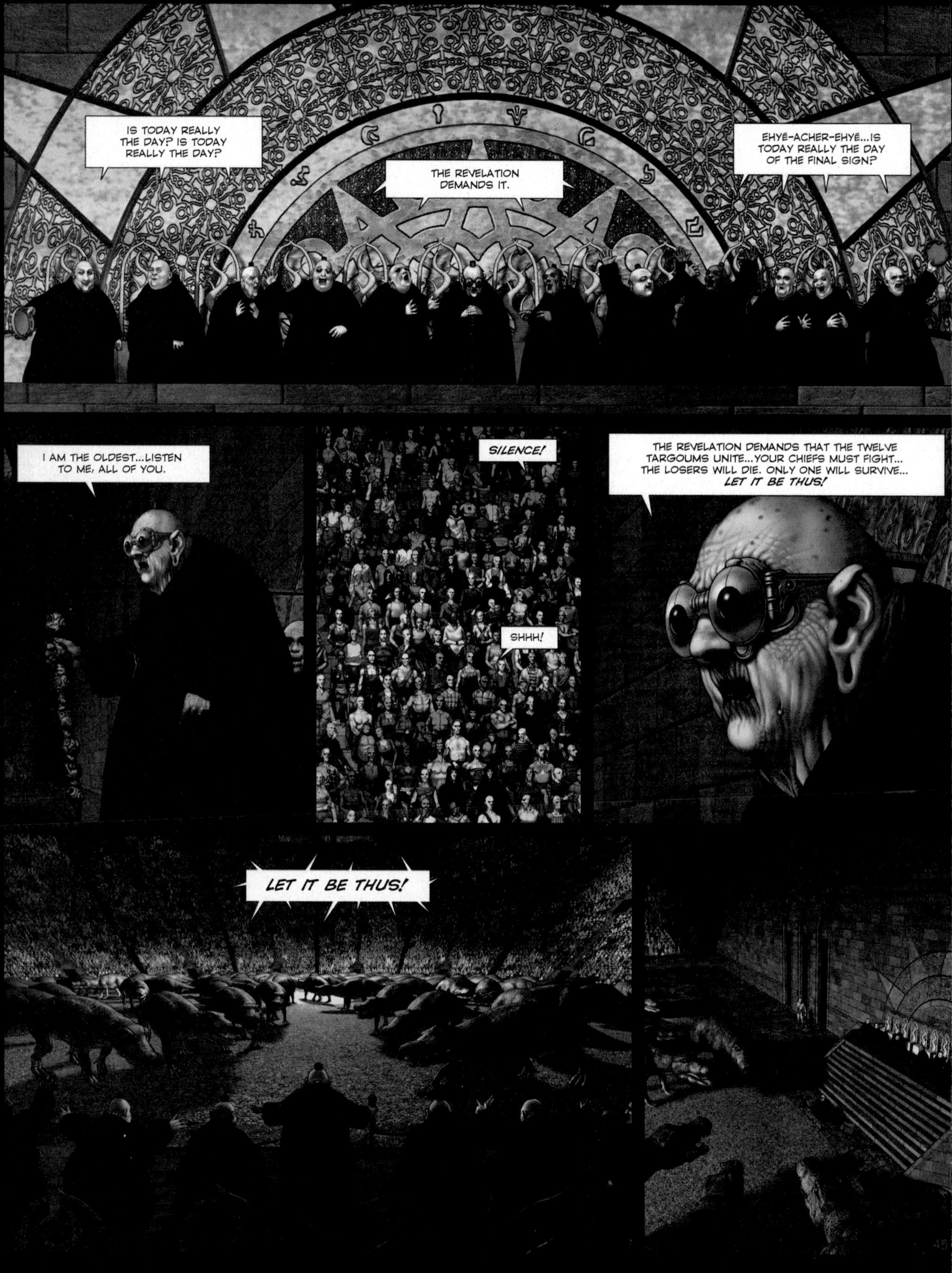
IS TODAY REALLY THE DAY? IS TODAY REALLY THE DAY?
THE REVELATION DEMANDS IT.
EHYÉ-ACHER-EHYÉ...IS TODAY REALLY THE DAY OF THE FINAL SIGN?
I AM THE OLDEST...LISTEN TO ME, ALL OF YOU.
SILENCE!
SHHH!
THE REVELATION DEMANDS THAT THE TWELVE TARGOUMS UNITE...YOUR CHIEFS MUST FIGHT... THE LOSERS WILL DIE. ONLY ONE WILL SURVIVE... LET IT BE THUS!
LET IT BE THUS!

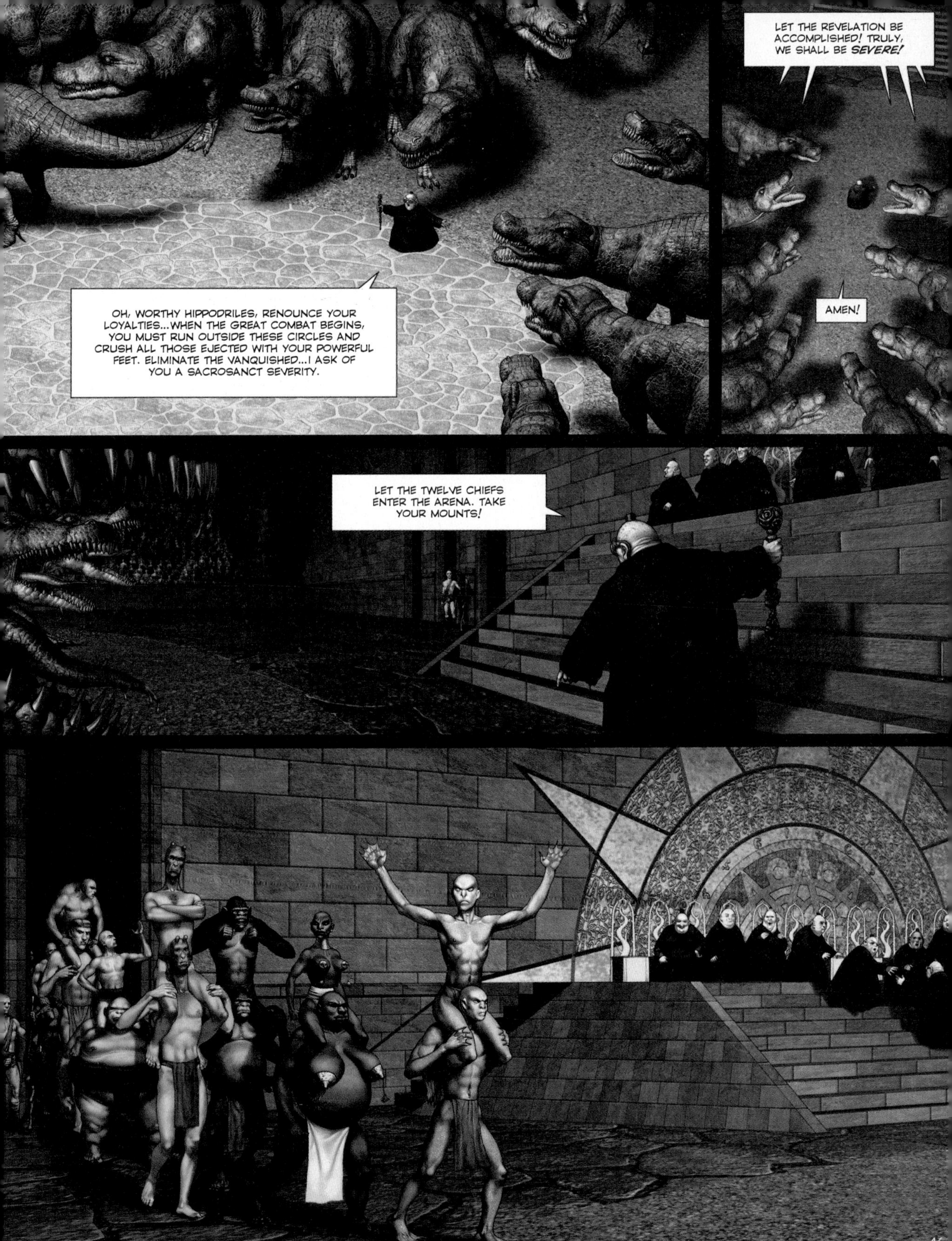
OH, WORTHY HIPPODRILES, RENOUNCE YOUR LOYALTIES...WHEN THE GREAT COMBAT BEGINS, YOU MUST RUN OUTSIDE THESE CIRCLES AND CRUSH ALL THOSE EJECTED WITH YOUR POWERFUL FEET. ELIMINATE THE VANQUISHED...I ASK OF YOU A SACROSANCT SEVERITY.
LET THE REVELATION BE ACCOMPLISHED! TRULY, WE SHALL BE *SEVERE!*
AMEN!
LET THE TWELVE CHIEFS ENTER THE ARENA. TAKE YOUR MOUNTS!

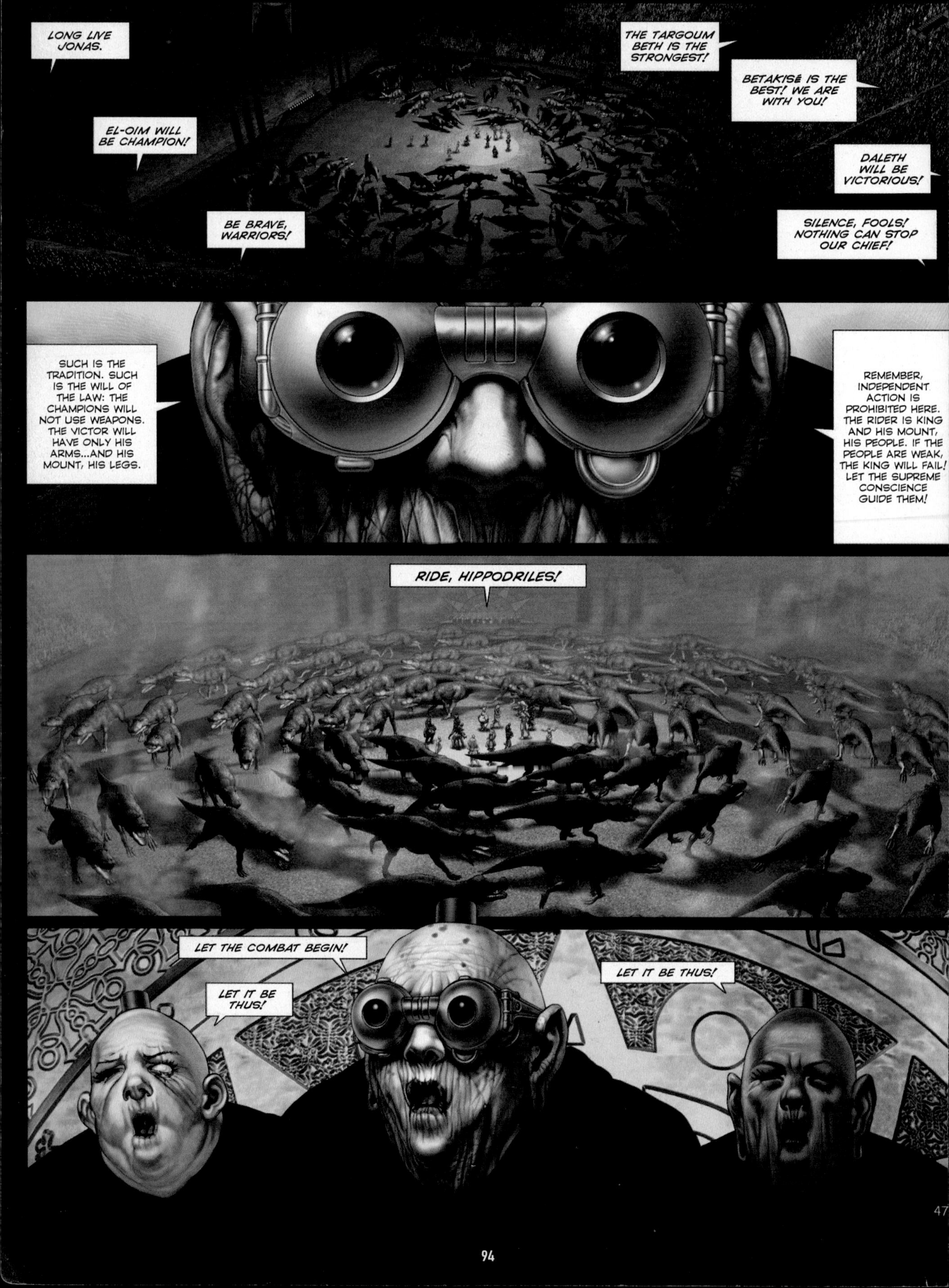
LONG LIVE JONAS.
EL-OIM WILL BE CHAMPION!
BE BRAVE, WARRIORS!
THE TARGOUM BETH IS THE STRONGEST!
BETAKISÉ IS THE BEST! WE ARE WITH YOU!
DALETH WILL BE VICTORIOUS!
SILENCE, FOOLS! NOTHING CAN STOP OUR CHIEF!
SUCH IS THE TRADITION. SUCH IS THE WILL OF THE LAW: THE CHAMPIONS WILL NOT USE WEAPONS. THE VICTOR WILL HAVE ONLY HIS ARMS...AND HIS MOUNT, HIS LEGS.
REMEMBER, INDEPENDENT ACTION IS PROHIBITED HERE. THE RIDER IS KING AND HIS MOUNT, HIS PEOPLE. IF THE PEOPLE ARE WEAK, THE KING WILL FAIL! LET THE SUPREME CONSCIENCE GUIDE THEM!
RIDE, HIPPODRILES!
LET THE COMBAT BEGIN!
LET IT BE THUS!
LET IT BE THUS!
47

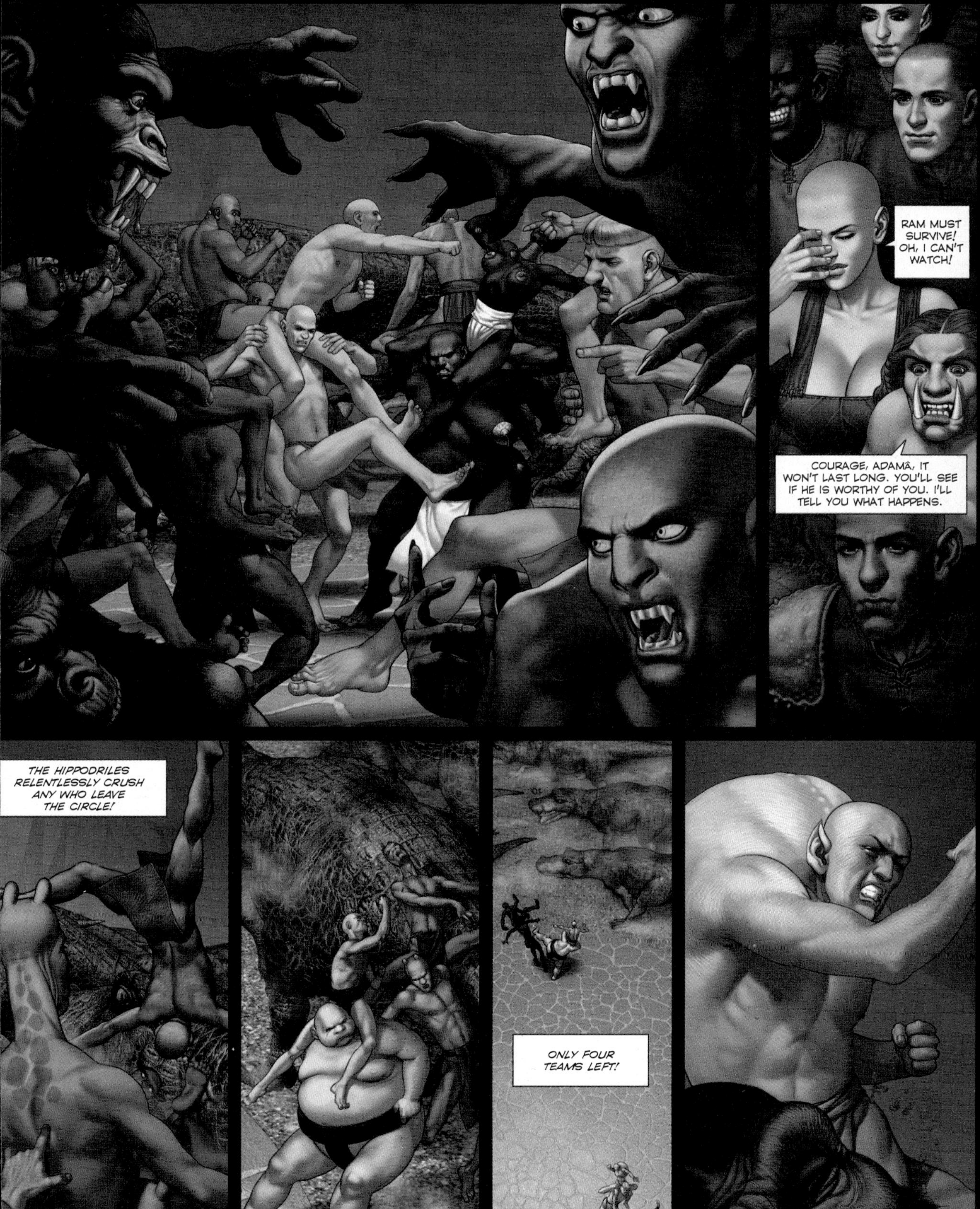
RAM MUST SURVIVE! OH, I CAN'T WATCH!
COURAGE, ADAMÂ, IT WON'T LAST LONG. YOU'LL SEE IF HE IS WORTHY OF YOU. I'LL TELL YOU WHAT HAPPENS.
THE HIPPODRILES RELENTLESSLY CRUSH ANY WHO LEAVE THE CIRCLE!
ONLY FOUR TEAMS LEFT!
48

NOW IT'S TWO...RAM AND ZERAIN ARE STILL IN...

REMEMBER, RAM, WHEN THE BEAST CHARGES THE ANGEL *FLIES*...

GO FEED THE HIPPODRILES, FATSO!

I WON! WE WON!!!

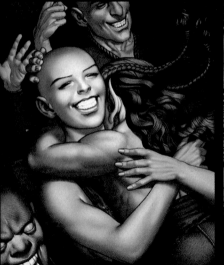

IT IS THE WILL OF THE SUPREME CONSCIOUSNESS! ZERAIN, CHIEF OF DALETH TARGOUM, IS THE *SACRED CHAMPION!*

FROM NOW ON WE WILL FORM A SINGLE, GREAT TARGOUM! ZERAIN IS THE EHYÉ-ACHER-EHYÉ! THE GREAT CHIEFTAIN!

THE GREAT CHIEFTAIN! LONG LIVE THE EHYÉ-ACHER-EHYÉ!

LONG LIVE ZERAIN!

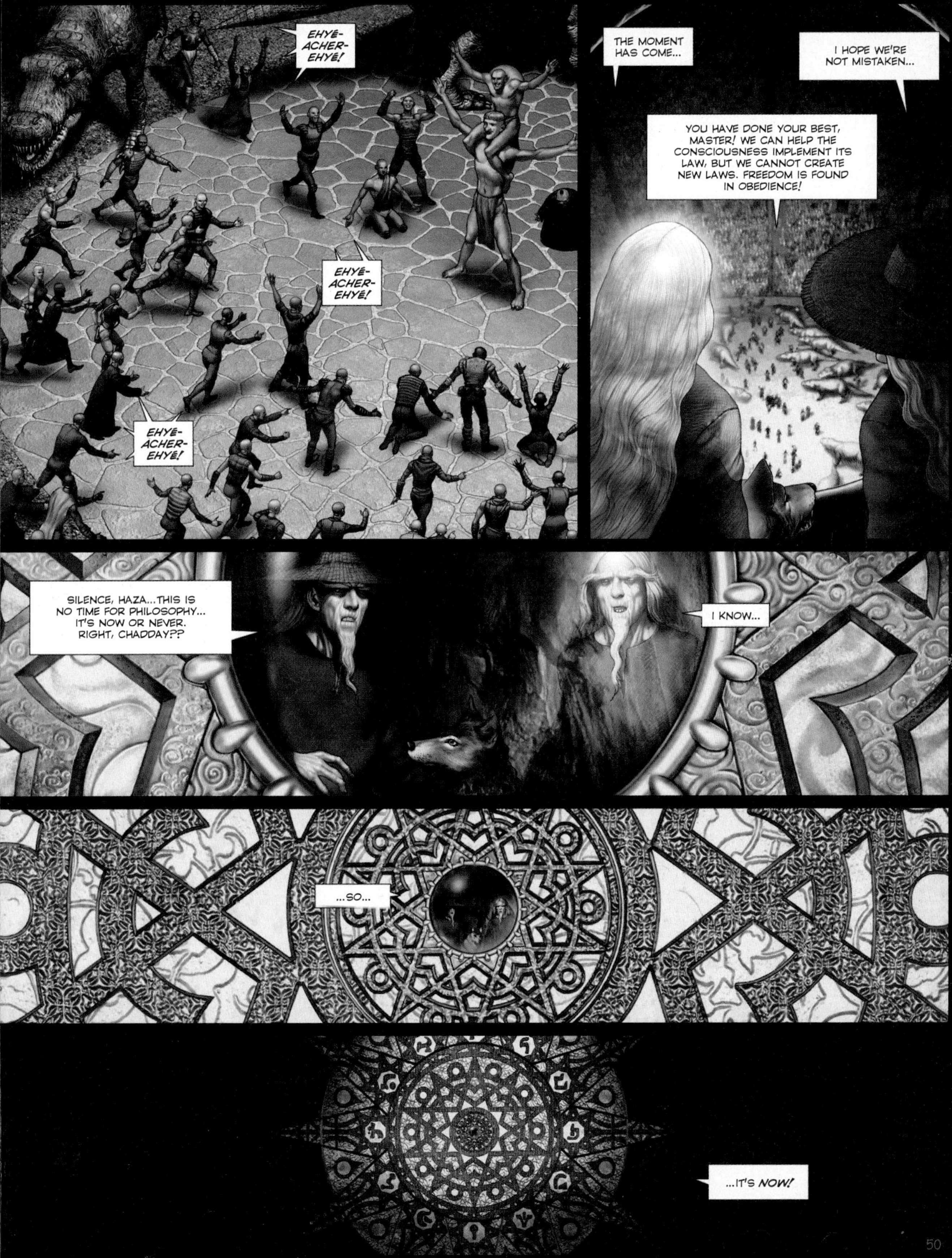
EHYÉ-ACHER-EHYÉ!
EHYÉ-ACHER-EHYÉ!
EHYÉ-ACHER-EHYÉ!
THE MOMENT HAS COME...
I HOPE WE'RE NOT MISTAKEN...
YOU HAVE DONE YOUR BEST, MASTER! WE CAN HELP THE CONSCIOUSNESS IMPLEMENT ITS LAW, BUT WE CANNOT CREATE NEW LAWS. FREEDOM IS FOUND IN OBEDIENCE!
SILENCE, HAZA...THIS IS NO TIME FOR PHILOSOPHY... IT'S NOW OR NEVER. RIGHT, CHADDAY??
I KNOW...
...SO...
...IT'S NOW!

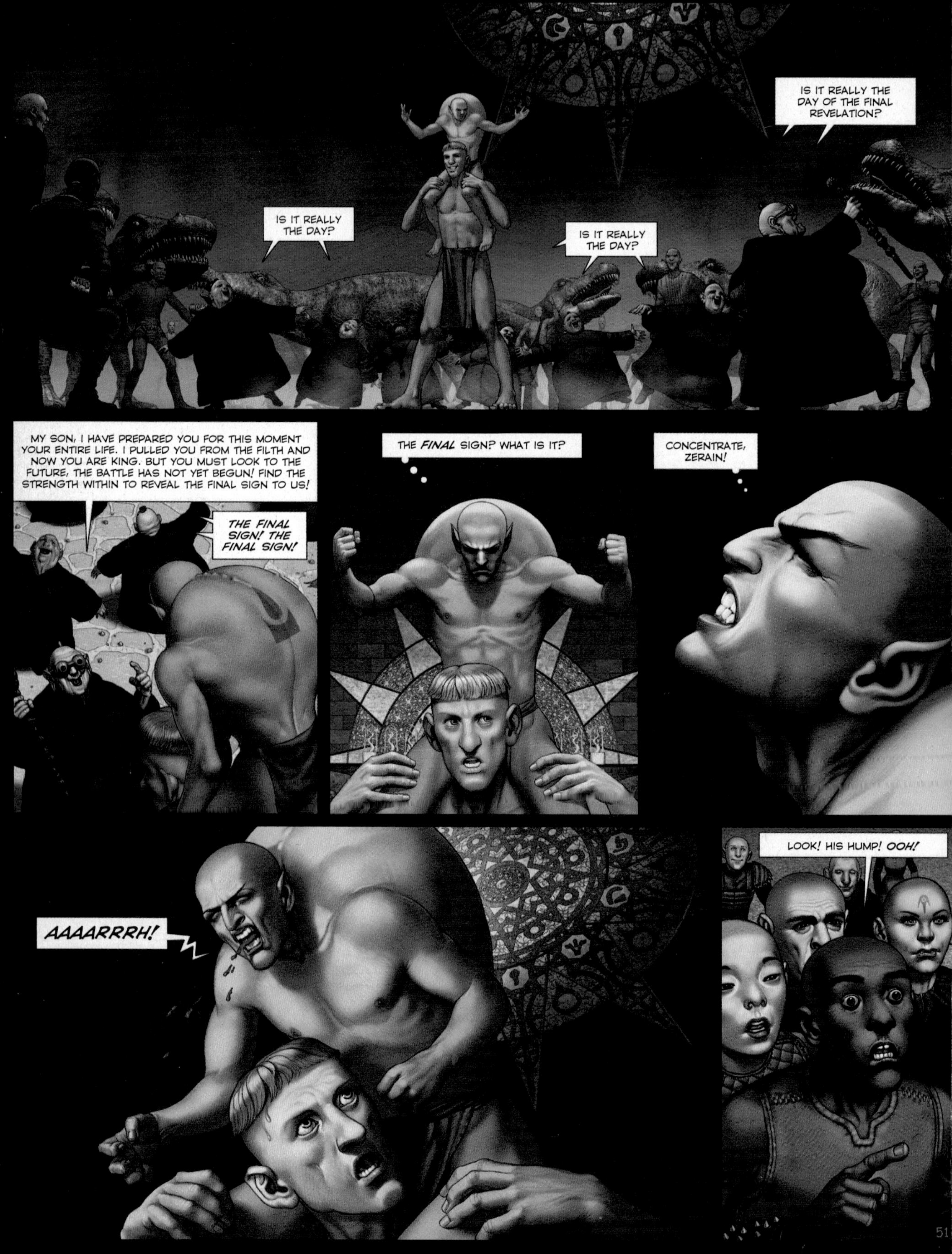
IS IT REALLY THE DAY OF THE FINAL REVELATION?
IS IT REALLY THE DAY?
IS IT REALLY THE DAY?
MY SON, I HAVE PREPARED YOU FOR THIS MOMENT YOUR ENTIRE LIFE. I PULLED YOU FROM THE FILTH AND NOW YOU ARE KING. BUT YOU MUST LOOK TO THE FUTURE, THE BATTLE HAS NOT YET BEGUN! FIND THE STRENGTH WITHIN TO REVEAL THE FINAL SIGN TO US!
THE FINAL SIGN! THE FINAL SIGN!
THE FINAL SIGN? WHAT IS IT?
CONCENTRATE, ZERAIN!
AAAARRRH!
LOOK! HIS HUMP! OOH!

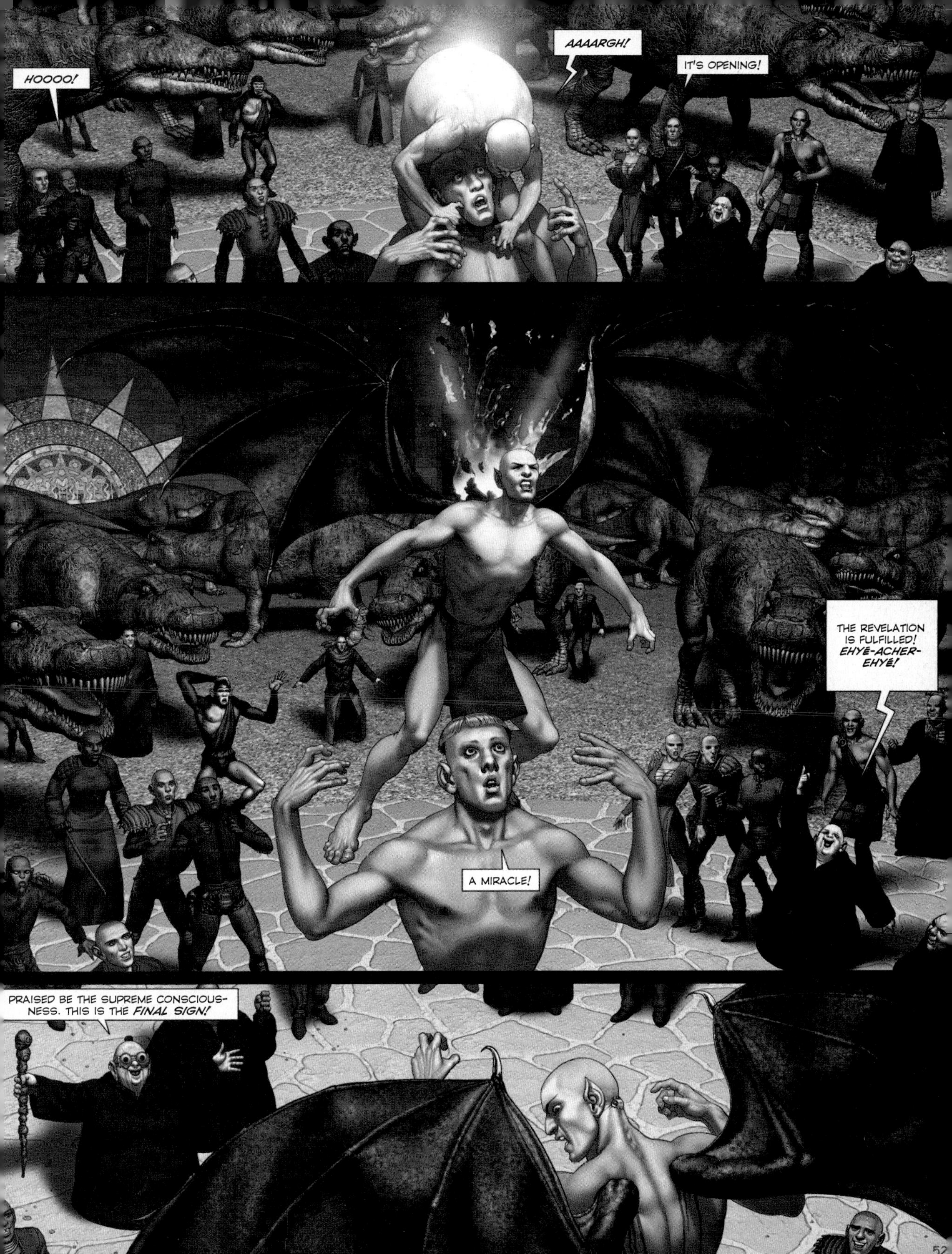
HOOOO!
AAAARGH!
IT'S OPENING!
THE REVELATION IS FULFILLED! EHYÉ-ACHER-EHYÉ!
A MIRACLE!
PRAISED BE THE SUPREME CONSCIOUS-NESS. THIS IS THE FINAL SIGN!

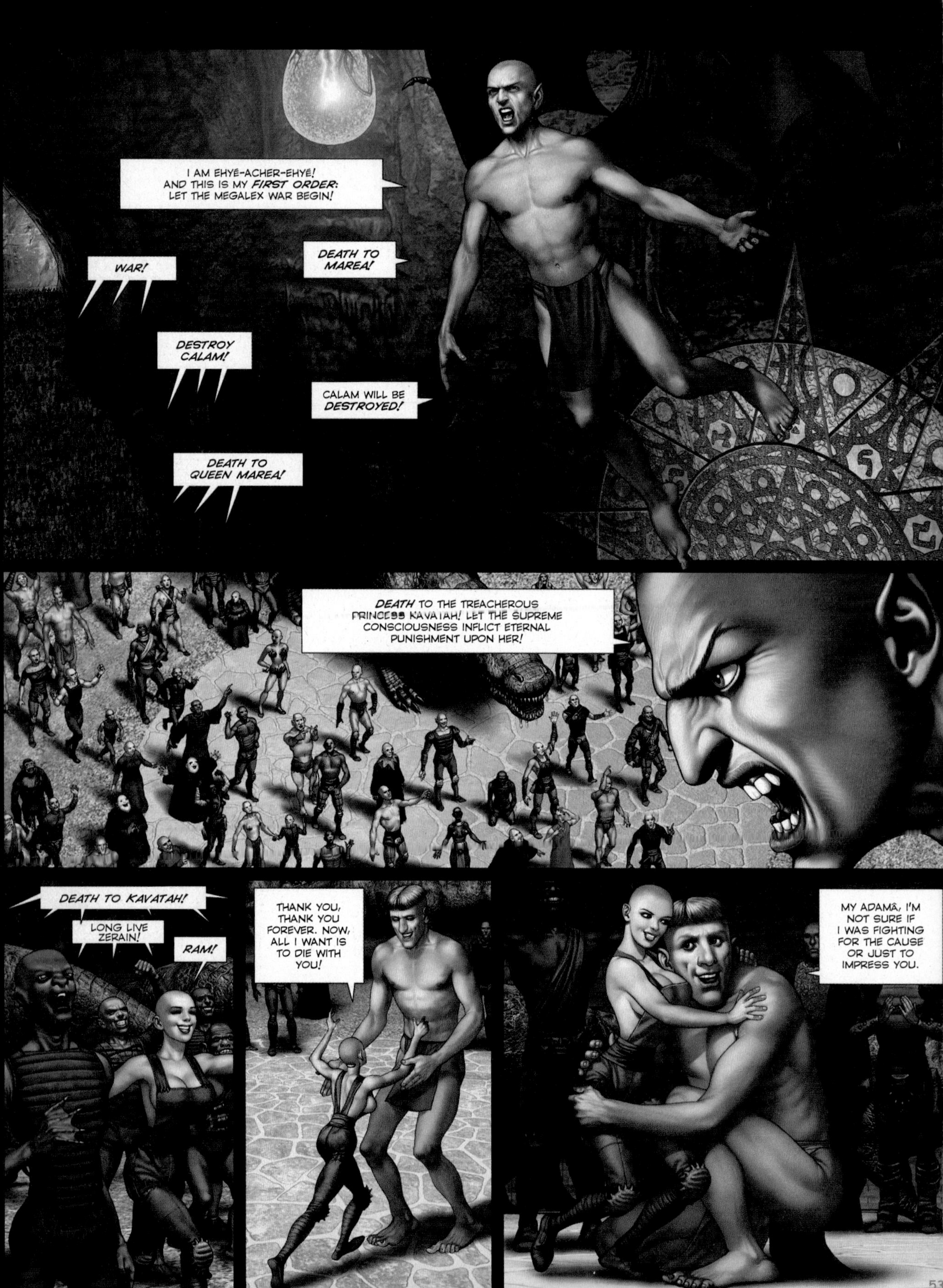
I AM EHYÉ-ACHER-EHYÉ! AND THIS IS MY FIRST ORDER: LET THE MEGALEX WAR BEGIN!
WAR!
DEATH TO MAREA!
DESTROY CALAM!
CALAM WILL BE DESTROYED!
DEATH TO QUEEN MAREA!
DEATH TO THE TREACHEROUS PRINCESS KAVATAH! LET THE SUPREME CONSCIOUSNESS INFLICT ETERNAL PUNISHMENT UPON HER!
DEATH TO KAVATAH!
LONG LIVE ZERAIN!
RAM!
THANK YOU, THANK YOU FOREVER. NOW, ALL I WANT IS TO DIE WITH YOU!
MY ADAMÂ, I'M NOT SURE IF I WAS FIGHTING FOR THE CAUSE OR JUST TO IMPRESS YOU.

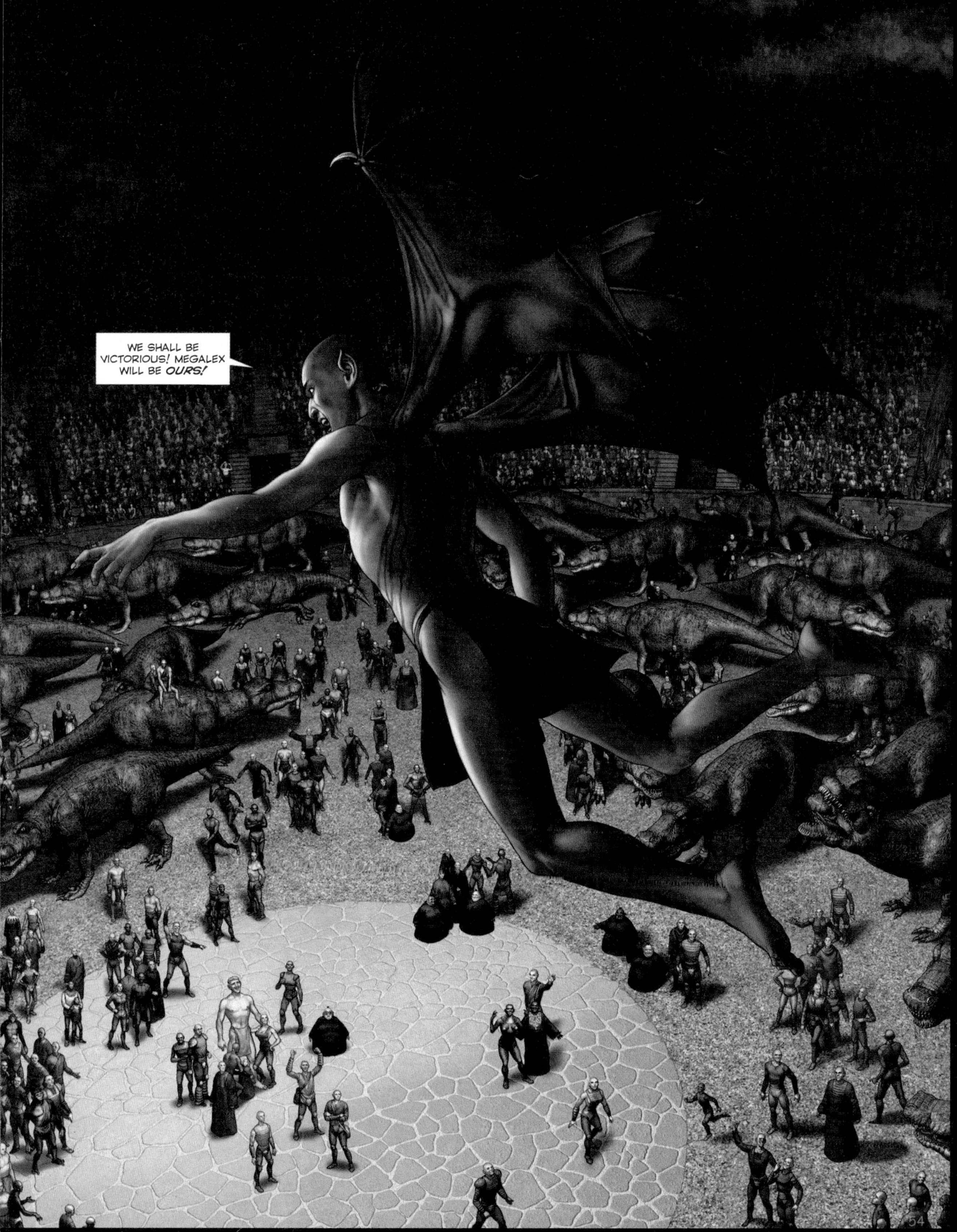
WE SHALL BE VICTORIOUS! MEGALEX WILL BE *OURS!*

TO BE CONTINUED.

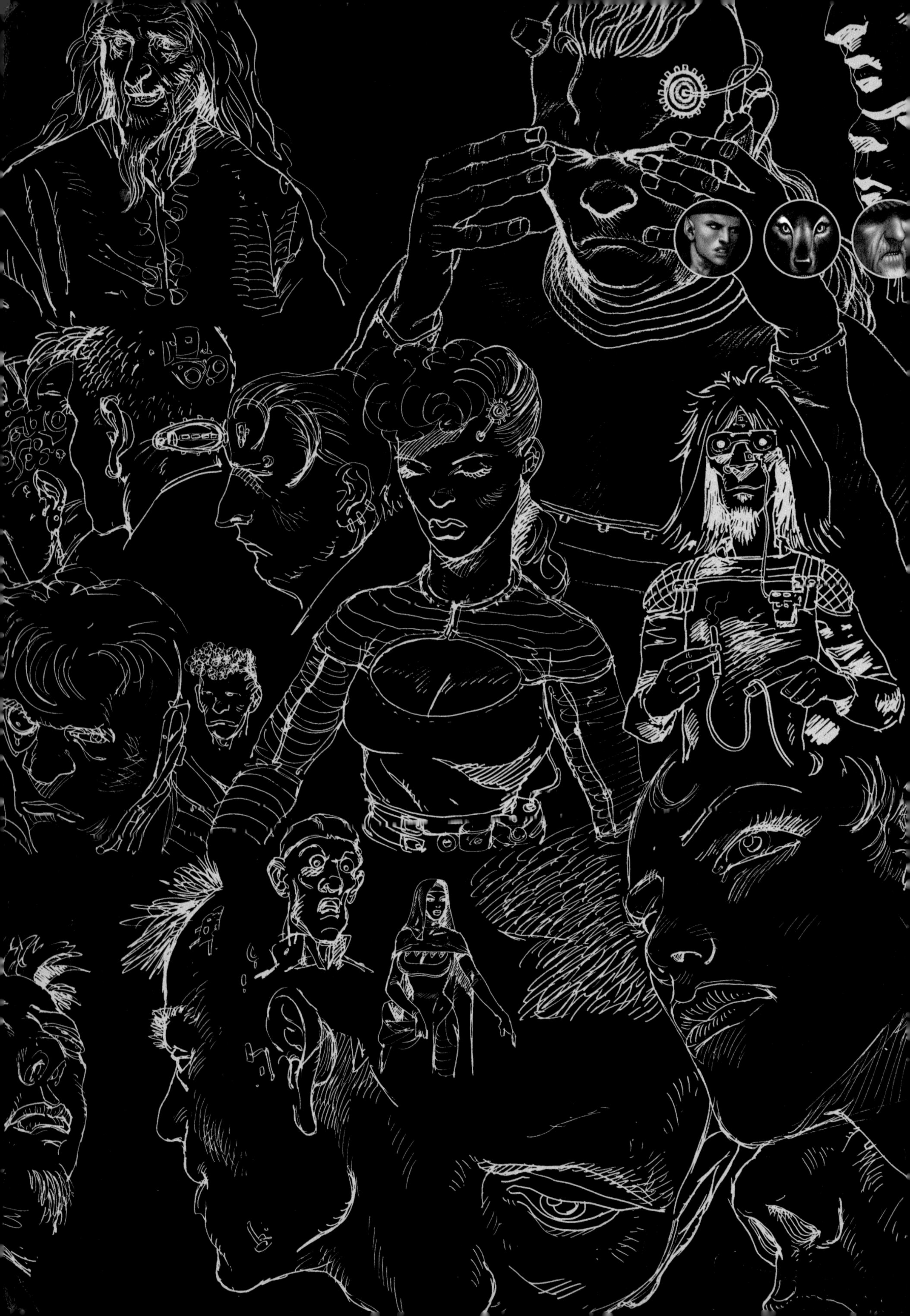

THE MAKING OF MEGALEX

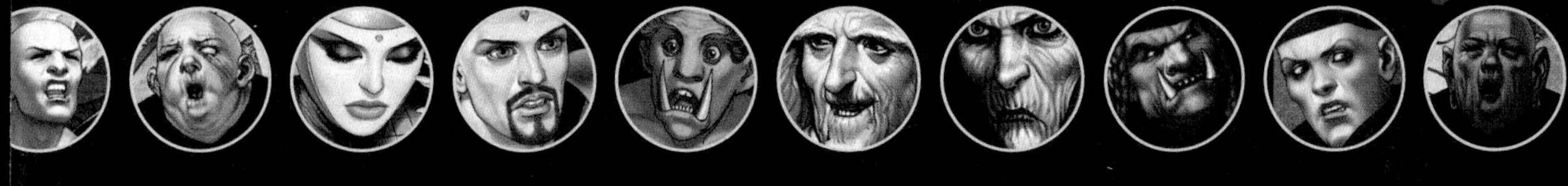

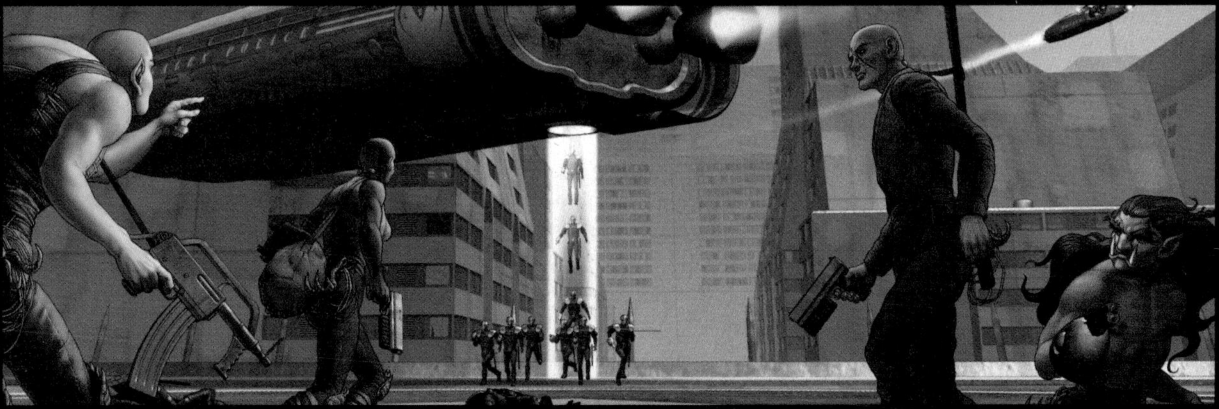

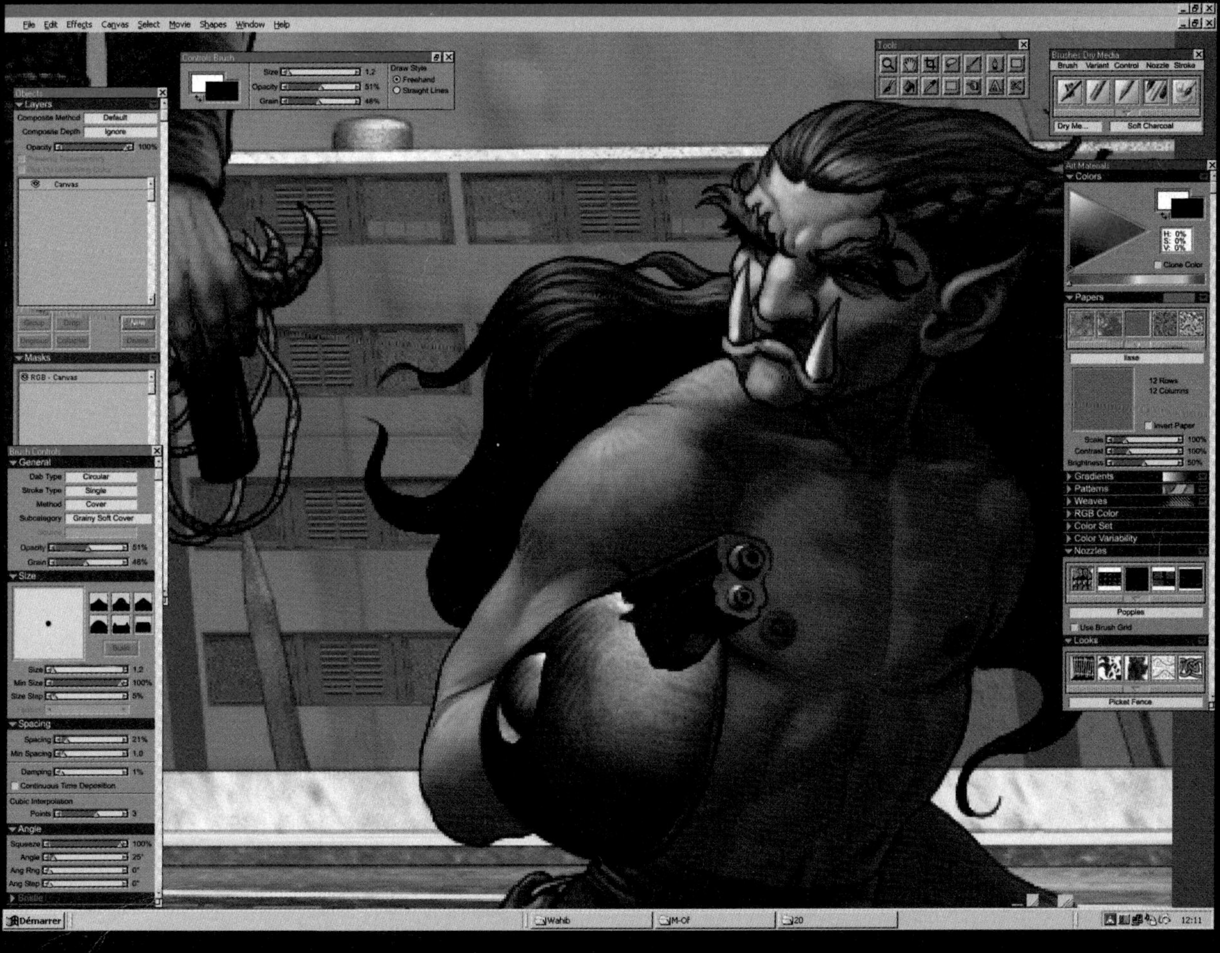
File Edit Effects Canvas Select Movie Shapes Window Help
Controls: Brush
Size
Opacity
Grain
Draw Style
Freehand
Straight Lines
Tools
Brushes: Dry Media
Brush Variant Control Nozzle Stroke
Dry Me...
Soft Charcoal
Objects
Layers
Composite Method
Default
Composite Depth
Ignore
Opacity
Canvas
Masks
RGB - Canvas
Brush Controls
General
Dab Type
Circular
Stroke Type
Single
Method
Cover
Subcategory
Grainy Soft Cover
Size
Spacing
Continuous Time Deposition
Cubic Interpolation
Angle
Art Materials
Colors
Clone Color
Papers
12 Rows
12 Columns
Invert Paper
Gradients
Patterns
Weaves
RGB Color
Color Set
Color Variability
Nozzles
Popples
Use Brush Grid
Looks
Picket Fence
Démarrer
Wahib
M-OF
20
12:11

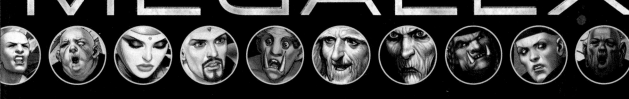

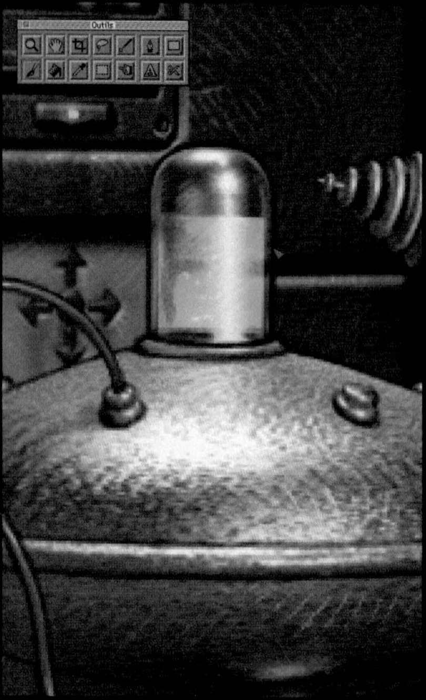

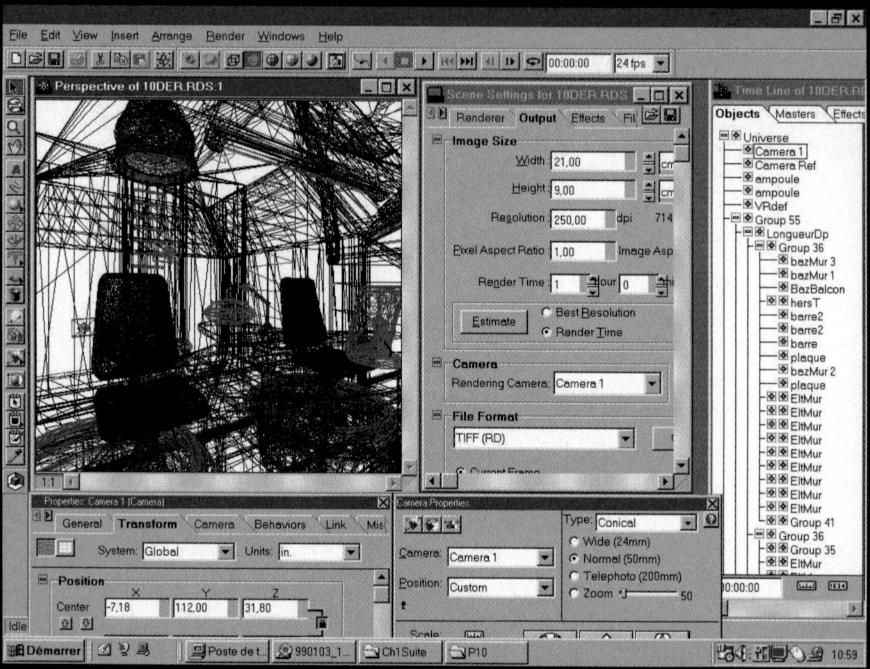

File Edit View Insert Arrange Render Windows Help
00:00:00
24 fps
Perspective of 10DER.RDS:1
Scene Settings for 10DER.RDS
Renderer Output Effects
Image Size
Width 21,00
Height 9,00
Resolution 250,00 dpi
Pixel Aspect Ratio 1,00
Render Time 1 hour 0
Estimate
Best Resolution
Render Time
Camera
Rendering Camera: Camera 1
File Format
TIFF (RD)
Objects Masters Effects
Universe
Camera 1
Camera Ref
ampoule
ampoule
VRdef
Group 55
LongueurDp
Group 36
bazMur 3
bazMur 1
BazBalcon
hersT
barre2
barre2
barre
plaque
bazMur 2
plaque
EltMur
EltMur
EltMur
EltMur
EltMur
EltMur
EltMur
EltMur
EltMur
Group 41
Group 36
Group 35
EltMur
General Transform Camera Behaviors Link
System: Global
Units: in.
Position
X Y Z
Center -7,18 112,00 31,80
Camera Properties
Camera: Camera 1
Position: Custom
Type: Conical
Wide (24mm)
Normal (50mm)
Telephoto (200mm)
Zoom 50
Idle
Démarrer
Poste de t...
990103_1...
Ch1Suite
P10
10:59

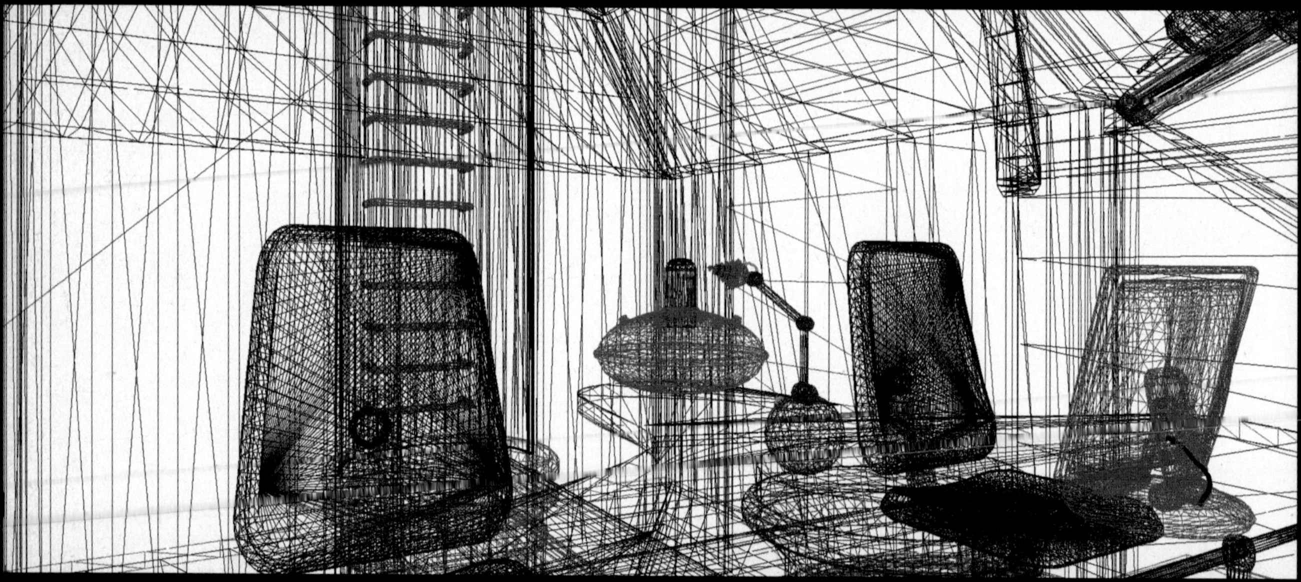

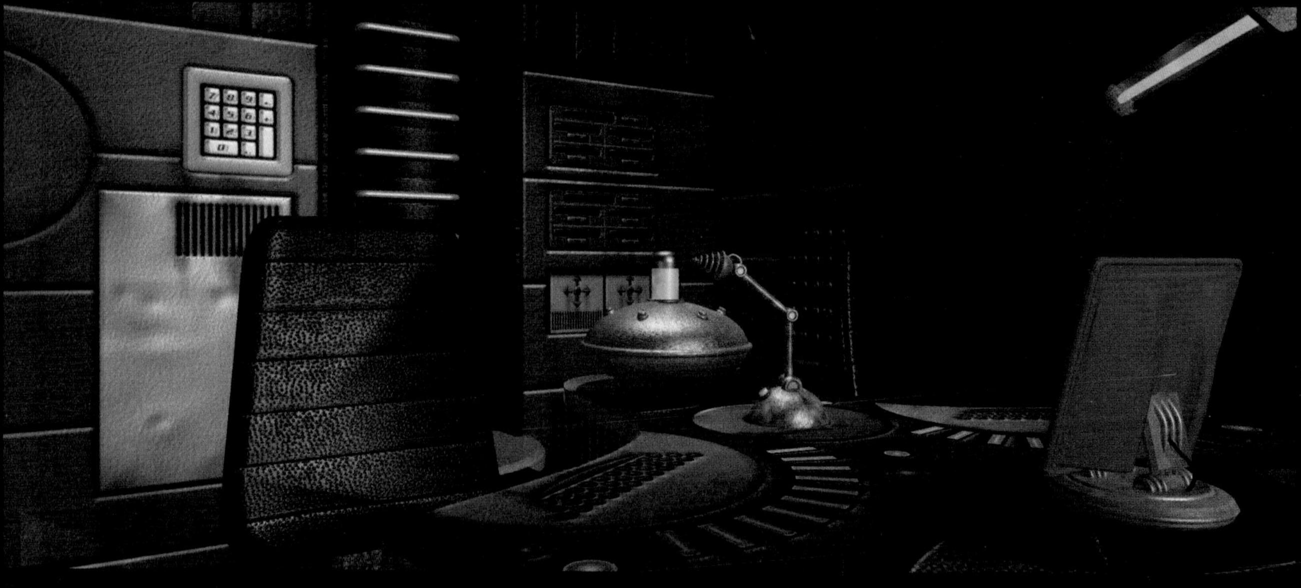

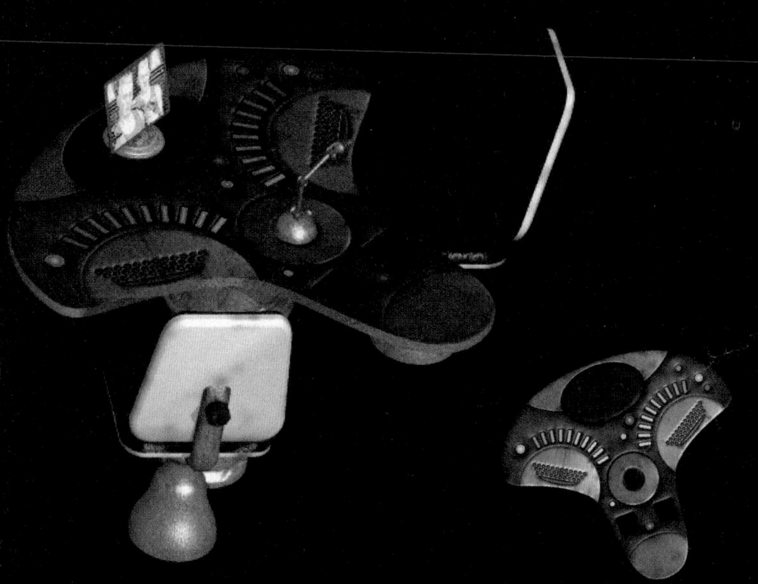

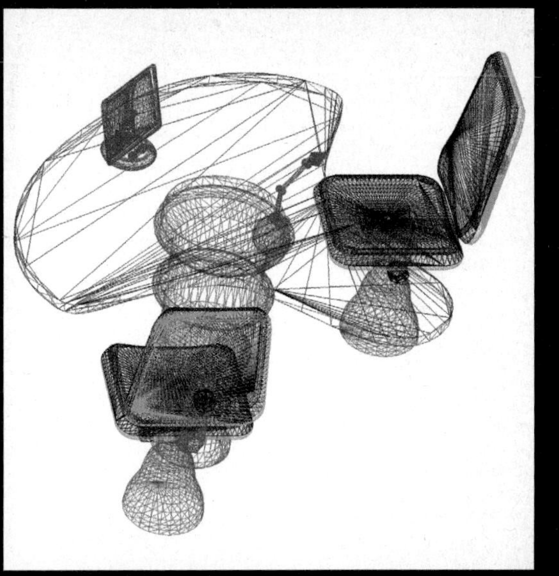

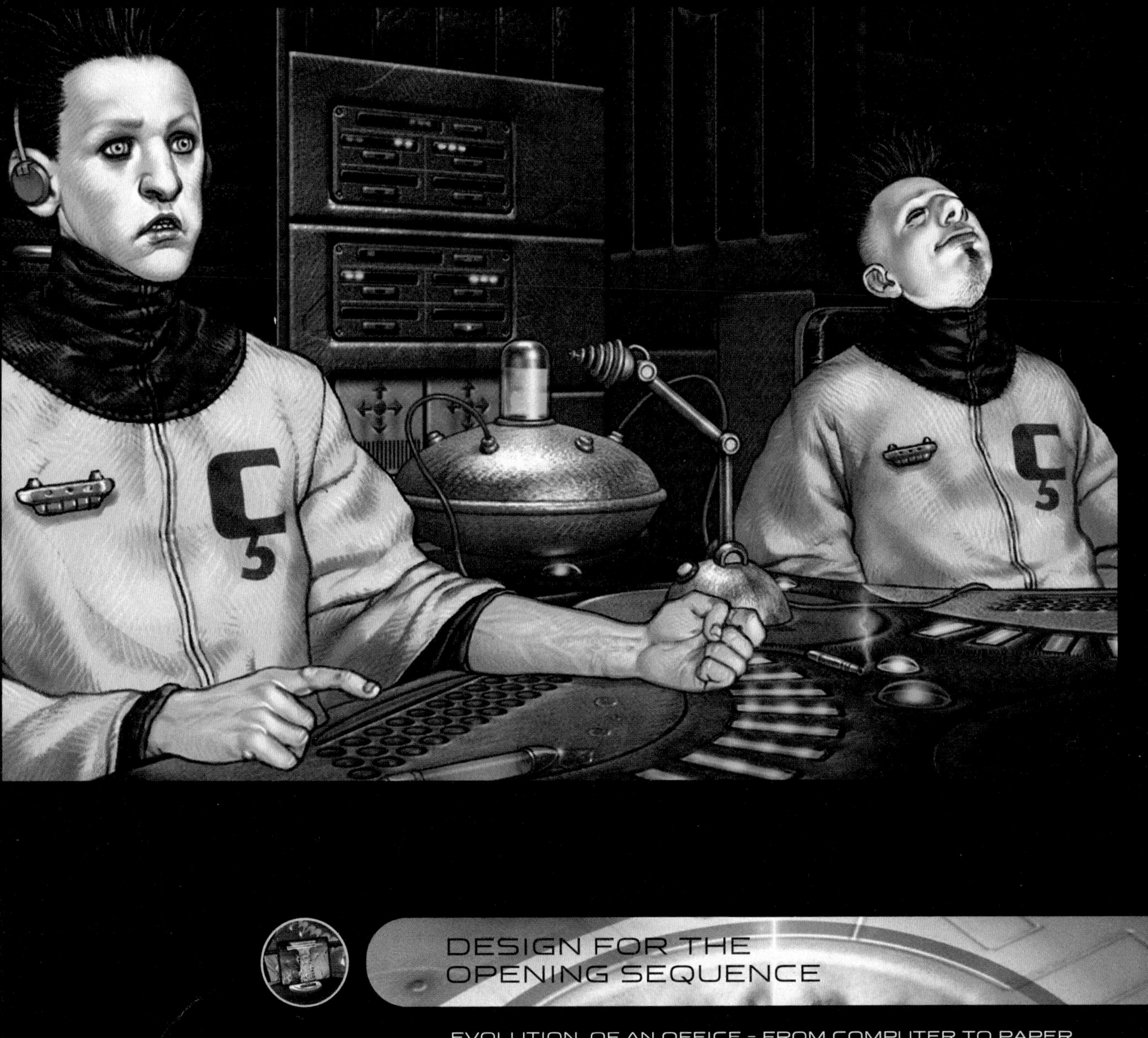

DESIGN FOR THE
OPENING SEQUENCE

EVOLUTION OF AN OFFICE - FROM COMPUTER TO PAPER

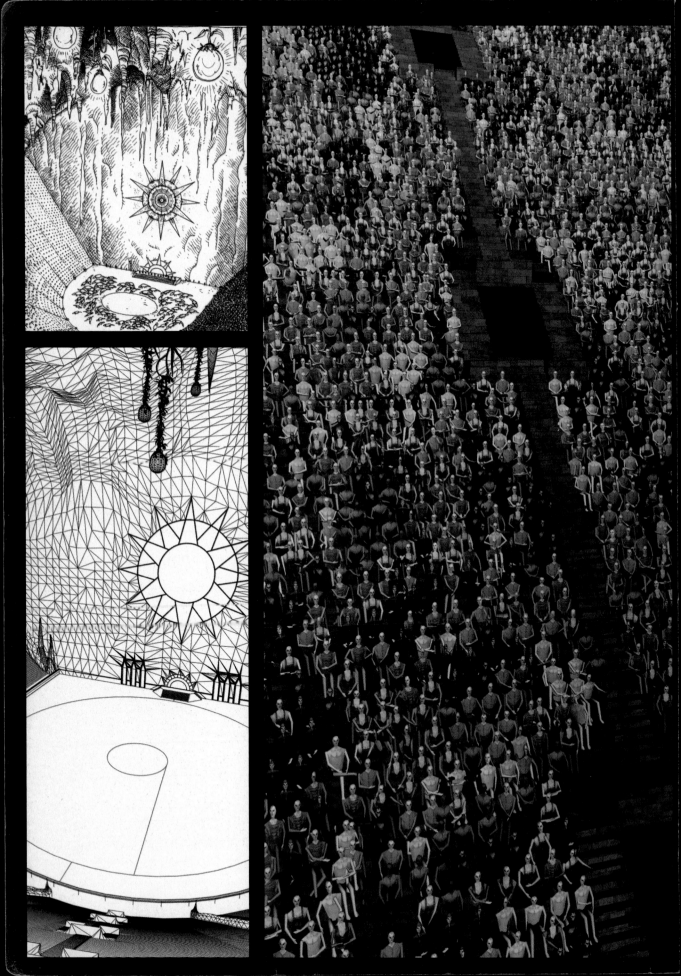

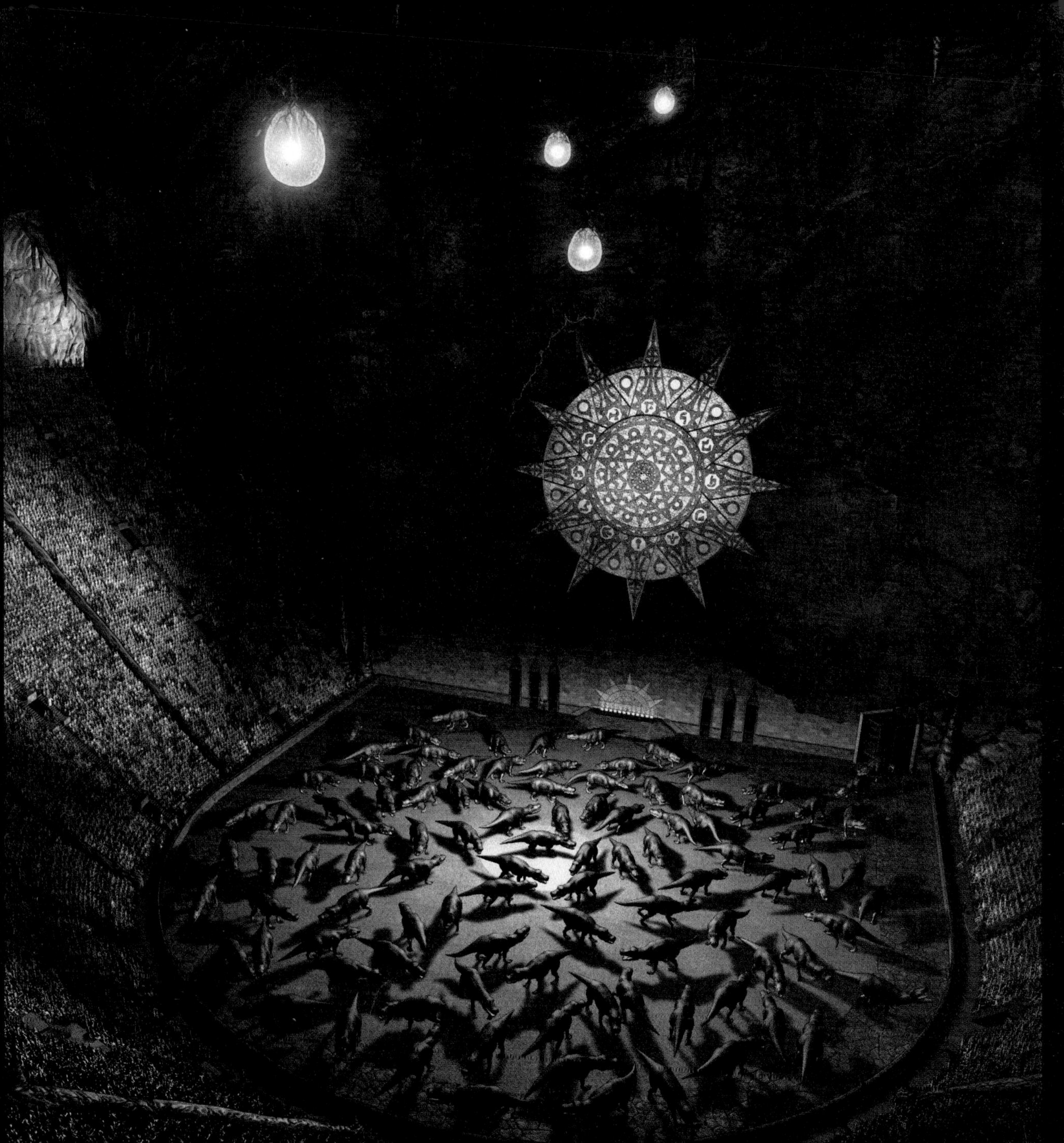

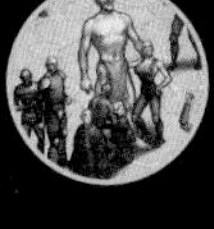

DESIGN FOR THE ARENA SEQUENCE

PENCIL STAGE - 3D STAGE - FINAL RENDER

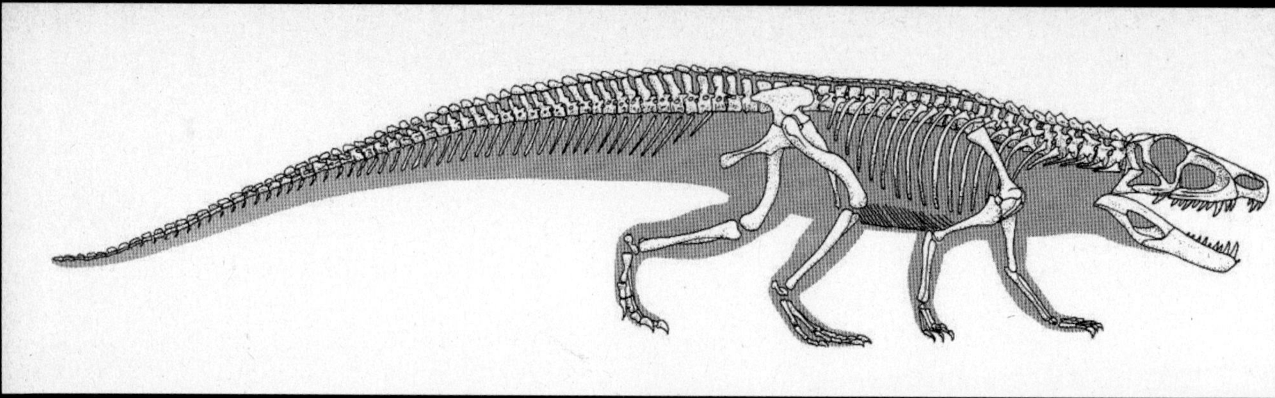

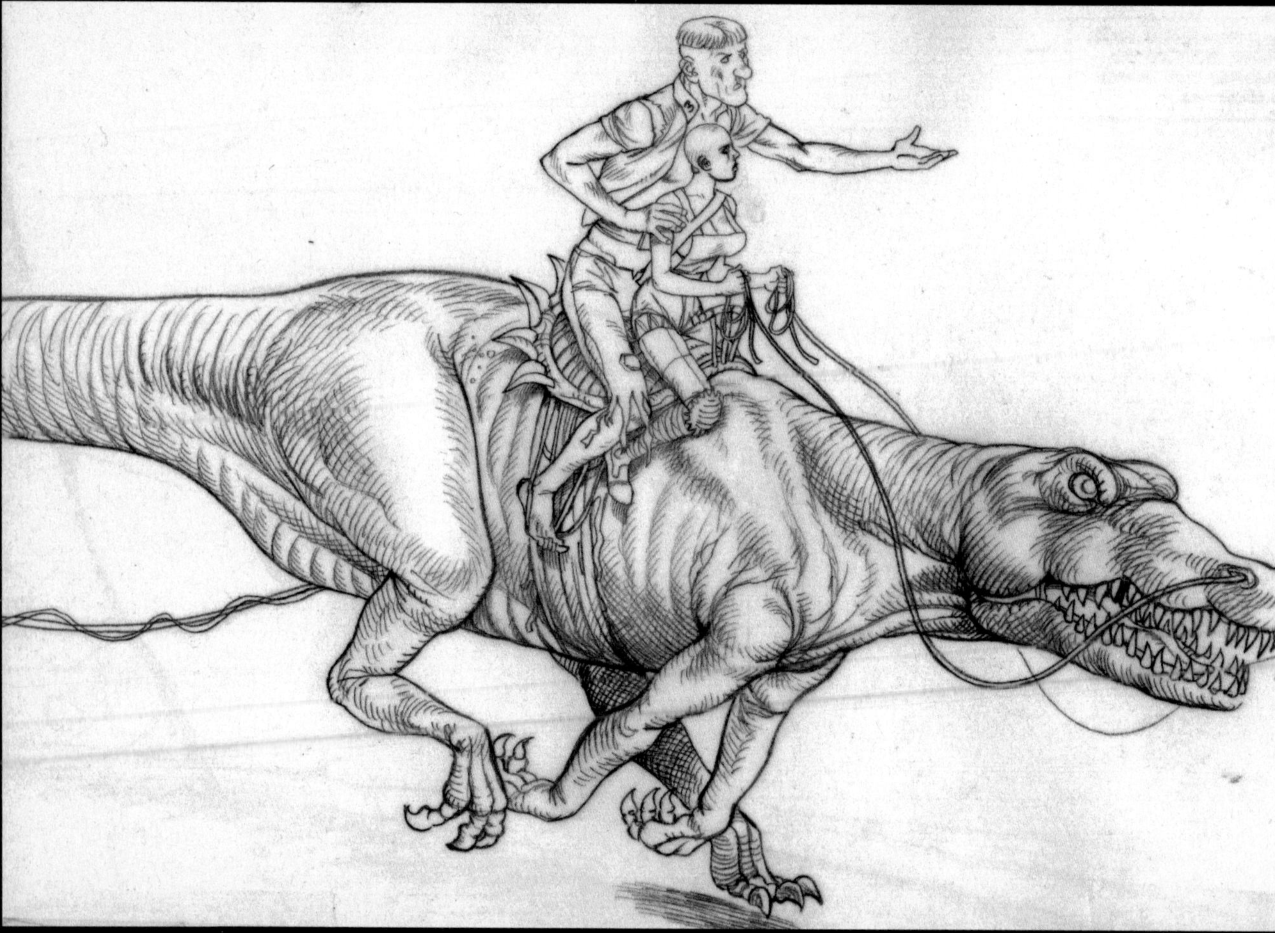

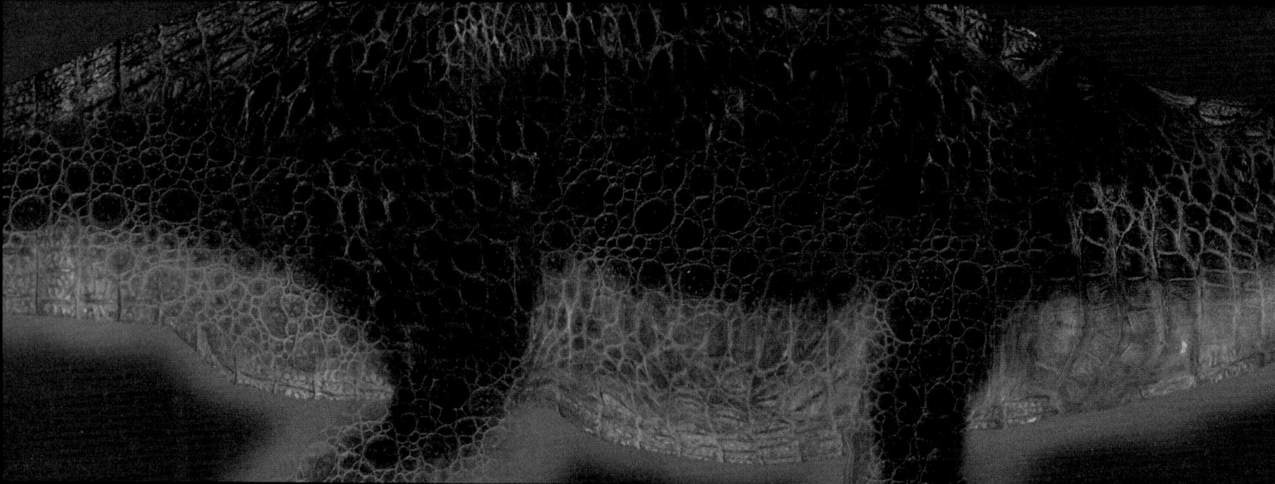

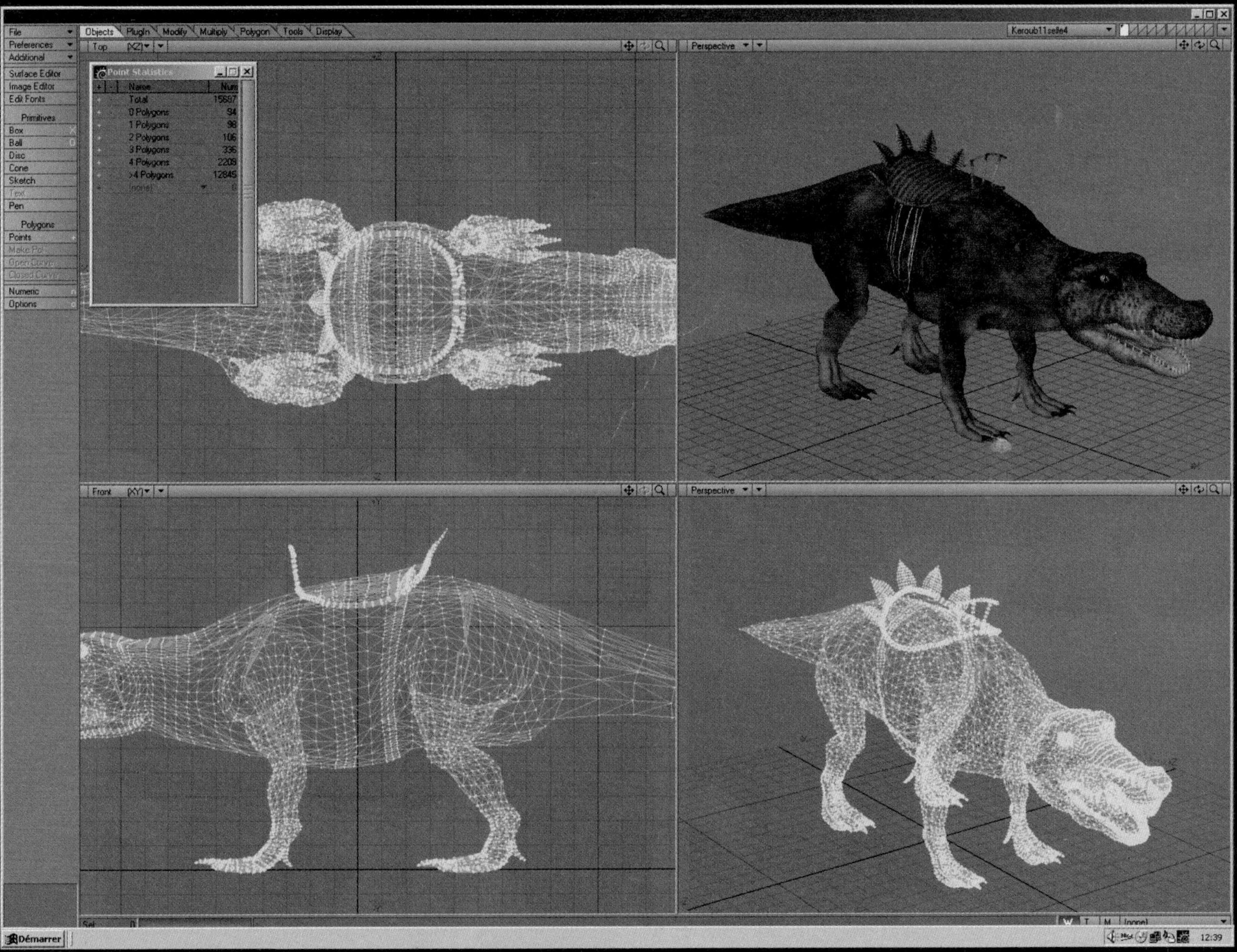

File
Preferences
Additional
Surface Editor
Image Editor
Edit Fonts
Primitives
Box
Ball
Disc
Cone
Sketch
Pen
Polygons
Points
Numeric
Options
Objects
PlugIn
Modify
Multiply
Polygon
Tools
Display
Keroub11selle4
Top
Perspective
Front
Point Statistics
Name
Total 15597
0 Polygons 94
1 Polygons 98
2 Polygons 106
3 Polygons 336
4 Polygons 2208
>4 Polygons 12845
Démarrer
12:39

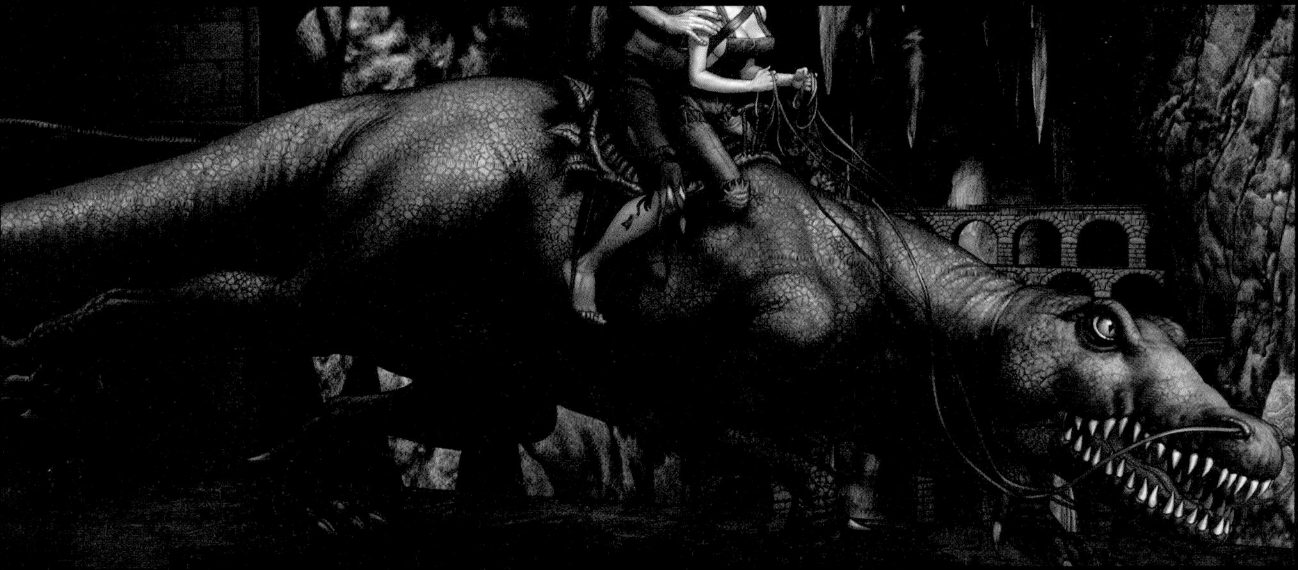

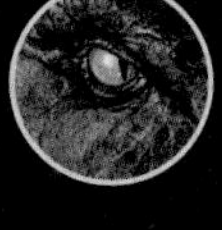

THE MAKING OF
A HIPPODRILE

RESEARCH - SKETCH - 3D MODELING - TEXTURING

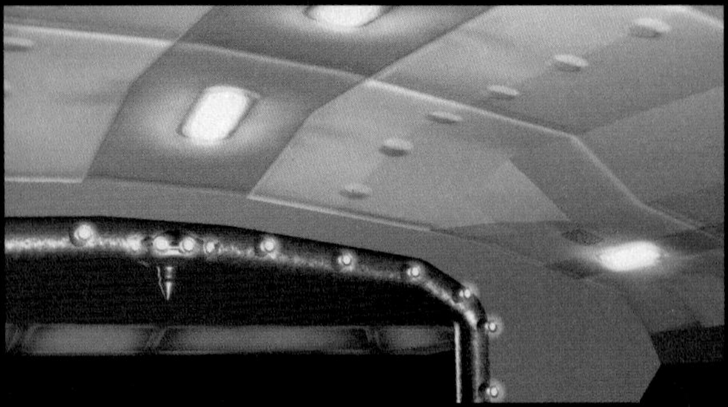

1

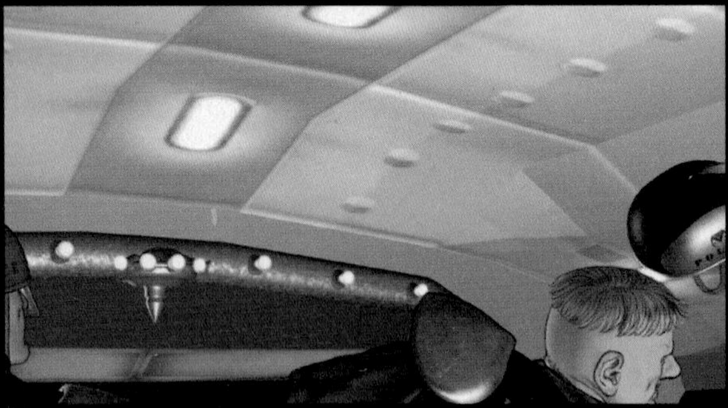

2

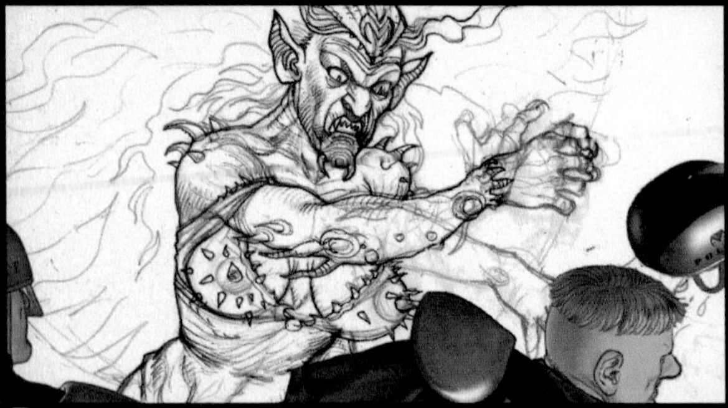

3

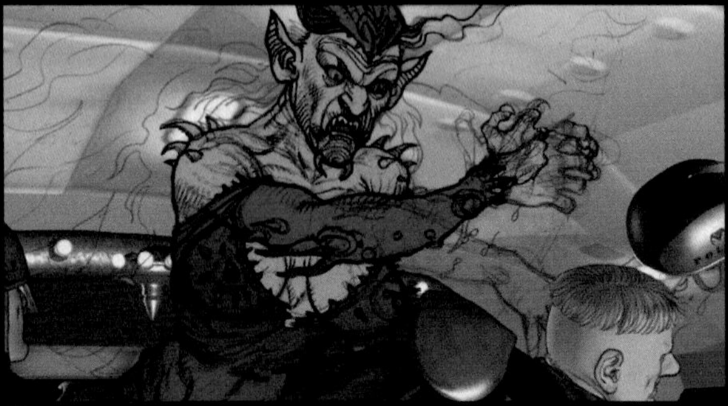

4

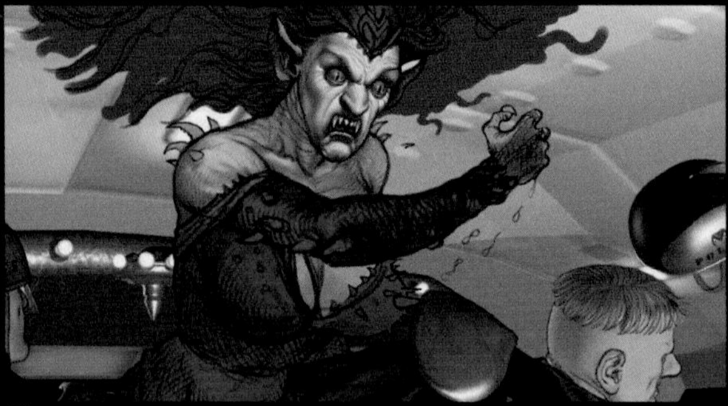

5

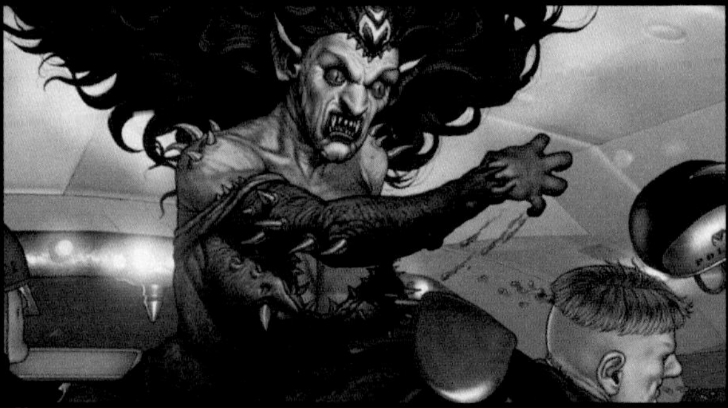

6

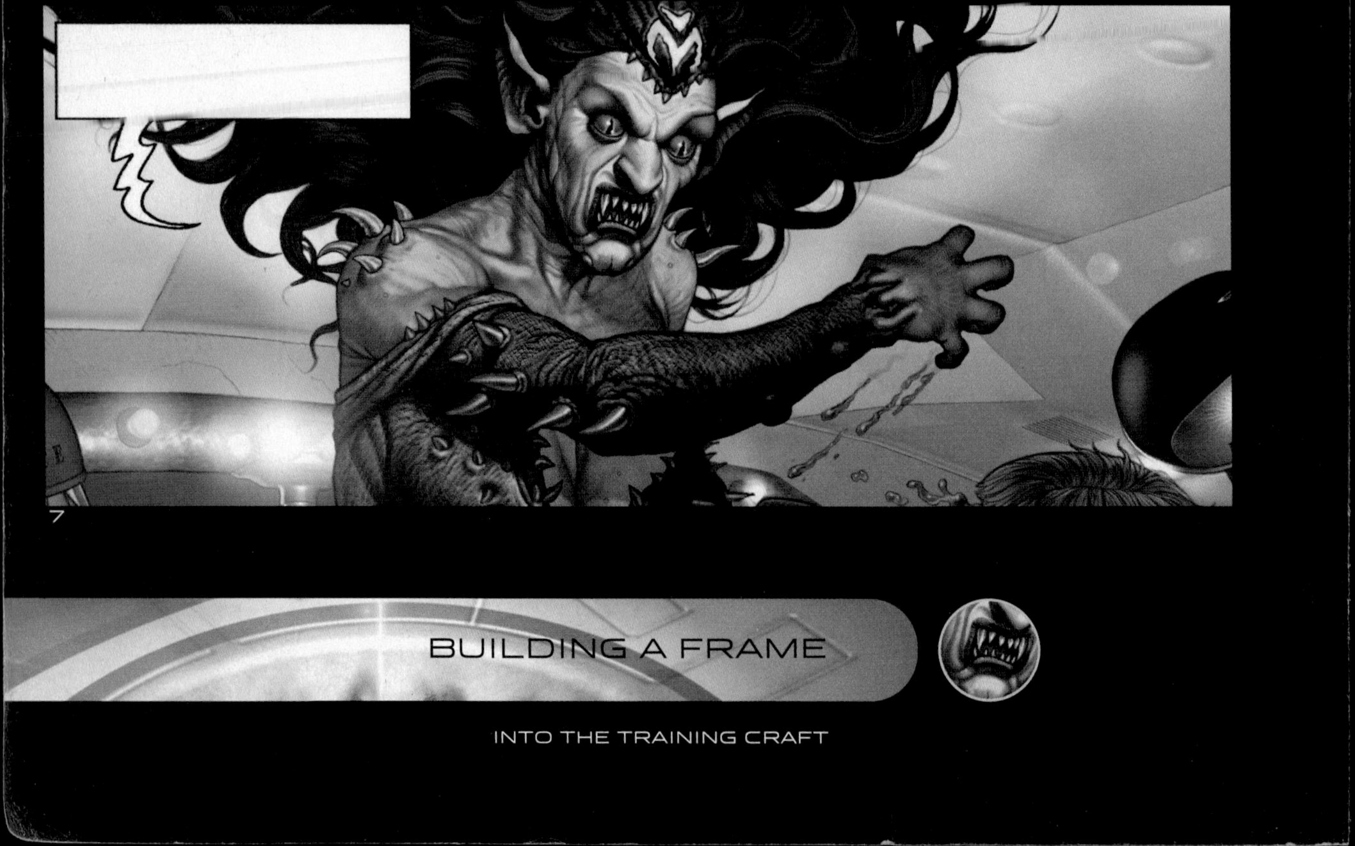

7

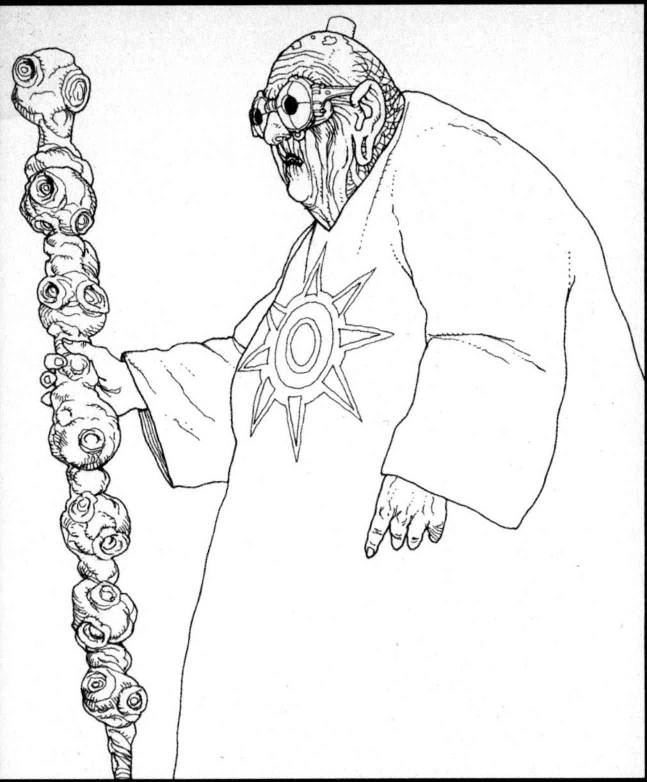

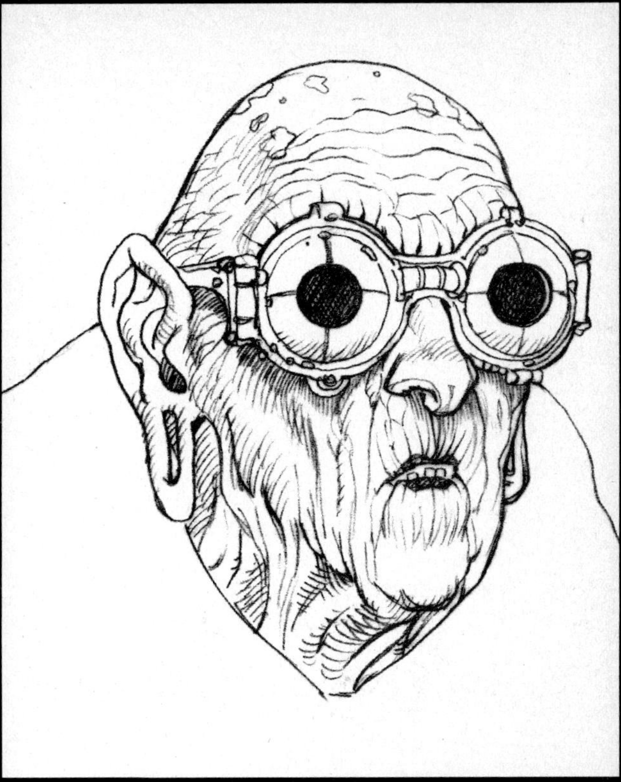

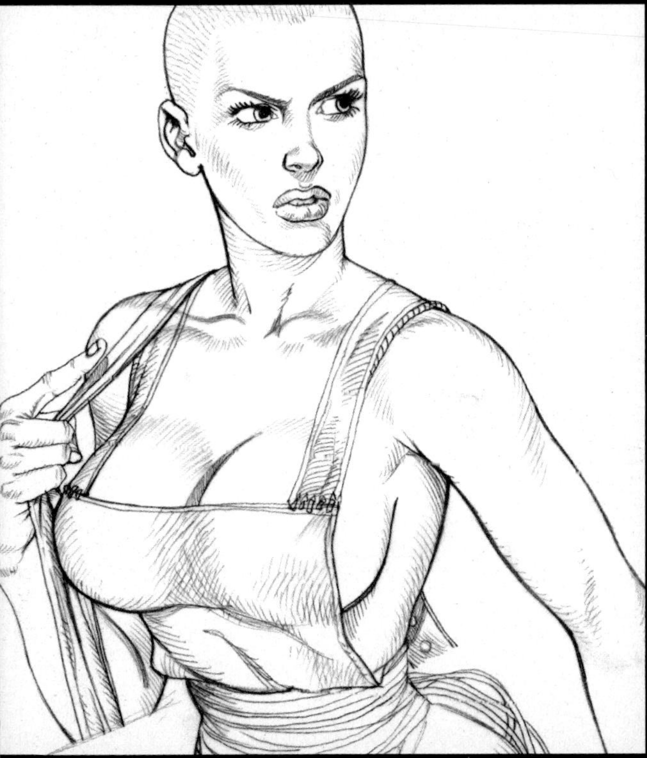

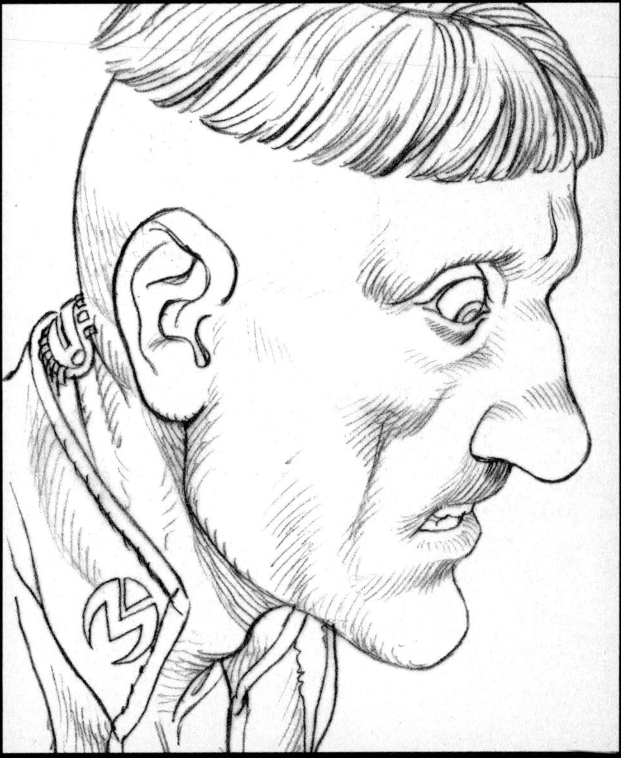

HUMANOIDS/DC COMICS
MORE WILD TALES FROM THE UNTAMED MIND OF ACCLAIMED WRITER AND FILMMAKER ALEXANDRO JODOROWSKY:

THE METABARONS #1: OTHON & HONORATA
THE METABARONS #2: AGHNAR & ODA
Follow the bloodline of the galaxy's ultimate warriors.
ILLUSTRATED BY JUAN GIMENEZ

BOUNCER: RAISING CAIN
A Western tale of a washed up, one-armed gunslinger and his nephew's quest for vengeance.
A complete story in one book.
ILLUSTRATED BY FRANÇOIS BOUCQ

THE TECHNOPRIESTS Book 1: INITIATION
THE TECHNOPRIESTS Book 2: REBELLION
More epic sci-fi from the creators of Megalex.
ILLUSTRATED BY ZORAN JANJETOV AND FRED BELTRAN

THE WHITE LAMA Book 1: REINCARNATION
THE WHITE LAMA Book 2: ROAD TO REDEMPTION
Mystical martial arts adventures. A complete story in two books.
ILLUSTRATED BY GEORGES BESS

THE INCAL: THE EPIC CONSPIRACY
The first part of the classic sci-fi comic book.
ILLUSTRATED BY MŒBIUS

SON OF THE GUN #1: SINNER
SON OF THE GUN #2: SAINT
A no-holds-barred tale of a modern day gunslinger's path through the darkest places in the human soul.
A complete story in two books.
ILLUSTRATED BY GEORGES BESS

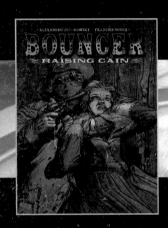  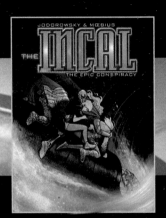 

LOOK FOR THESE OTHER BOOKS FROM HUMANOIDS/DC COMICS:

THE HORDE
The spirit of Genghis Khan is used to create a new Russian Empire.
A complete story in one book.
BY IGOR BARANKO

SANCTUM
Technology battles ancient evil.
A complete story in one book.
WRITTEN BY XAVIER DORISON
ILLUSTRATED BY CHRISTOPHE BEC

CHALAND ANTHOLOGY
#1: FREDDY LOMBARD
#2: FREDDY LOMBARD
Eisner-nominated series from one of Europe's greatest cartoonists.
BY YVES CHALAND

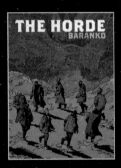  

TO FIND MORE HUMANOIDS GRAPHIC NOVELS, CALL 1-888-COMIC BOOK, VISIT DCCOMICS.COM OR GO TO YOUR LOCAL BOOK STORE.